Jane Cumberbatch's

Jane Cumberbatch's

PURE
style LIVING

photography by Pia Tryde

A DORLING KINDERSLEY BOOK

LONDON, NEW YORK, MUNICH, MELBOURNE and DELHI

Book Design and Art Editor: Vanessa Courtier
Design Assistant: Gina Hochstein
Text, Photographic Art Direction, and Styling:
Jane Cumberbatch
**Co-ordinator, Research, Design of Projects,
and Styling Assistant:** Kate Storer

For Dorling Kindersley:
US Editors: Gary Werner and Margaret Parrish
Project Editor: Neil Lockley
Art Director: Janis Utton
Category Publisher: Judith More
DTP: Sonia Charbonnier
Production Controller: Louise Daly

First American Edition, 2001

02 03 04 05 10 9 8 7 6 5 4 3 2

Published in the United States by
Dorling Kindersley Publishing, Inc
375 Hudson St.
New York, New York 10014

A Cataloging in Publication record is available from the
Library of Congress.

ISBN 0-7894-8015-8

Reproduced by GRB, Italy
Printed and bound in Spain by
Artes Gráficas Toledo

see our complete catalog at
www.dk.com

contents

sources

live

directory

Introduction

Pure Style Living is about trying to live more simply and efficiently: it is a **blueprint for living** in the new millennium. This is a book about homemaking in a **down-to-earth**, **practical**, and **realistic** way. It's a **fresh approach** to making a home **stylish**, **sensual**, **and peaceful** that will work for any domestic setup – single, married, shared, or any other kind of permutation of the contemporary household.

Pure Style Living is timely because life is tough these days. Our consumer society has led to high expectations, but do we really need all of these consumer props? And although we live in a super-technological age where emails and computers react instantly, working hours are increasing and chipping away at precious free time.

This sentiment is echoed in the poem *Leisure*, by W.H. Davies (1870–1940), that begins:

> *What is this life if, full of care,*
>
> *We have no time to stand and stare?*

Although it was written years ago in a cozier English age, it is perhaps more startlingly relevant today. When slaving away on the consumer treadmill it's easy to lose sight of the simple things in life, such as appreciating a walk in the fresh air or having a picnic feast with friends.

I have written **Pure Style Living** from the viewpoint of a working mother of three children who is trying to make life more **balanced** and laid back in the face of all the pressures that make up contemporary life. For me, **home** is at the **heart** of daily life; it is the one place where we can communicate our honest feelings and be our real selves, and this is reflected in the colors and furnishings that we choose to decorate with, in how we sleep, bathe, garden, or in what we choose to eat. Whatever else is going on in the outside world, **home is grounding**, a refuge, and our main source of **warmth and security**. It should be **light and airy**, a living breathing environment furnished with **natural textures** and **uncomplicated designs** that minimize the daily grind.

Of course, there's no escaping the fact that money has to be earned in order to have the means to buy or rent, and decorate and run a home, however large or small. But we're beset with a bewildering choice of ideas and goods in the stores. This book aims to show the reader how important it is to go back to **basics** when picking the best ideas for the home. It illustrates that there are ways to make a **stylish home** in an economical way – **without skimping on essentials** like good food or a decent bed.

Pure Style Living is about using **functional** yet **good-looking design**. There's no point in having tricky gadgets or fancy furnishings if they're not well made, and **easy to use and maintain**; for example, in the kitchen a dozen inferior knives are worth less than **one really good steel blade**, and in the living room a fussily trimmed velveteen upholstered sofa would be more good-looking and practical if covered in an **honest, plain-cotton loose cover**.

Pure Style Living is also about **paring down** and **sorting out clutter** to make the home more **organized**. Having less things to look after and worry about cuts down on stress levels. Cupboards, open shelves, boxes, and drawers can all make life easier to run. It is also about **being practical** and **doing things yourself** that are **achievable**, not impossible. **Transform a chair** with a coat of paint. If you can sew, **make basic cushion covers**. Make your own cards and decorations. Be **resourceful** and equip your home with **affordable** ideas from chain stores, **secondhand shops**, and flea markets.

Fresh, sensual living is a part of **pure style**; paint rooms in light tones of **whites and creams** with **crisp injections of color**, and use natural textures of **cotton, linen, and wool** for loose covers and curtains. It's also about having **gorgeous scented** flowers such as **hyacinths** and narcissi, or delicious soaps and **natural candlelight**.

And **Pure Style Living** also concerns **health**. We are what we eat, and our well-being depends on **good food** from **local and dependable** sources. There is growing dissatisfaction with mass-produced and packaged food that is high in additives and low in nourishment.

The approach is about putting back the **rituals** into preparing and eating food, and about using **fresh ingredients** and simple techniques. It isn't difficult to prepare a fresh salad of crisp lettuce leaves or to grill a piece of meat, and it is so satisfying to set a table simply with a cloth and to take the time to sit down and eat.

Pure Style Living is also about being **eco-friendly** around the **home** and knowing that because the earth's resources are finite we should put less strain on an already beleaguered environment. As well as avoiding processed and packaged food, we should buy fruit and vegetables that are grown without harmful pesticides and fertilizers, or even **dig a little patch**, make a **compost heap**, and **grow our own produce**. In the home we can **recycle** everything from old clothes to newspapers, let clothes **dry naturally** to save electricity, and use cleaning products with fewer chemicals.

Pure Style Living aims to make life more **sensual**, **practical**, and **balanced**.

Jane Cumberbatch 2001

sources

Nature

Smell

Texture

Eat

Architecture

Function

Order

Homemade

Fabric

Color

Nature

Man used to live **at one with nature**, and the pattern of his existence was defined by the **rising and setting of the sun**, and by seasonal changes. However, technological advances have long overridden our co-existence with nature. Because of electric lights, we can work at all hours, but early man had no choice but to sleep when it got dark. Similarly, in traditional societies the heat of midday dictated repose and rest, but nowadays in hot months air-conditioned offices and factories ensure that the workers continue working.

Commercialism has also eroded the meaning behind **seasonal rituals** – both religious and secular – that are linked to the **natural cycle of the year**. Christmas – which replaced a pagan festival to celebrate the passing of the shortest winter day – has become a cynical marketing opportunity, with plastic Christmas trees and Christmas songs appearing in shopping malls as early as October.

Getting back in touch with nature and the passing seasons, and enjoying life in a simpler way, can help us steer away from materialistic concerns.

In **spring**, the lengthening evenings and **flowering bulbs** that push up through the grass are tonics to the eye after the long dreary winter days. At home it's time to spring clean and push the windows wide open for fresh air. At Easter, we blow out eggs and decorate them with paint for Easter baskets (see pp.206–207) and pick little posies of primroses. In **summer**, I head for the sea or park and we **picnic outside**, taking every possible opportunity to enjoy the outdoor elements when they are at their most clement. Summer is when **children learn to swim**, to cook sausages on the grill, and to **grow brown and strong** from running wild. Picking strawberries and eating creamy fruit desserts made from fat gooseberries or raspberries are summer highlights. **Fall** is a voluptuous season, with **smoky November evenings**, ruddy sunsets low in the sky, walks through thick mounds of **papery fallen leaves**, and the earthy and **woody smell of mushrooms**. This is the time to make **jack-o'-lanterns out of pumpkins** for Halloween, to **roast chestnuts** on the fire, and to make delicious preserves from apples and cranberries.

Celebrate the **long dark days of winter** with candlelight, **warming stews**, rich puddings, and indoor games like charades and cards, and set aside time to catch up on reading. Get out into the elements and **experience the chilling and crisp air** of an open field, or the white snow-covered ground in the **bright winter sun**. We go and **gather greenery** to make a Christmas wreath for the door, and pile the table high with **clementines and nuts**. The children grow a **hyacinth bulb** in a glass of water and watch it sprout and produce **spring color** and scent.

Smell

Smell is the most direct and **evocative** of our senses. Damp scented pines, **sea-salty air**, honeysuckle, cut grass, **toast in the morning**; a whiff of any of these might conjure up a scene or conversation that happened years ago. Smells are **nostalgic** because they trigger images and emotions before we have time to edit them. The fresh **scent of a yellow peace rose** encountered in the park will take me **back to childhood** and the memory of playing barefoot in my mother's garden, where she had a bed of these blooms that flowered throughout the summer. Smells fall into a few basic categories: minty – peppermint; floral – roses; ethereal – pears; musky – musk; resinous – camphor; foul – rotten eggs and acrid vinegar.

We don't need to use our sense of smell to survive anymore except to taste and sense danger, but there seems to be a need to surround ourselves with artificial outdoor smells, perhaps to remind us of how we used to live at one with nature.

Scented artificial camouflages are not desirable, but neither are unwashed bodies, unwashed clothes, or a room stale with cooking smells. Again, it's a question of balance. Of finding simple ways to make ourselves and our homes smell good.

Start by choosing cleaning products that are unperfumed or that contain as little perfume as possible. And practice simple rituals such as opening the windows to **circulate air**, letting the laundry

dry naturally, or washing down surfaces with hot water to keep them fresh. Keep clothes fresh in

drawers with sachets of **dried lavender** or blocks of earthy **cedarwood** for deterring moths.

Fresh flowers are an instant way to bring **natural scent** into a room. Scented hyacinths or

narcissi are a joy to the senses in the middle of winter, when you can have a reminder in your bedroom

or living room that spring is on its way. In summer, raid the garden for **sprigs of rosemary**, lavender,

rose blooms, stems of jasmine, or tuberoses and bring them to the table in vases for intoxicating scent.

Scented potpourris made with dried flower petals and scented candles are also ways to refresh

your home. The general rule is to buy the best you can afford for the most authentic and appealing

smells. Cheap scents smell just that – cheap and nasty.

The **kitchen** is a place where we can also indulge our nasal receptors each time we prepare food

to eat. Enticing scents include **chopped garlic**, mint thrown in with a pot of new potatoes, **grated**

lemon or orange rind, and ground coffee brewing on the stove.

In the bathroom buy good-quality soaps and colognes for simple beauty routines. Also use **simple**

lavender or rosewater, which can be bought from drug stores and put in a bottle to splash

on after baths and showers. Invest in some outrageously exotic lotions and potions for the days

when extra pampering is necessary.

Texture

We are **energized by touch** – without the chance to hug, or be hugged, we humans become withdrawn, cynical, and grumpy. It is imperative that we experience the **tactile elements** around us and replay them as visceral memories to **remain healthy in body and mind**. There is nothing more sublime than feeling the **breathy gentle nuzzling** of a newborn baby, the hot sand trickling through toes, the **tingling and breathtaking iciness** of the first swim of the year, or the **enveloping** soft warmness of bedding. But legislation and efficiency-obsessed corporations care little that our lives are becoming more sanitized, preventing connection with our instincts and natural surroundings. How I wish to fling myself among sweet grass and wild flowers after spending a day traveling through static-loaded, plastic-furnished airport lounges, or sitting in the meeting rooms of an air-conditioned, windowless office.

Health and hygiene rules are also dehumanizing. "Don't touch," said the fierce woman (perhaps anticipating a visit from the health and safety inspector) standing behind the crates of fruit and vegetables as a small child **ran her fingers** over the furry bloom on some plump peaches tantalizingly displayed at eye level at our local market the other day. It is also depressing to have more of our food presented in characterless and antiseptic plastic wrap or molded polystyrene. (Kudos to the stores that still **hand wrap** their goods in **smooth waxed or brown paper**.) At least we have the power to make our homes living breathing spaces, a second skin filled with **natural** and **sensual** textures.

In the kitchen, work with tools and surfaces **in wood**, or honest metal textures, ceramic tiling, marble, or **smooth utilitarian stainless steel**. Eat real food – raw salads, natural cheese, good meat, homemade cakes – to teach taste buds that overprocessed, oversalted, or sugared goods are unhealthy and unsatisfying.

Sleep like a baby among **soft wool** blankets and **crisp cotton** sheets that have flapped dry on the line, or luxuriate in **linen** that is the coolest texture on hot summer nights.

Curl up on the sofa in front of a **blazing fire**, and keep toes warm with a **wooly** blanket. Bring in logs from the woodpile and stack them in **rough woven baskets**. Use natural textures underfoot – **tough hairy sisal**, rough terra-cotta, or **scrubbed wooden boards**.

Bathe in scented water and **rub down skin** with a **loofah** or pumice, and wrap up and wind down in a soft towel or cotton robe.

Eat

We should buy the best food we can afford: **fruits and vegetables** that are **in season** from **local sources**, not waxed and polished, and not flown out of season at great expense from far-off locations; **fresh bread made with unrefined flour**; chocolate high in cocao solids; good-quality coffee; **natural cheese** made on a farm and not in a factory; and meat from **small-scale producers**. Food that is grown **organically** is produced with farming methods that avoid the use of synthetic pesticides and most artificial fertilizers; instead, organic farming methods use crop rotations and good husbandry to promote the health of crops and livestock. Genetic engineering is not allowed in organic systems. **Animals reared on farms certified as organic** have **access to space and natural light**, are protected by rigorous **animal welfare** standards, and are not raised in cramped conditions and fed on antibiotics and other drugs.

I know how wonderful **home-produced** meat can be after we kept some of the local **Iberian black-footed pigs** at our farm in Spain and fed them on a diet of **acorns**, **chestnuts**, and **apples**. This produced the most succulently sweet air-dried ham – **jamon** – which the Andalucia region of Spain is noted for, and the most mouthwatering tenderloins that were barbecued on the fire.

Architecture

Home is a notion as old as the human species. For the vast majority of people – whether they live in caves, as many still do in Cappadocia, Turkey; in mud, stone, or straw huts; or in apartments or houses – home is the fixed point in their lives, both emotionally and physically. Our homes should be **comfortable**, womblike and **enveloping**, but **simple in proportions and function** to cope with the frantic demands of contemporary life. A large bank account is useful, but doesn't guarantee instant style, as anyone browsing through the pages of celebrity magazines can see. Getting back to basics with ideas that are **simple and functional** is more likely to make your home **stylish and sensual** without costing wads of money.

For inspiration take a look at different buildings around you. **Vernacular buildings** have a pleasing **simplicity** and **unself-conciousness**. They are the result of generation upon generation continually defining and redefining function, working within the means at the disposal of their builders, and transcending poor ingredients. The appeal of a cottage in Scotland, of a modest schoolhouse building, or of a hut for storing food and animals in rural Spain, is visual; the appeal is also in knowing that its shape has evolved from pure necessity.

Nowadays, when the traditional family setup is being replaced by more fluid family groupings, we need to be increasingly **flexible** in our living arrangements. Borrow from vernacular principles such as using **natural materials**, keeping detailing simple, and **maximizing storage space** to make the most of space, **light**, and **proportion** in a modern home. For example, a small row house can be improved by carefully knocking out walls and simplifying the interior.

In recent years, the **conversion** of many sturdily built and well-proportioned disused inner-city **industrial warehouses and factories** into **domestic living space** – or **lofts** as they have become known in real estate jargon – has allowed many people to enjoy the benefits of living centrally in environments that are more **spacious and airy** than conventional city houses or apartments. Three years ago we left a five-story home and traded the grueling stairwork for horizontal space in a fourth-floor warehouse space on the edge of the city of London. **Remodeled** to accommodate five of us, it has proved to be a workable and comfortable **multifunctional home and office**, with solid walls and good-sized windows that allow large amounts of daylight to flood in.

Homemade

In contemporary England we're not used to the notion of being **thrifty** and **economical**, when so many mass-produced goods are available that are cheap to buy and often disposable. It's worth reminding ourselves, as we throw away another razor or pair of holey socks, of the incredible **resourcefulness** of people during the last world war. With the make-do and mend approach encouraged by the wartime government, everything was made into something else. Curtains and wedding dresses were sewn from the materials available – parachute silk, butter muslin, and blackout materials. Flour sacks and sugar bags became cushions and loose covers. And the fabric used to fill broken windows after air raids was found to be useful for making tea towels. During the summers of 1941 and 1942, women's charity organizations made 1,500 tons of jam from surplus fruit.

No doubt, my need to be economical has been influenced by **growing up in the 1950s** with parents who had experienced wartime rationing of food and other household staples and who encouraged my sister and me **to sew, cook, and make our own presents**. In adult life, although my credit card yields to some retail therapy – an expensive dress or coveted pair of shoes – my conscience

generally asks me why should I waste money on store-bought things such as cushion covers or

Christmas cards if I can make them myself? To be resourceful, buy **cheap utilitarian fabrics**, such as

canvas and **cotton**, and look out for bargains and sale items. **Collect** a bag of **remnants**, bits of **ribbon**,

and other trimmings, and use them to freshen up a collar or the hem of a skirt, or to trim a plain napkin.

There are many stores selling renovated and painted furniture, but why not buy your own

secondhand chair or table from a flea market, strip it down, and **paint it yourself**.

When cooking it's quick to throw together **easy-bake items** such as **scones**, flapjacks, cookies,

or a **simple cake**. With a basic recipe it is quick and simple to boil up a batch of **jam** with summer

strawberries, or to make **marmalade** from tangy Seville oranges.

At Christmastime, when funds are stretched, make your own decorations, cards, and labels with

supplies of colored paper, pens, and paint from an art shop or stationery store. A batch of **homemade**

cookies packed in a box and tied with bright ribbon couldn't be a more appreciated present.

Fabric in natural cotton, linen, wool, and silk used to trim and decorate windows, sofas, beds, cushions, and other home furnishings is one of the simplest ways to make your home comfortable, colorful, and textural.

plain hardworking **basic utilitarian** fabrics, used for sails, tents, awnings, sacks, and other commercial purposes can be bought from specialized stores and used to make **textural** and **tough** home furnishings. Art suppliers are a good source of artists' canvas, which can also be transformed into chair covers or curtains. Burlap, which is normally used as a canvas backing, could equally be used to make a textural curtain or seat cover. Theatrical and film set suppliers sell very cheap muslin, which can be tied with loops onto a pole or even just stapled up at the window. Felt, generally used for commercial backdrops, is useful and comes in wonderful colors, including pinks, greens, oranges, and lilacs. There are also quite a few companies that specialize in various basic materials, such as sheeting that you can use to make your own duvet covers and pillow cases, or bright orange, yellow, or green canvas to make chair slings and cushions.

Dry goods or army surplus stores are good sources of rope for making cord to use in heavy-duty laundry bags or beach bags made from tough canvas.

florals   Back in the 1970s, girls in my senior class floated from class to class in romantic **Laura Ashley** floral-sprigged cotton frilled shirts and patterned milkmaid smocks, bought with Saturday job money from her small shop on the Fulham Road, London. Ashley's vision of the English country look, inspired by **floral-printed chintzes**, dried potpourris, and roses climbing around cottage doors, was cleverly interpreted in both her clothes and furnishings. After her sudden death, the sweetness and clarity of her designs was never quite recaptured in successive collections. During the get-tough, get-rich 1980s aspiring bankers and other moneymakers paid interior decorators to recreate the grand English country house, in mansions and houses alike. Swathes of chintzy wallpaper and extravagant curtains with swags in bold floral patterns appeared in every interior-decorating magazine. During the 1990s, the country look went out of fashion to be replaced by more pared-down and modern trends in interiors. **Florals have come back again** as **pretty details** for home accessories, but in a much more restrained manner, and in some gorgeous **retro-1940s styles**. When used sparingly, florals can look **fresh and crisp** in a contemporary interior.

checks and stripes are **simple patterns** that have been used for centuries in commercial and domestic environments. Blue-and-white striped **cotton ticking** is a traditional mattress covering that has become a stylish curtain, cushion, or chair covering in its own right. Cotton tickings are **tough and good value**, and can be found in black, terra-cotta, brown, and yellows, as well as blue.

Striped linen, used for roller towels in hospitals and institutions, can be bought by the roll from the suppliers and cut to make table runners, or sewn together to make chair covers. Classic striped linen tea towels can also be given the same treatment.

Checks are basic and **uncomplicated** and provide a **sense of order and neatness**, that's why they are used for table linens in restaurants and cafés. I adopt the restaurant principle at home and use either bright **blue-and-white check cotton** cloths or wipe-down checked plastic that is highly practical. I also use checked cotton fabrics for cushions and blinds, against a backdrop of plain walls and furnishings. A local Spanish supermarket is my source for coveted mesh shopping bags – ordinary, dirt cheap, and stylish carriers for my bread and vegetables.

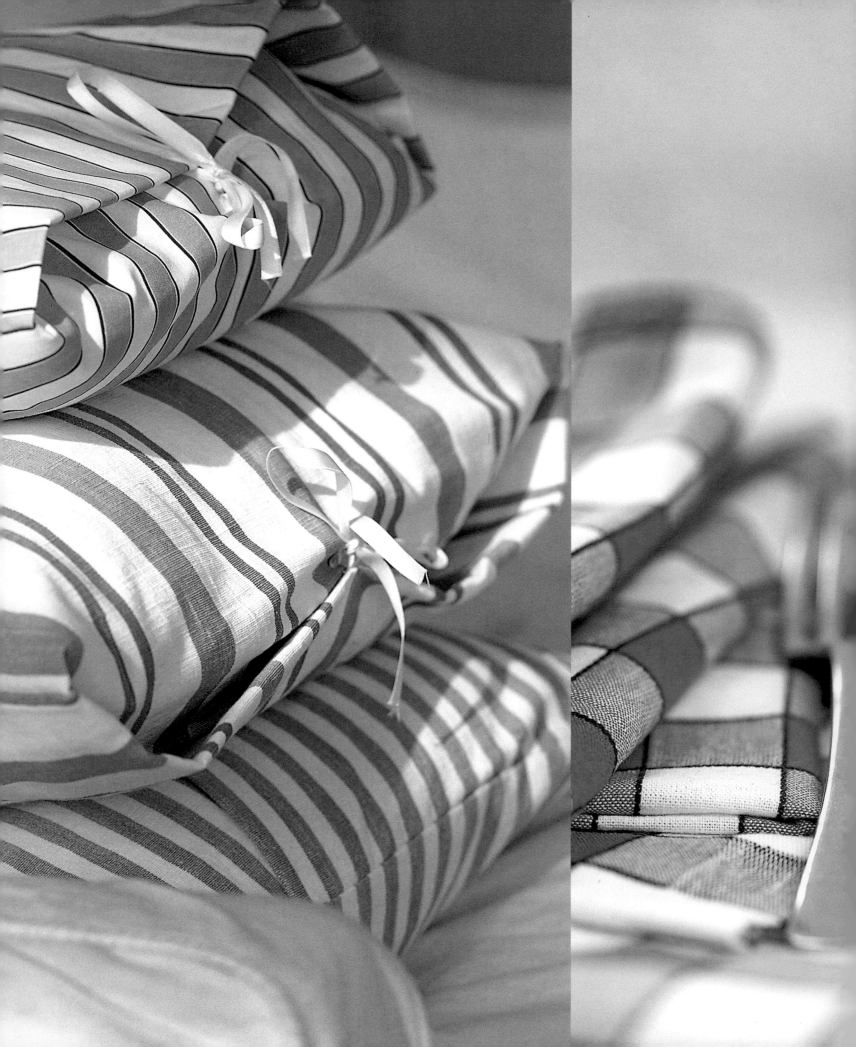

Color

How do I choose the colors that I want to live with? I resist examining color wheels or remembering which colors are supposed to go with which. I use my **instinct** for colors that feel right – a **sentiment**, not born of any particular logic. This belief in an intuitive sense of color is echoed in the theories of Li Edelkoort, who predicts new trends in fashion and business. My instinct has no doubt been developed by being brought up in the drab English climate, where the very absence of color during the winter has stimulated my desire for it.

I look to **nature** for **inspiration** – the sea, the sky, and plants and flowers. And, of course, I am influenced by **art** – the Scottish colorists and the Bloomsbury group of artists are favorites. Two years ago, on a rain-swept January day in Paris, I was lifted out of the gloom by the soft, luminous rectangles of color on the expansive canvases by Mark Rothko.

I constantly **observe** and **appraise** colors around me: the **detail** of a cardigan trimming, or a painted door, or the color of the fabric of a child's dress. I store these visual fragments in my mind like a mental bulletin board of samples, to bring into my work as a stylist and as ideas for my home.

I prefer to live with a **backdrop of calm**, wraparound color – such as white or a country cream – that serves as a **canvas** onto which I **inject color** in the form of fabric – a bright throw or cushions, plants, a terra-cotta pot with blue hyacinths, or a pitcher of pink tulips.

white   Think of things that are white – a stark, snow-covered landscape, a smooth ovoid duck's egg, a worn and weathered creamy beach pebble, or a sun-and-saltwater-bleached clam shell. White is **pure**, **calming**, and **soothing** for the soul. White decor is eminently livable, making white eternally popular with architects and designers, who use it in the simplest beach houses, as well as the hippest ultramodern hotels. White is **light-reflecting** – the white huddled village houses of Andalucia, Spain, and homes in other hot climates are painted in white limewash because of this quality. If you adopt this principle in a grimy urban area and paint a south-facing interior in white, the space will be infused with luminous light even in the gray of winter. White is **rejuvenating** – think of freshly washed white linen flapping on a clothesline; use white to spruce up tired pieces of old furniture or for simple slipcovers. White is also **seductive** – there's nothing more **cooling** than white linen clothing against tanned summer skin, or more freshly pretty than a present wrapped simply in filmy layers of white tissue paper.

earth Terra-cotta and various shades of brown are basic **back-to-nature** hues that evoke rural images – furrowed and plowed fields, bare trees silhouetted against the winter sky, **brown peaty earth floors**, rough burlap sacking stuffed with hay. In medieval England, the clay soil itself colored mud-and-wattle huts a dull brown. And in parts of rural Spain, red oxide is still mixed with limewash to color village barns or hut walls a pinky terra-cotta inside and out.

In the home, **earth colors** and textures are **grounding** elements that add a certain **honesty** and down-to-earth quality to make an interior an **organic environment**. These can be **tough coir and natural matting in brown shades**, natural wooden floorboards in scrubbed bare pine or richly worn oak, or **linen in oatmeal or natural brown** for slip covers and simple blinds. Roughly woven log baskets filled with cut logs by the fireside and irregular hand-thrown worn and weathered terra-cotta flowerpots planted with bulbs can bring nature in from the outside. If renovating an old house, search for irregular **brown-and-plum-colored handmade traditional bricks**, rather than using mass-produced bricks of uniform texture and color.

yellow is a **warm and positive** color. It varies in hue from the **pale cream of straw** to the **brilliant yellow** in the petals of a **sunflower**. **Strong yellow** walls are **sunny** and **exuberant** and are good for **enlivening** dark north-facing rooms. Avoid using citrus-colored yellows on walls as they are too harsh on the eye. The natural pigment **yellow ocher** is a wonderfully rich yellow that can be added to **limewash** to make the rich sandy colors (which include white, green, and terra-cotta) seen on the elegant, faded townhouses that line Seville's narrow streets. One of the most beautiful yellow-painted rooms I have seen is the sunny and airy drawing room of English architect Sir John Soane (1753–1837), in his house in Lincoln's Inn Fields in London. **Paler country cream colors** work in most interiors – they can **look really fresh in a modern apartment**, but also appropriately **authentic on old wood paneling** in a 19th-century house. **Creamy yellow-colored mixing bowls** and dishes are an alternative to whiteware in the kitchen. A **sunny yellow-and-white checked chair cover** or blind is a good choice for brightening up a child's bedroom which is painted in white. And what could be more spirit-lifting and easy on the wallet than a bunch of daffodil buds from a flower stall for spring color on the supper table.

pink and lavender colors are **inspired by hedgerows** and garden borders. Purple **lavender**, scented heads of **lilac**, **foxglove** bells, dusky pink **roses**, and pinky **tulips** are nature's ideas that can be copied and translated to paint and furnishing colors. **Fuchsia-pink felt seat cushions** for a pair of recycled chairs, or a **fuchsia-pink wool throw**, are useful **color injections** in an all-white interior. But such is the power of this color that it would be a psychedelic experience to have to live with it as an all-over room color. **A bedroom painted in pale lilac** with white bedlinen and a vase of pink tulips would be easier on the senses and look simple and fresh; lilac is a good choice for living rooms, too. Sprigged and floral pink-printed cottons can also look clean and contemporary as slip covers, cushions, or simple blinds. And on a sartorial note, I love to wear pink. It looks great – a bright rosy pink scarf or shirt in winter when everyone is muffled up in winter browns and blacks. In summer, strong fuchsia pink looks good against healthy tanned skin – a plain cardigan with jeans, a pair of silk fuchsia-pink, 50s-style cigarette pants with an orange shirt, or a Liberty of London floral pink cotton skirt. Finally, for a cheap and colorful idea, wrap up presents in bright pink tissue paper or use pink ribbon on lime-green tissue paper for a more contemporary look at Christmastime.

live

Eat

Work

Garden

Rest

Play

Wash

Sleep

When I married in the early 1980s, a **food processor** was a kitchen status symbol and was at the top of my wedding list. I used mine to rustle up many a delicate nouvelle cuisine sauce or fancy terrine – *de rigueur* at the time – for meals that went on into the early hours and were a feature of childless social life. Seventeen years or so later, it's still sitting on the worktop, a little battleworn, but it has never broken down and is now used to help fill small, hungry tummies with quick-to-prepare hearty and wholesome soups, puddings, cakes, and pastries. My other long-standing kitchen companions are two **cast-iron enameled saucepans** that my mother bought cheaply on a trip to France. After rigorous use for over fifteen years they have only a few chips. Even though they are heavy, I rely on them when making stews and sauces, steaming vegetables, and doing countless other tasks. I've learned through bad buys that cheap, light pans tip over, thin ones warp and cook unevenly, soldered handles fall off, and non-stick coatings eventually peel.

I am always on the lookout for kitchen tool bargains in London markets or seaside junk shops; I keep my eyes open for items such as **old-fashioned** glass lemon squeezers, nicely worn breadboards, or collectible 1940s green-and-cream ware items like pots, pans, and tins for storing dry ingredients.

New additions to my basic kitchen gear include a couple of rather good **shallow aluminum baking sheets** for shortbread, pizza, or chocolate brownies, and a **catering toaster** for chunky slices of toast. I add to my supply of **cream-colored mixing bowls** (see p.91) because every now and then there's a breakage when the children are making one of their famous cakes or batches of cookies. If anyone wants to give me a present, I would ask for another heavy kitchen **knife** with an excellent blade and a very well-designed handle.

making marmalade   The season for Seville oranges – the only oranges for making marmalade – lasts only a few weeks, from January to mid-February. Rows of stocky, bushy trees **laden with little orange orbs** can be seen on the huge estates around Seville in Spain. **Fragrant skinned** but too bitter to eat raw, the fruit has been made into marmalade since the 18th century. I use my friend Emma's recipe, which, unusually, involves boiling whole oranges to make a rich, **aromatic**, tangy addition to the breakfast table.

1 Cover 2–3 lb of Seville oranges with water in a large saucepan and simmer with the lid on for up to 3 hours or until soft. If using a pressure cooker reduce cooking time to 1 hour. Seville oranges can be frozen if you want to make marmalade later in the year but defrost them before following the recipe.

2 Remove the oranges from the pan and put into a bowl; retain the liquid in the pan. Cut oranges in half and remove the seeds. Return seeds to the pan, and boil rapidly for 10 minutes. Strain into another bowl and discard seeds.

3 Cut up the peel into pieces – the size depends on personal preference but I like my marmalade to be chunky. Use scissors rather than a knife to make cutting the pulpy oranges easier and less messy.

4 Measure the strained liquid and peel.
Add 1 lb peel to 2 cups liquid and 1¾ lb sugar. Bring to a boil slowly and then boil rapidly until setting point is reached (see Step 5). (Any liquid left over makes delicious orange jelly. Add 2 cups juice to 1 lb sugar and boil until setting point is reached.)

5 Test by pouring a spoonful onto a plate
that has been cooled in the freezer. If the marmalade or jelly wrinkles when pushed with a finger or spoon it is ready.

6 Leave to stand for 15 minutes – then stir and pour into sterilized jars. Cover with waxed paper and lids while marmalade or jelly is still hot. Makes about 5½ lb of marmalade and a jar or two of jelly. Customize with homemade labels – an idea that will appeal to children.

setting the table   In an age of snatched sandwich breaks and microwave dinners, it is very important to sit down and appreciate good food when there is time available. An everyday meal of breakfast, lunch, or supper can become a feast with a **simply laid table**. I start by spreading an **ironed, white cotton or linen tablecloth** – a white cotton sheet will do. **Table components** include **simple tumblers** or plain wine glasses, **plain white china**, classic cutlery, and plain white or **blue-checked napkins**. I always put a pitcher or glass of **flowers** on the table. In Spain, they could be wild peonies, daisies, tuberoses, or herbs, and in London, tulips, naricissi, or sunflowers, depending on the season. **Hunks of bread** are cut to pacify the very hungry before plates of grilled fish or a simple salad arrive.

Plain simple tableware and china lets the food speak for itself. Soup swirled with cream and a few chopped herbs looks magnificent in a shallow white bowl (see p.97); similarly, salad leaves, a batch of chocolate cupcakes, or even hash browns look more inviting on a white plate. For daily use and eating outside, I have **basic white** plates and bowls from a department store or catering shop because they are cheap to replace. For suppers when friends come around, or weekends when the whole family sits down and eats together, I use my favorite large, white, bone china plates and bowls in a classic shape (see p.96). If I'm lucky, I can usually stock up during the sales in one of the large department stores because they're expensive when new. **Storage** for my linen and tableware is in slim custom-made cabinets – the width of the largest dinner plate – which I designed versions of for both my London apartment and the house in Spain (see left and opposite).

making a table runner   A narrow table runner spread along **the length of the dining table** is a simple way to add texture and color. I first came across the idea in **Sweden** where freshly scrubbed tabletops have lengths of crisp linen – either plain or decorated with a plain stripe – placed along them. The runner shown below and opposite is made in a **straw-colored**, **loose-weave cotton** and is trimmed with a pink, cotton **velvet ribbon**. Experiment with different colors and textures but check that the fabrics are washable.

1 Measure the length of your table and add about 16 in to give the length of fabric required for your runner. A suitable width for a runner is 14 in, but bear in mind the table it is to go on – one-third of the table width is a good guide. The length of ribbon required is 2 x length plus 2 x width of the runner plus a bit extra for overlap. Overlock raw edges of the fabric, and hem about ½ in all the way around.

2 Pin a piece of ribbon to the length of the runner. Turn the beginning of the ribbon under to make a hem, and cut the other end, leaving a bit extra for the hem. Sew along the outer edge of the ribbon. Take one end of the loose ribbon and tuck under the end of the length just sewn to make a neat corner. Pin this piece along the width of the runner, remembering to turn the far end over, and sew along the outer edge.

3 Continue to attach the ribbon until all four sides are trimmed. Tuck the final end under the first piece of ribbon and fasten. Now sew all the way around on the inside edge of the ribbon to finish off. Press flat, and place symmetrically along the length of your table (see right).

4 Matching napkins can be made in exactly the same way. For each napkin you will need a square piece of fabric measuring 14 x 14 in, and 5 ft of ribbon. Hem the napkins and attach the ribbon as described in Steps 1–3.

Small spaces When small kitchens in an apartment or studio double as eating areas, it is essential to keep clutter to a minimum and to take advantage of space-saving ideas.

Put up **shelving** so it almost reaches ceiling height; space the shelves so that they are further apart at the top for bigger and less frequently used items, such as a turkey roasting pan or large meat dish. Have a lightweight folding aluminum stepladder to get to things high up. Stick to a **minimum number of essentials**; be strict and give gadgets or china you don't use to relatives, friends, or a charity shop. Likewise, **pare down your pantry** to necessities and don't hoard food you are unlikely to use. I couldn't live without black pepper, good sea salt, saffron, virgin olive oil, lemons, and garlic. My staples also include chickpeas for instant houmous; canned tomatoes – good in winter when tomatoes are out of season; cans of tuna – for pasta and salads; tomato puree; pesto; rice – for risottos and paellas; couscous; pasta; and dried mushroms for risottos and pasta sauces.

A countertop with either integral cupboards and drawers beneath or space for **freestanding furniture**, such as a dishwasher, is practical. If money doesn't stretch, a curtain can be hung to hide cleaning equipment and other kitchen paraphernalia beneath.

Buy a **narrow dishwasher** – 18 in rather than 24 in – and use for storage as well as washing. There are even smaller machines that sit on a worktop. If you don't need gadgets, a folding wooden drainage rack does a pretty good job at storing the evening's load of dishes (see pp.84 and 87). Miniature electric stoves with one or two rings and toaster ovens have kept alive generations of hungry students in studio apartments, and are great in cramped kitchens. A full-size fridge is a good way of storing food, and most have racks for holding bottles flat. Folding or stacking chairs are best in a small space. **Extra table space** can be created with a collapsible card table, that can be stored flat against the wall when not in use.

When the temperatures rise and the days lengthen, it's time to head outside for **al fresco eating**; each hour of the day has its own special possibilities in the open air.

It is a **hit to the senses** to drag oneself from sleep and feel the grass bristling with dew in the cool of morning, a sweatshirt tugged on over pajamas for warmth, a cup of hot, steaming coffee clasped in one hand and a thick slice of buttered toast with honey in the other. Everything is hot and cold all at once, with the sun just warming up. Have lunch outside under a shady awning in the midday heat with a cold beer coursing through your limbs and munching a crisp, thirst-quenching, leafy summery salad, served with the morning's fresh bread and slivers of salty, nutty cheese from a slab protected by a mesh net. At the end of the day, sit with **bare feet** nuzzling warm stone, and nibble almonds with a glass of fino sherry as long shadows creep in the setting sunlight,

and the air is **warm like velvet**. As night approaches, candles and nightlights flicker, and the heady fragrance of sweet jasmine wafts across from over the wall.

On the more practical aspects of **outdoor feasting**, use an old table that can be left outside in case of summer storms (see opposite). Better still, devise a collapsible eating surface from a piece of fiberboard, or even an old door or planks of pine stuck together, and rest it on a pair of folding trestles (see pp.104–105). Everything can be whisked away when the sky threatens. Spread a cloth in gingham, or white for special meals, and buy those useful clips that cafés use for anchoring down tablecloths when it's windy. **Candles and nightlights** can be contained in glass or metal lanterns so they don't blow out. For comfort, folding director's chairs are good for relaxing in. Take out extra seat cushions, and blankets or throws if there's a nip in the night air.

Lolling on the back seat of my dad's Ford Corsair, eating cold sausages, spreading crumbs, and not being scolded for it, was the highlight of the long monotonous preradio car journeys of my childhood. **Eating on the move**, eating out of special lunch boxes, baskets, or carefully wrapped greaseproof paper packages, rather than sitting up straight at the table and being correct with cutlery was bliss to a seven-year old. I still **embrace the informality** of picnicking, tearing bread apart with hands and licking fingers clean.

I keep anticipatory **pantry stocks** just in case. Slabs of chocolate, a few cans of soup, cans of sardines, tuna, and olives, plus jars of tapenade and of grilled peppers. Gear includes a **plastic wine cooler** in the freezer, **thermoses** in the cupboard, and a **backpack** with a permanent **corkscrew** in one pocket. Simple robust foods are best for **eating al fresco**, and the secret is not to take too many ingredients. What could be more comforting than a **picnic** of smoked salmon sandwiches and a bottle of ice cold bubbly (pour into small tumblers), especially when enduring the unpredictability of an English train journey.

In the winter, **slabs of fruitcake** and a thermos of hot chocolate warm everyone when taking a break on a brisk walk. On the beach, Italian sausages cooked up on a little barbecue to wedge between buns, with cups of hot soup, is the sort of nostalgic, sand in the sandwiches, **sand between the toes**, experience that is exhilarating for adults and kids alike — better than being shut in with the video and a sense of cabin fever on a dark winter's weekend afternoon.

For the beach in summer, I put a bottle of water in the freezer to throw in a cool bag with bagels or bread buns stuffed with slices of tomato, cucumber, tuna, mint, or basil. The buns are filling and tasty after a cooling dip in the sea, and drinking lots of water keeps dehydration at bay. Heat doesn't agree with sticky cake or chocolate so we stop for ice cream on the trek back home.

campfire cooking   For my children, making a campfire and cooking their own grub is a high point of vacations in Spain. In summer, the fire risk is too great so our cookouts are restricted to the cooler months. The children pick a spot and **make a circle of stones**, having cleared away any dry grass and leaves. Georgie is dispatched to **gather kindling**. Tom lays a few **dry logs** on the pile. Keeping a match alight is testing, but soon the blaze gets going. Once it has died down, we start cooking. **Sausages** are all-time favorites, wedged hot dog-style between bread (the adults cook field mushrooms in garlic and butter). **Plastic plates**, paper towels, and tongs are useful. For a wickedly sweet treat, we lay bananas in the embers to soften, then slit them open and fill them with butter and brown sugar.

Homespun Christmas   By simplifying Christmas, I keep my sanity intact. The rule is not to start too early or be too ambitious, and to **get key tasks done in advance**, such as stocking up on wine (we buy champagne, cava, lots of red and white riojas, plus some port and sweet dessert wine while we are in Spain); buying olives and ham (for cutting in slivers for tapas); making and freezing stock for soup; and creating homemade ice cream to eat with desserts.

Stir-up Sunday in mid-November is traditionally the latest date for making English **Christmas pudding** so that it matures in time. Everyone in the family has a stir with the wooden spoon to mix the wet ingredients: raisins, suet (buy it fresh from the butcher or use shortening), figs, walnuts, and all the other fruity additions. Dark brown sugar will give the pudding a richer color and flavor and if you want to deepen it further, you can increase the quantity of stout. It doesn't matter if you throw this treat together at the last minute – steaming it for an hour or so longer than the normal 4–5 hours will help to give it more texture and taste. I also try and make **mincemeat** a couple of weeks beforehand, adding pine nuts, walnuts, orange liqueur, and orange peel, and stuff it into little mince pies to give as presents, or freeze to eat over Christmas, served with *crème fraîche* flavored with vanilla sugar or dollops of cream.

Table ingredients include candles in clear glass jars or plain candlesticks (see opposite) and, for scent, bowls of hyacinths, amaryllis, or white narcissi, which shoot up quickly and flower for a couple of weeks. Other essentials to get us in the Christmas mood are mounds of clementines with their citrus-smelling peel walnuts to crack and eat with cheese and slabs of membrillo (quince paste), Christmas crackers, indoor fireworks, and chocolates wrapped in tissue paper.

I decorate my **Christmas tree** (see opposite) with iced cookies in heart and star shapes, rag balls made from strips of fabric remnants (see p.198) – bright green is this year's theme – and white candles in cheap brass holders that have been camouflaged with white paint (the candles are lit only when adults are present, and the tree is never left unguarded in case of fire). The black pot that the Christmas tree came in has been given a similar disguise with white latex paint. If the tree has roots and has been watered, it's worth planting in the yard for use again next Christmas.

Christmas food can be simple and quick to make, producing yummy treats for the festive table. **Potatoes and parsnips** are delicious roasted in olive oil. Peel, chop, and parboil before tossing in hot oil. Roast in a pan or place around the chicken or whatever meat is being served. Turn regularly to ensure even crisping. As an alternative to traditional Christmas goose or turkey, I like to serve **roast chicken** with the breast stuffed with lemon and herb butter, and trimmed with some sprigs of fresh rosemary. When the meat is finished, boil up the bones with bay leaves, onions, and carrots to make a delicious stock that can form the base of a seasonal chestnut soup or be frozen for later use. Serve a big platter or dish of **mixed seasonal vegetables**, such as leeks lightly fried in butter; Brussels sprouts with bacon, shallots, chestnuts, and pine nuts; and carrots sautéed with the juice and grated rind of an orange for an aromatic twist. Other vegetables that might feature on my menu include steamed broccoli or cabbage, and roasted onions, peppers, eggplants,

and whole garlic cloves for a more Mediterranean flavor. Cut out star shapes with pastry cutters to make pretty **mince pies**, and finish

with a dusting of confectioner's sugar. If you don't have time to make your own mincemeat, buy the luxury version from a gourmet food

shop and pep it up with extra brandy, a little grated orange or lemon peel, or a few chopped almonds and walnuts. I find that the earthy,

slightly tart flavor of **walnuts** is perfect with cheese, fruit, fresh dates, or membrillo (quince paste) at the end of a meal. Invest in a good

pair of nutcrackers. For the perfect finale to go with coffee, serve homemade chocolate **truffles**. Buy the best chocolate you can afford,

melt and combine with cream, butter, and rum or brandy, cool, and then roll teaspoonfuls in cocoa powder. Chill in the fridge and serve

on small white plates, or put in a little box lined with greaseproof or tissue paper, and wrap with a bright ribbon for an edible present.

Work   Create order in a home office or workspace to help your thoughts flow. Find an

area that is calm and peaceful, with adequate desk and shelf space, and invest in a comfortable chair

and a good work light. Thank goodness for vacuum cleaners, dishwashers, and washing machines,

that help to make light work of domestic chores. Cut back on chemical cleaners and detergents and

use more eco-friendly ideas such as hanging the washing out on an old-fashioned clothes rack, or

cleaning surfaces with beeswax polish or plain hot water.

Home work   Now that email, faxes, and computers enable us to work from home, **work space** and time vie with the needs of daily family life. Since giving up an office-based job as a design editor twelve years ago, to be **home-based** while the children are growing up, I have become expert at writing books on the kitchen table, jockeying for space with children's paintings, and working alongside the newspapers and clutter of everyday life. Despite the domestic pressures, I'd never go back to the hectic daily commute or office politics.

My work room (see p.127), shared also by a husband and, after school, children doing their homework on the computer, has a **long work table** and **lots of shelves** for books and papers. It's small but **light and airy** and **quiet** (essential when living in a largely open-plan space). With a folding metal bed set up, it doubles as a spare room when friends come to stay.

Artists, and other workers with small home-based businesses, need larger studios or office spaces. One way around this is to buy or rent a commercial property, such as a small shop with living quarters above it or a large **loft-style space** in an industrial building that can be **divided** into living and working areas. In the average home, the work space possibilities can be solved with a bit of **flexible thinking and planning**. A photographer friend of mine uses the ground floor of his house as a studio. It has a glass extension – housing the family's kitchen – overlooking the backyard. Another photographer I know works from an apartment, using her kitchen/dining/sitting room by day as a **studio** (see p.126), and in the evening the big work table is pulled out and used for eating dinner.

My **dress designer** sister-in-law lives in a small row house and has put aside the largest of the three bedrooms for her **work studio** (see pp.122–124), where she designs, makes, and fits her stylish creations. Most of the room is taken up by a **large cutting table**, which houses **tools, bolts of fabric,** and other **sewing paraphernalia** underneath.

Practical, space-saving ideas for home work spaces (see pp.126–127, and above) should stay within arm's reach. Old **baked bean cans**, painted in smart colors are good storage ideas for pens, pencils, thumbtacks, paper clips, and other office supplies. A **slab of raw cork** is a new take on the traditional bulletin board made from processed cork. Also, try covering a piece of particle board with felt for a new look (see the step-by-step instructions on pp.132–133). Push pins are best for securing things. **An angled desk lamp** will direct the light where it's needed and stop shadows from falling over work. Clip-on lights are useful when space is limited; most halogen bulbs are smaller, more efficient, and give off a bright white light compared to the standard yellow tungsten type. For work requiring realistic daylight, use special daylight bulbs, which give a near natural light; these can be bought at art or lighting shops. **Make a bulletin board** to run the length of a wall (the one above right is in plywood) and use it for cuttings, postcards, and inspirational

images. I have a bulletin board made of white painted plywood in my office and another in the hallway created from stick-on cork tiles.

The cork bulletin board measures 10 ft x 2 ft and is divided into sections for each child to tack up drawings, party invitations, and anything

else they wish to stick up. Make full use of wall space with **overhead shelving**. I have lengths of painted pine, measuring 8.5 in deep

and 1.5 in thick, that are wide enough to accommodate my magazines and box files. Shelving that is any deeper takes up unnecessary

visual space. I have a lightweight folding stepladder to get to less-used folders that are out of arm's reach. There are many stores selling

off inexpensive **office filing equipment** now that paper files are redundant in computerized companies. I bought two rather ugly gray

metal ones that I revamped in white eggshell paint, and they now look fresh and modern. Go to a good old-fashioned stationery store and

buy some **plain brown paper envelopes** in which you can store fabric samples, papers, photos, and other things that need to be filed.

Whatever type or size of space you set aside to work in, even if it's just a curtained-off alcove containing a desk with a phone and fax, it's important to make the area a **comfortable** and **pleasing environment** (see opposite).

Ideally, a work surface should be 5 ft long x 2.5 ft deep. If it is any deeper, things lurking at the back of the table won't be within easy reach. When considering **desk height**, make sure it is high enough so you **don't slouch** over it. There should be enough clearance underneath the desk for your legs when the chair is pulled up close.

The more time you spend sitting, the more adjustable the chair should be. A chair with adjustable height can be used by all the family. Your **feet** should be **flat on the floor** so that there is no pressure from the chair on the back of your knees. Also, make sure that the chair has adequate back support to avoid back problems in the future.

Choose your **workspace** to let in as much **natural daylight** as possible. Internal windows, glazed or open, between rooms can help spread the available light. However, working in bright sunlight is hard on the eyes and devices such as opaque white blinds can remove the glare.

The correct **temperature** (ideally between 65°F and 75°F) is essential for keeping the thought processes working. Trying to work in hot stuffy conditions is as bad as shivering in a cold drafty room. In summer, open windows for ventilation, and in winter, dress in warmer clothes to avoid having to turn the central heating up too far.

A **healthy body** helps to create a **stimulated mind** so avoid coffee and **drink plenty of water** to stop dehydration at your desk. When chained to a computer screen for long hours, it's sensible to take a break and go for a walk or a swim. The fresh air and exercise will boost ideas. When energy levels run low, eat healthy snacks such as dried fruits and nuts, rather than reaching for the potato chips and chocolate bars. Bring nature into your work space with a vase of flowers and make the place a little more sensual by burning a scented candle.

Making a bulletin board   A felt-covered bulletin board is a **colorful and inexpensive** way to brighten up a home office. Felt is cheap and available in a **stunning array of colors** – try fuchsia pink, lavender, apple green, white, or the rich sky-blue shown below and opposite. Re-cover an existing cork bulletin board or buy particle board from specialized home improvement stores. Use your bulletin board for **important dates** and telephone numbers, or make it more artistic with **favorite postcards** and children's drawings.

  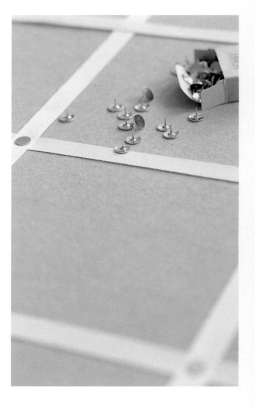

1 Assemble the materials: 23 in x 31 in board; 27 in x 35 in felt; 20 ft cotton ribbon; scissors; staple gun; thumbtacks; and string. Lay the board on the felt and cut around it to leave a 2 in edge. Fold the felt around the board and staple, leaving the 2 in edge behind the board.

2 Make sure the felt is pulled tight – not so tight that it stretches, but so that there are no creases or wrinkles. Position the lengths of cotton ribbon every 8 in in a checkerboard pattern.

3 Pin the cotton ribbons where they cross with the thumbtacks or any type of pin, such as map pins. Pull the ribbons taut as you secure each one. You could use pins of matching colors or a variety of colors to make a pattern.

4 Turn the board over and attach the ends of the ribbon to the back using the staple gun. To attach a hanging cord, cut a length of string the same width as the board and tie a knot at each end. Measure 10 in from the top of the board and attach the string across it using the staple gun. You may need a couple of staples at each end for added strength. Hang your board on a wall or leave it freestanding.

It is tremendously useful to have a **utilitarian washing area** for heavy-duty jobs such as removing mud from dirty boots, cleaning paintbrushes, and descaling fish. Plastic cleaning **bowls** in bright colors and **metal buckets** are also useful for handwashing delicate sweaters, or scrubbing a bag of mussels for supper. One of the most practical shapes for a sink is the freestanding stone type with a built-in sloping ridged surface for scrubbing clothes on; you see these in the open courtyard wash areas in southern Spain and Portugal. Shallow stone sinks, or double **butler's sinks,** can be bought new or picked up quite cheaply in reclamation yards and can be used in conjunction with either modern or old faucets. I am particularly fond of the simple brass faucets that can be attached to the wall with their pipes exposed. Walls of **tongue -and-grooved** planks look basic and utilitarian in a washing area, and if painted with a durable eggshell finish will be quite waterproof. Floor surfaces should be equally durable and nonslip, with linoleum, rubber, wood, or stone being good choices.

Recycling ideas   Think before you throw anything away. Be less wasteful around the house and recycle everything from vegetable peelings to jam jars and help take the pressure off the environment. **Recycle packaging** – make the most of reusable items, such as envelopes, that can be used again and again; I particularly like to keep those bulky padded bags for sending breakables since they are rather expensive to buy new. Cover old postmarks and addresses with an adhesive label or a piece of plain paper. This is also a good way to keep down costs if you're running an office from home. **Egg cartons** made out of recycled cardboard can be saved and returned to the store for further use or collected with your other recycled paper (or they can be used by children for cutting into creative shapes). Always try to avoid unnecessary packaging – especially goods like shrink-wrapped individual portions – and buy as many loose items as you can. Create **compost buckets** – save organic matter from kitchen tasks to put on a compost heap; this will make a nourishing

compost that will enrich the soil in the organic vegetable garden. Vegetable peelings, eggshells, bone, coffee grounds, and small pieces of cardboard are all good composters. **Build a compost heap** in the corner of the yard (see p.336). Surround the compost with wire or a wooden frame with holes for ventilation. Turn the compost regularly. **Sort recyclable materials** into different boxes and bins: glass, paper, metal (aluminum cans are recyclable), organic matter, and plastic soda bottles (reused to make fleece clothing) can all be recycled. Also, put old clothes into boxes and garbage bags to donate to a charitable organization. **Save glass jars and wide-necked bottles** and reuse them for homemade jams, chutneys, and other preserves. Always clean out thoroughly before use and sterilize with boiling water or in a hot oven and seal carefully. Also, keep plastic receptacles, such as fresh cream and soup containers, that can be used for all sorts of different things from freezing homemade soups and other foods, to holding sewing materials and pens and pencils.

ecologically friendly Look for ecologically sound products and more **natural** ways to keep the home clean.

A little bit of dirt never did anybody any harm; in fact, some research suggests that children brought up in squeaky clean surroundings don't build up as much immunity against certain illnesses as their peers who live in homes that aren't kept clinically pristine. However, in our fussy, overprotected society we seem to be obsessed by cleanliness and germs, and so manufacturers cater to the popular demand for whiter-than-white whites or sparkly clean floors with chemical cleaning products that, while effective, have a high cost – that of damaging the environment.

For example, chlorinated bleaches and disinfectants certainly do their stuff, but they also disrupt the balance of microorganisms in septic tanks and sewers. Equally damaging to the water supply are the enzymes, bleaches, whiteners, and abrasives contained in laundry detergent.

It's really important, therefore, to use products that are **phosphate-free** and chlorine-free; these are available in the growing ranges in organic shops and some forward-thinking supermarkets. There are also a number of more benign and natural ways to keep things clean. To **handwash the green way**, use bar soap and sodium carbonate dissolved in hot water instead of detergent; and add a tablespoon of white vinegar to the rinse water to prevent soap scum.

And if you want to **get rid of the limescale stain** in the bathroom, don't use one of those nasty chemical cleaners with bleach and caustic agents; instead try a strong solution of **vinegar** to remove it. Equally basic and natural is **beeswax** – unequivocally the best thing for **polishing** wood – rather than something that comes out of an aerosol can that calls itself furniture polish and is artificially perfumed and full of solvents and synthetic silicones.

The **control** of household **pests**, such as flies, ants, bugs, and mice, is another area where heavy-duty insecticides and rodent killers not only have unpleasant effects on the environment but can also cause serious damage to humans and pets. Insect sprays are particularly unpleasant, and their chemical residues can be left on food and the skin. Eco-friendly ways to deal with pests include fly swatters, electronic bug zappers, citronella candles to keep away mosquitos, jars containing a tempting morsel and a makeshift ramp to lure cockroaches, and gruesome, but instantly effective, old-fashioned mousetraps. Remember, too, that adhering to **basic hygiene** rules, such as covering food and cleaning away food scraps, will deter many household predators.

Hanging out the wash to flap on the line is a wonderfully satisfying job, especially on a bright and **breezy** day. If it has been raining, I wipe the line before pinning on the clothes; I use either **plain wooden** or brightly colored plastic clothespins from the local hardware store. Whites – sheets, towels, underwear, and T-shirts – are **naturally whitened** and freshened by the effects of the sun. Remember to turn jeans and brightly colored clothes inside out to prevent fading (even though I like the worn look of some of my favorite T-shirts). The summer sunshine is more efficient than any electric clothes dryer and the whole wash is crisp and warm within a couple of hours. In **wintertime**, when there are long bouts of heavy rain, I often have to resort to drying things in front of the **fire**.

Flowers in brilliant colors, which grow from seeds or bulbs with little fuss, are enormously gratifying for any gardener. One small packet of **nasturtium** seeds yields an amazing show of flowers. Plant the knobby seeds straight into the ground, and remove dead blooms regularly for repeat flowering. Nasturtiums can be grown up wigwams made of sticks, or allowed to freefall from containers. They look pretty in a vase, and the flowers and peppery leaves can be added to salads. Try Tom Thumb, a dwarf variety (height 12 in) in bright oranges, yellows, and reds, or Tall Mixed, a rapid climber (height 6 ft). **Tulips** look good planted randomly in clumps. Flowerpots with five or six blue or white parrot tulips look great in the garden, or on a window ledge or balcony. Plant bulbs in a well-drained, sunny position sheltered from cold winds. If bulbs are left in the soil, as an alternative to lifting and replanting the following year, add bonemeal to help further flowering. The trailing character of **convolvulus** is useful for disguising water tanks, sheds, or fences. Although each voluptuous,

trumpet-shaped flower lasts only a day, the various shades of pink, purple, and blue come in perennial as well as annual varieties. Try Heavenly Blue with sky-blue flowers (height 10–13 ft). **Sunflowers** naturally turn their yellow heads to the sun. They can be grown straight from seeds planted in the ground, or potted singly and transplanted. Cut sunflowers in big pitchers make good table decorations. Large-headed varieties, such as Russian Mammoth (height 8 ft) are the most dramatic; plant in a row in front of a fence. Or try Big Smile, a dwarf variety (height 16 in), which is good for pots. The round fluffy heads of **allium** provide good architectural shapes for the garden. Members of the onion family, they like sun and well-drained soil. In pinks, purples, blues, and whites, they grow between 18 in and 39 in high. Try Caerulum, a small hyacinth-blue variety (height 24 in), or Globemaster, which sways on wiry stems at head height. **Narcissi** come in many varieties. I plant dwarf yellow tête-à-tête in pots and buy a forced white variety that flowers indoors in time for Christmas.

I find it deeply satisfying to **garden**, whether it's nurturing a few pots of herbs on the windowsill in my London apartment, or digging up potatoes, pruning the roses, or planting bulbs in my garden in Spain. Trying to tame nature and be close to it is an innate part of our makeup, originating from a basic necessity to grow food for sustenance. In an increasingly frenetic and technological existence, having a vegetable plot or garden to tend is literally a **grounding experience**, giving us the opportunity to bring a little more order into a world that is largely out of our control. It allows us to experience the simple **pleasures** of being outside in the **open air**, cooking on a hibachi or barbecue, or reading a book under a **scented**, climbing plant on a balmy evening.

You don't even need much space: some of the most sensual, **intimate**, and personal gardens that I have come across are little more than cultivated postage stamps. An example is transatlantic gardening pal Dean Riddle's **vegetable and flower plot**, which is a magical retreat from New York City in the Catskill Mountains; it is surrounded by **stick fencing** and planted with a patchwork of ornamental cabbages, herbs, **marigolds**, and other everyday plants.

Neither do you have to be based in the country to enjoy the peace and tranquility of a room outside, as in the secret leafy **urban oasis** (pp.150–151) where owner and artist Marianna Kennedy has painted her tiny, shady backyard in light-reflecting white, furnished it with textured **weathered York stone** flagstones and a nicely battered wooden garden table, and filled it with pretty, **low-maintenance** lilies, **nasturtiums**, and luxuriant, shade-loving **hostas**. This is a lush, still, **calm place** that belies its location just a few feet from the busy city street outside.

Making the most of even the tiniest **roof space** (see opposite) with sensible wooden decking and simple twig fencing for privacy and to support climbers, such as roses and honeysuckle, allows the busy owners of a food shop to escape from business and enjoy a quick rest in the sun on the roof.

renovate junk chairs from a secondhand store or flea market, and paint in a garden green eggshell finish to use around the table for outside feasts. I found four of the same chairs (see below and opposite) in a London junk shop, but it's not essential to have matching shapes. In fact, mismatched simple chairs painted in a unifying color will look just as good and add a rustic touch. When the chairs are not being used outside, they can provide extra seating for parties and at other times when there are extra mouths to feed.

1 You will need newspaper to protect the floor, sandpaper of assorted grades, a small can of wood primer, and a can of eggshell paint in the color of your choice. You will also need a ¾ –1½ in paintbrush, and, if your primer or paint is oil based, some paint thinner or turpentine substitute to clean your brush. If you prefer, however, you can use a water-based eggshell and primer.

2 Sand down the chair to get rid of any loose flakes of old paint or varnish; start with a medium grade of sandpaper and finish with a fine grade. Wrapping the sandpaper around a block of wood will make it easier to apply pressure. Always try to sand along the grain of the wood and not across it. Once the chair has been sanded you will need to give it a good wipe to remove all the dust before applying the primer.

3 Apply a coat of the primer using plenty on the brush, since it should not be spread too thinly. Allow the chair to dry if you have removed dust with a damp cloth. Try to coat the chair as evenly as possible, even though it will end up looking streaky. Always read the instructions on the can and allow the primer to dry for the correct amount of time.

4 Apply the first coat of paint when the
primer is dry. Try to follow the lines of the chair
with your brush strokes. You may need to apply
another coat once the first one has dried,
depending on how even the finish is. Eggshell
paint gives a durable matte/satin finish (see right).

Gardening in pots is a simple and effective way of bringing natural color and scent to tiny patios and other small spaces where having flower beds is not possible or desirable. Worn and weathered **terra-cotta flowerpots**, old ceramic kitchen sinks, wooden tubs, **galvanized buckets**, old tin cans, even old paint cans can all be put to use, and a surprising number of plants and flowers will flourish in such limited spaces provided they are fed and watered well. Create a miniature garden in pots on a windowsill or balcony; the **window garden** (see opposite) is a typical sight in the white villages of Andalucia, Spain and is an idea that can be transplanted anywhere. A traditional wooden **window box** always looks good, whether planted with mixed herbs for the kitchen, with **bulbs** such as tulips, hyacinths, and narcissi, with a hedge of purple-headed **lavender**, or with bedding plants such as pinks, marigolds, and pretty, scented, **old-fashioned geraniums**.

Pots can be massed together and planted with a variety of annuals or bedding plants for color in a back garden, or they can be arranged to look more **formal**, for example, a pair of **leggy bay trees** or **box standards** in metal pots placed on either side of a doorway. Small orange or lemon trees grown in big terra-cotta pots are another favorite in my garden in Spain, where they can flower and fruit in sheltered spots without falling prey to frost. A row of containers holding the same plant can look dramatic. I tried it with twelve giant blue **agapanthus** that I planted in three wide, **shallow, terra-cotta** bowls on the edge of the sunny patio at my Spanish home. They flowered for months, growing to about 5 ft. In my previous house in England, I achieved an equally successful visual effect using foxgloves and delphiniums planted in deep, terra-cotta pots on the roof terrace. On a smaller scale, a shallow, **stone sink** is a good container for miniature plants such as camomile, thyme, and small succulents.

The essential requirements for successful container gardening are **good drainage**, the right type of soil, and regular watering and feeding. Ensure that containers have a central drainage hole that is covered with a few stones before being filled with soil (see pp.160–161). For **a well-balanced potting medium**, use soil that is light, friable, and nourishing. You can mix heavy soil with sharp river sand to lighten it, and supplement light soil with rich loam and granulated peat to help retain moisture. With regular watering and additional nourishment in the form of compost, bonemeal, and other organic plant foods, most potted plants, including climbers such as clematis, passionflower, honeysuckle, and some roses, will remain healthy in the same soil for years.

My **indispensable garden kit** starts with a pair of **well-worn boots** with a special thermal lining that are parked next to the front door. In **winter**, I also pull on **extra-thick socks**, and an old waterproof coat for garden tasks. In **summer**, there's no need to dress quite so defensively, but a large wide-brimmed **straw hat**, a long-sleeved T-shirt, and suncream (SPF 40) for the face are sensible measures against burning, especially in the intense Andalucian sun. Whatever the time of year, I always make sure that there is a pair of really **tough gardening gloves** – thick rubber or tough cotton – lying around the place. I don't mind getting my hands dirty but unprotected they are prone to painful thorn pricks, allergic rashes from the leaves or sap of some plants, or insect bites received when rummaging around in the bushy undergrowth.

I'd be lost without a pair of **pruning shears** – for pruning, trimming, and cutting flowers and stems for decoration in the house. I keep these in a little **Sussex trug** – a functional wooden carrier used by many generations of English gardeners – along with a **trowel** (invaluable for digging and planting), a **little fork**, **string**, and **wire** for supporting and training plants, and a package of bonemeal, which is used as nourishment for the plants. I have two or three **watering cans**, of which a small, galvanized metal one with a short spout is the easiest to handle. I use a **hose** for the heavier watering jobs. Stored under the lean-to shed, along with the wood pile, are heftier tools including a couple of good **stiff brooms** for sweeping up dust, leaves, and other debris, and a **pitchfork**, **shovel**, and **wheelbarrow** for **weeding**, **digging**, and **planting** down at the vegetable patch.

In the **basement** of my Spanish house, along with the drying hams and jars of homemade jam, are numerous paper bags of **old bulbs and seeds** saved from previous years. I am wild for the mouthwateringly sweet, local **Spanish tomatoes**, and since they're not available commercially I **dry the seeds** and keep them in foil in an airtight plastic box for sowing the following year. There are also stacks of old, worn, hand-thrown, **terra-cotta flowerpots** for bulbs, which were brought in the moving van from England.

plant bulbs to create brilliant color for pots and window boxes. Once a year, I make a pre-breakfast visit to the local Sunday morning flower market to buy **bulging bags of bulbs** – feathery white parrot tulips, scented white hyacinths, deep blue grape hyacinths, and delicate, miniature, yellow tête-à-tête narcissi. I plant these in old, weathered flowerpots rescued from the run-down potting sheds of country estates. Line the pot with **terra-cotta shards** or stones to help drainage. Fill half the pot with a **loam-based compost**. Sit the bulbs on a **layer of fine grit or sand** to improve drainage. **Evenly space about six bulbs** per 10 in pot. **Cover with compost** about two to three times the height of the bulbs and then water. Continue to water sparingly to keep the bulb fibers moist.

Dig a vegetable patch in the garden for the simple and earthy delights of lifting **sweet**, **succulent carrots** to chop up and make into a crisp salad, or **new potatoes** that taste divine when **boiled with mint** and smothered with melting butter. If you don't have a garden, grow garlands of tiny tomatoes in growbags of organic compost in any available outside space, or plant a box outside the kitchen window with **herbs** – tarragon, basil, thyme, and chives – for a permanent herb garden within arm's reach. **Urban gardeners** can feed their families with **fresh organic produce** by applying for a little growing plot in one of the communal vegetable gardens found in towns and cities or by being inventive with any outside space, even a tiny window ledge. In the suburbs and countryside, however, there's much more scope for creating vegetable patches in the backyard.

A good example of organic vegetable gardening in **urban London** is John Matheson's vegetable and flower patch (see pp.164–165). This oasis is tucked away among a patchwork of communal gardens on a windblown hill; wedged between high-voltage towers, scrapyards, and factories, the plot boasts an unexpected view of a sliver of a tributary of the Thames River, where herons come to feed and frilly cow parsley grows head high in the summer. Only those with highly detailed instructions and a key are able to gain access to this little **inner city haven**, where retired pub owners and railroad employees tend their dahlias, feed the foxes, and offer gardening advice alongside families with young children who spend the weekends weeding, planting, watering, **manuring**, and harvesting homegrown produce. Like all good organic gardeners, John Matheson works with nature, not against it, and so in the absence of harmful insecticides, his garden is **busy with wildlife** – bees, hoverflies, butterflies, scuttling beetles, and thrushes that tap snails out of their shells.

A thick **rosemary hedge** divides flowers off from vegetables; the flower garden is planted with **alliums**, **euphorbias**, and **lavender**, all good for attracting pest-eating insects. There is also a little **toolshed** for stowing garden gear and deckchairs, which are brought out for rest and relaxation. In late spring the vegetable garden bears the young leafy tips of **beets**, **rutabagas**, and **parsnips**. There are some good-looking shallots, climbing **white beans** that are starting to curl around the wigwam made of peasticks, and flowering **broad beans**, which will start to produce their crop in a few weeks' time. Throughout the growing season, Matheson's plot also yields an impressive six types of potato, three types of onion, three types of pumpkin, two types of French bean, broccoli, corn, arugula, mizuna, lettuce, and zuchinnis. One fall day, John knocked on my door carrying a heap of tender **Jerusalem artichokes** fresh from the patch, which I chopped up and fried with butter to form the basis of a delicious, velvety, winter soup – this earthy offering from so local a source couldn't have been more appreciated.

Homegrown produce is fresher than anything you can buy, and many herbs and vegetables are easy to grow. You don't need much room: reserve a small patch in the garden for herbs, or in a backyard clear a patch to grow zuchinnis, or on a balcony, plant tomatoes in pots. **Lettuces** (see opposite), for vitamin-packed salads through the year, will even grow on a sunny windowsill. **Outside**, sow the seeds thinly in shallow troughs 12 in apart, in the shade of another crop, such as peas, if possible. Water well for a good crop.

Young crops from an urban garden raised in **rows from seeds** under a **glass cloche** (from top: beets, spring onion, early little gem lettuce, leek, early carrots, mature little gem lettuce, early carrots, and broccoli rabe). Forced under a terra-cotta cloche, **rhubarb** is delicious in desserts and fruit crumbles, but remember that the leaves are poisonous. A single package of seeds can give you two basketfuls of **climbing beans** that will grow in any good garden soil. Dig a trench before planting and fill with organic matter – my grandmother has used seaweed for decades. Grow in a double line supported by stakes or a wigwam made out of sticks.

Rest   We live such a stressed existence that it's important to rest and relax. On long hot summer days flop under shady trees, doze, or read a book. Inside, use light-reflecting whites to create a light and airy living room. Furnish with a well-upholstered sofa, the largest you can afford, and soft feather cushions. In winter, build a blazing log fire, light candles, and keep drafts at bay with woolly throws in checks and stripes.

Bundled up in layers to protect winter-chapped skin, I look forward to summer days in the fresh air on a beach or relaxing under the dappled shade of a tree in the park. I am all in favor of the **siesta** – still a feature of life in the hot Andalusian summer, where between the hours of 2 and 5 every afternoon, very little human or animal life stirs, the sheer ferocity of the heat sending everybody to the nearest horizontal surface. Daily, during our vacations at the *finca*, I drift into afternoon sleep in the cool of a shuttered room, lulled by the bees humming in the eucalyptus tree and the smell of hot, dry grass outside.

Practical, **hardworking fabrics** are vital for making cool furnishings on which to chill out. Tough **cotton** is useful for a **shady**, **collapsible canopy**, to be used either on the beach (see pp.170–171) or at the park. Constructed on the tent principle – with a cover, poles, nylon guy ropes, and wooden tent pegs – the canopy can be folded up and carried under the arm or in a lightweight basket or bag.

Also easy to make are **cotton-covered mattresses**, stuffed with foam (which dries more easily than feathers) to lie on or sit on by a swimming pool or on a patio (see pp.172–173). Use bright stripes or plain colors in green, orange, or hot pink and make **removable covers** for the mattresses in different sizes suitable for adults and children.

One of my most exciting recent fabric discoveries is **seagreen**, **heavy**, **waterproof canvas**, the kind used for old-fashioned tents; this has been made into **awnings** for the front and back of my house in Spain (see opposite). The fabric is thick, and the amounts required are bulky to work with on a normal sewing machine, so it is best to have a curtain or blind specialist make your awnings. For easy removal when it starts to rain, mine were constructed with Velcro fastenings. Also, note that it's wise to **choose dark colors for shade**; I once made the mistake of making awnings in thin, pale creamy fabric which let the sun through and caused bare skin beneath to burn.

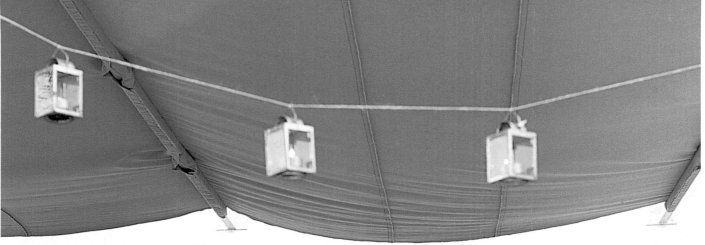

Blues, greens, and whites are cool, relaxing colors for summer rooms inside and outside. With little spare time, and practicality at the top of my list of priorities, I used ordinary exterior white paint for our patios in Spain (see pp.172–173 and 175), but purists are likely to choose more traditional paints. For example, our friends Nick and Hermione Tudor used traditional limewash at their seaside retreat in Southern Portugal (see opposite). Rustling up a supply of limewash is time-consuming, but worth it for the matte, chalky texture that you can't achieve with other types of paint.

Limewash – or *cal* – is still made in the traditional way in the village where the Tudors live, by boiling marble chips and pig fat in outside ovens for 24 hours; this technique dates back to Roman times. After being cooled for 24 hours, the calcified chips are then added to water and mixed to give the thin white liquid typical of old-fashioned limewash. The chips are caustic and, therefore, they should be handled carefully and always be stored in metal containers.

Stirring a very small amount of *azul-oscuro* (a blue pigment) into a metal bucketful of wash, Nick and Hermione mix up varying shades of blue from a very pale lavender for the walls, to darker shades for door frames, benches, and baseboards. If the rain has damaged the surfaces in winter, the Tudors revamp the house with fresh coats of limewash at the beginning of the summer.

Other elements to make an outside space textural and sensual include rough terra-cotta or ceramic tiles underfoot and light, floaty fabrics, such as muslin, hung in a doorway to draw in a cooling breeze. Plants are key ingredients in my view: climbing jasmine grows in most conditions, and the white flowers release their headiest scent in the night air; passionflower is a fast grower, and, although unscented, produces extraordinary flowers; and architectural agapanthus – tall green stems carrying white or blue flowers – is my favorite summer bloom. Finally, candles burning in lanterns on the table or strung on a wire are best for natural lighting.

making a curtain   A basic curtain with looped headings is simple to make in any kind of fabric – lightweight muslin, heavier canvas, or wool. The curtain width should be 1.25–1.5 times the width of the window, depending on how full you want it to be. Striped patterns (see below and right) look fresh and work well in bedrooms and living rooms. This curtain design also looks good across alcoves used for clothes storage. Hang the curtain on a wooden pole included in a kit or made out of doweling from a hardware store.

1 Cut fabric to required length, allowing an extra 6–8 in for top and bottom hems. Measure and cut the curtain to the required width, allowing about 1 in for side hems. If your windows are very wide you may need to join two widths (take care to match pattern repeats). Overlock or zigzag stitch the raw edges. Cut a strip of iron-on interlining, about 2–4 in wide and as long as the curtain width. Iron the strip onto the back of the top edge of the curtain.

2 To make the tabs, cut strips twice the width and length that you require the finished tabs to be. Our finished tabs measured 1½ x 7 in, so we cut strips that were 3 x 14 in. Fold each one in half lengthwise with the right sides facing and sew the long edges together. Turn each one inside out and press flat so that the seam is in the center at the back. Now fold to form a loop, making sure that the seam is on the inside, and stitch the two ends together.

3 Position the tabs at regular intervals along the top edge of the curtain on the right side, with the edge of the tab level with the edge of the curtain. Pin and then sew along about a ⅜ in from the edge, fixing the tabs into position.

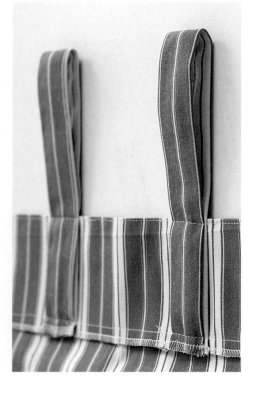

4 Turn a hem at the top edge the depth of the interlining and press flat. Now sew along the fold, fixing the tabs into position. At either end of the curtain sew down the depth of the hem. Hang the curtain and pin up the bottom hem to make sure the length is correct. Remove the curtain, sew the pinned hem, and press. The curtain is now ready for hanging (see right).

Keeping **cool** inside in summer isn't easy when it's hot and sticky outside and there's barely a breath of wind in the air. It helps to have **light-colored natural cotton or linen fabrics** which can be whisked off sofas and chairs and given a wash to keep them fresh and crisp. Remember that strong sunlight fades fabrics ruthlessly; I have found that cushions brought to Spain from England have become much paler than their original color, so it might be worth having one set of **pale slipcovers** for summer and another set in brighter colors for winter. Invest in a portable electric fan — they can be enormously effective. When the temperatures begin to soar, it's wise to **close the shutters** during the day and open them as night falls; in this way, the strong heat of the day is kept at bay. Our sitting room in Spain (see opposite) also has a **lofty ceiling**, which helps to keep it cool in summer. In winter, the underfloor heating is kept turned on to maintain a comfortable temperature.

Natural textures in **pale colors** accentuate a sense of **light and spaciousness**. The color of flooring is a particularly important factor: choosing a dark oak or a highly varnished finish doesn't give the same sense of space as a paler surface, such as the **solid natural oak** strip flooring (see opposite) that has been treated with an environmentally friendly matte sealant. Cream and oatmeal-colored throws, blankets, or cushions in linen or wool add **sensual layering** to chairs and sofas, which I like to cover in white cotton or linen covers (see left, and p.184). **Plain white cotton roller blinds** are an economical, simple, and stylish window dressing, and unless you're expert at hanging them, it's far cheaper in terms of time and hassle to let the supplier install them. White blinds can also help to **diffuse the light** on a particularly bright day (see left).

one chair, four looks

For centuries, loose slipcovers have been used to protect upholstery. In the **pure style** home, unfitted covers are the key to revamping old chairs and updating upholstery. My preference is for white covers – I choose robust, machine-washable textures to cope with the frequent washing. An old armchair (opposite and below) has been dressed in four easy-to-make covers for different effects. To make at home, allow about 13 ft of preshrunk fabric per chair; if necessary, add 5–10 percent for shrinkage.

A pretty, vintage-style floral cotton cover with side pleats and ties creates colorful detail in simple white decorating schemes – good for bedrooms and living rooms. Striped cotton ticking with side pleats and stitched bands is stylish and classic, and suits both traditional and modern interiors. A soft green cotton cover has pleated sides and button detailing. Green is calming and looks good with pink details, such as flowers or cushions – try it in a sunroom or bedroom. A plain white cotton cover with a side zipper is suitable for any room in the Pure Style home. With white or pale colors, make sure the material is thick enough to conceal darker upholstery beneath.

building a fire   For a glowing retreat on damp, blustery days at my Spanish *finca*, I make a fire first thing in the morning that burns all day. **Logs of encina-scrub oak and chestnut** are kept under cover and we collect kindling that has fallen from the cork trees. Combustible pine cones are gathered from nearby trees and bundled into sacks. I clean out the grate and scatter the nutritious ashes around the young fruit trees in the garden. I lay two largish logs 20 in apart and parallel to the sides of the grate with four or five **balls of newspaper**, three or four **pine cones**, and a **bundle of kindling** in between. On top of this pile I lay five or six logs wigwam style. If the wood is dry, a lit match produces **roaring flames** that catch the logs to produce a warm and comforting focus to the house.

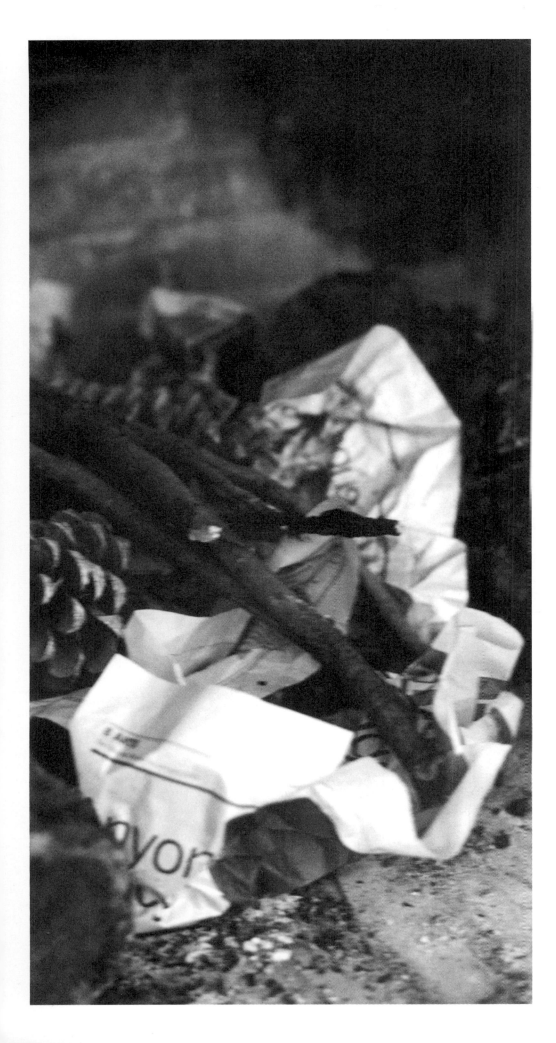

Even on the most foul wind- and rain-swept day, a **blazing log fire** warms and revives flagging spirits. We crowd around our fire (see opposite) to dry off damp feet, **roast chestnuts**, and **toast marshmallows**. In cities with smokeless zones, for example London since the Clean Air Act of 1955, you must burn a **smokeless fuel**, such as **anthracite**. Alternatively, although they can't recreate the heat and energy of a real fire, flame-effect gas fires are worth considering, and modern types with no grate or obvious gas source are more stylish-looking than the kitsch log-effect fires from the 1970s. Multifuel **cast iron** and **aluminum stoves** in plain shapes for burning wood briquettes, logs, and smokeless fuels, or gas versions if you don't have a chimney, are easy to maintain and a good substitute for a real fire.

Being someone who much prefers bare floors with **rugs and mats** to the more insulating qualities of deep pile wall-to-wall carpeting, it has been exciting to experience the warming benefits of **underfloor (or radiant) heating**, which we have installed in our house in Spain. Laid underneath the terra-cotta floor, the heating system circulates hot water through a series of plastic pipes to create an even temperature over the whole surface of the floor. It produces a very pleasant sensation, which enables us to walk over the tiles with bare feet. In our previous home, we used the same underfloor heating system below the wooden floorboards, but it wasn't nearly as effective because gaps beneath the boards and a poorly insulated house led to heat loss and barely warm floors.

Another comfort factor for surviving long winter nights **curled up on the sofa with a book** is a collection of plump feather-filled cushions and woolly rugs to snuggle into when it's really chilly (see pp.190-191). **Soft pools of light** from table lamps are more soothing and easier on the eye than harsh overhead lighting. Dark nights are good times for sticking all those photos from last year's summer vacation into an album, or listening to music, or watching the videos that you didn't have time for when the days were longer.

Bring nature and its tactile, organic qualities into the home with collections of shells picked up on beach-combing expeditions. Pebbles have wonderful organic shapes, as beautiful to look at, if not more so, than many works of art (see opposite). We have a collection of old plant specimen jars from a botanical garden that we bought from a local antique dealer; the children fill these up with their nature finds: pieces of cork, acorns, lichen, seeds, shiny black stag beetles, a silvery snake skin, a dragonfly for an unusual display.

Stick shells with extra-strong adhesive glue into shadow-box frames and mount on the walls, or leave flat, museum style, to look at on a table. Razor shells also look good displayed in this way. Old botanical specimen jars filled with nature finds can be grouped together for an eye-catching and educational exhibit. Discarded birds' nests are simple, twiggy sculptures that provide an original and natural arrangement when stacked in a simple white bowl.

Inspiring children to choose **creative play** activities, such as painting, reading a book, doing a puzzle, or play acting can be a battle, especially with older children who have to be steered away from television and computer games. It really pays to be **organized** and to have a good stock of **materials** immediately at hand. I save fabric cuttings for collages and dollhouse furnishings; cardboard boxes for numerous imaginary homes; and I ensure that there is a good supply of **plain white paper**, colored tissue paper, and bottles of poster paints. A small chest of drawers on a shelf in the kitchen is completely stuffed with pens, **crayons**, **glue**, **scissors**, pencil sharpeners, erasers, and other equipment. Projects with edible incentives, such as chocolate prizes, are popular; you could try an **art competition** with subjects such as vegetables or flowers from the garden (see left and opposite), or the family cat or dog. Asking children to make things for a special occasion is a good way of attracting interest, for example **baking a birthday cake**, making tissue-paper penants for a party (see pp.200–201), or preparing cookies, fruit tarts, and tree decorations at Christmas (see pp.216–217).

Painting eggs   for the Easter breakfast table is a tradition my children look forward to each year. **Pierce a small hole with a pin** at either end of an egg, making one hole slightly larger than the other (this is tricky and requires a steady adult hand). Holding the egg over a bowl, **Gracie blows through the smaller hole** so the yolk and white slip out of the other end (use later for an omelette or scrambled eggs). Gently rinse the empty shell in water and leave to dry. With **poster paints** or **watercolors, paint a design** on each egg – **spots and stripes in bright pinks, blues, and greens** are good combinations (see pp.204–205). To dry the paint, put the eggs in a low oven. When dry, pile them into a **basket with straw**, tiny **foil-wrapped chocolate eggs**, and chicks for **Easter Sunday**.

Making space for children to **paint and play** doesn't mean you need a separate playroom. Even though we were lucky to have a lot of space in our previous house, I found that my children literally played under my feet whether I was at the sink or working at my desk. Despite the sophistication of modern life, it seems that humans, especially young ones – although I am not so sure about moody teenagers – have the inbuilt herding instinct of our cave-dwelling ancestors who all squashed together under one roof. We muddle along in a communal way in our London apartment, where there is one large **kitchen/eating/sitting space** in which everyone congregates. One child might be playing with the dollhouse on the floor, the others reading or doing homework at the **big kitchen table**, while I am cooking. My only irritations about this arrangement are the noise levels – whether it's high-spirited yelling, the television, or one child's latest music craze. When I get my way, I like the comforting tones of news and reviews on the radio.

Practical ideas to accommodate children's toys and materials in an open play/living area are essential. One example is making a **blackboard** area for messages and artwork: buy special blackboard paint and apply to a flat wall painted with latex paint; the area can be left open, or framed in painted wood with a useful shelf for chalk and a blackboard eraser below (see right). Bulletin boards made out of cork tiles or painted plywood (see pp.128, 132–133) are also useful for displaying paintings, and tacking up invitations, school telephone lists, and other day-to-day information. Allow small children a corner for a **child-sized table and chairs**, and a couple of baskets filled with toys or dress up clothes. A few pillows on the floor and a rug are also a good idea if the children want to read, sprawl, or have a nap.

Dressing up   Weary with the routine of wearing their school uniforms all week and jeans on the weekend, Georgie and Gracie are always eager to experiment with the **dress up box**. The gypsy theme is their favorite, and they love to dress up in authentic **frilly and flouncy flamenco dresses** (*trajes flamencas*). Georgie has one in bright pink and yellow (see pp.210–211) – genuine bull-fighting cape colors – and Gracie's is blue with white spots. We bought them from one of the many flamenco shops in Seville. **Ironed and pristine**, this gorgeous finery is normally reserved for **Spanish fiestas, ferias, and romerias**, but my daughters can't resist putting them on to **swish, twirl, and stamp their feet** when they hear the strains of a *gitano sevillana* dance on the compact disc player.

potato prints are fun for adults as well as children; they are an easy way to make prints on paper for **stylish wrapping ideas, cards, and labels**. Cut a potato in half – the size depends on your design, but we used a medium-sized one (see opposite). Outline the design on the cut surface of the potato with a pencil; cut away the potato with a kitchen knife outside the outline to a depth of about ¼ in. **Soak the stamp in poster paint**, not too thick or runny, on a plate for a few seconds and print onto paper, construction paper, or even paper bags.

Two potato halves ready for printing. For design ideas use **trees** and **stars** for Christmas, **hearts** for **Valentine's Day**, and **pumpkins** at **Halloween**. Stamp out the initial of the person receiving the present for a really individual touch. Single motifs printed on pieces of construction paper for labels. Small paper bags printed to make unusual packages; print rows of the same motif on plain paper for wrapping paper. Take it a stage further and **decorate** printed cards.

Homespun Christmas decorations are so much cheaper and more original than store-bought ornaments. Children can take part in trimming a tree with offerings such as **fabric balls** (see opposite). Decide on your color theme and **cut strips of fabric** from a remnant bag; checked and striped patterns in blues and greens look good, or experiment with your own color and print ideas. **Wrap the strips** of material around a florist's oasis ball or a plain polystyrene ball that you can buy from a craft store. Secure the fabric with a pin at the top of the ball, and add a ribbon or string loop, secured in the same way, to hang the ball on the tree (see p.198). **Iced cookies** decorated with tiny silver balls (see right) have a **fairylike quality** as they dangle from the branches of a twinkling tree. Their tempting aroma means they won't last long, but they can easily be replaced with a fresh batch as they are eaten. Make them speedily with ready-made pastry or prepare a delicious buttery version yourself (see p.393). Roll out the pastry and cut out the **heart shapes** with a pastry cutter, which you can buy from a kitchenware store or supermarket; pierce a hole at the top for a hanging ribbon or piece of yarn. After baking, let the biscuits cool, then ice, decorate, thread with a ribbon, and hang on the tree.

Wash

Washing is both cleansing and rejuvenating. Efficient delivery of hot and cold water, waterproof and wipe-down surfaces, and warmth to keep towels dry are key features in the contemporary bathroom. Bolster your mood at bath time by using scented soaps, moisturizing lotions, and potions.

Water is essential for life, but it also has sensual qualities – water cooling hot skin, the freedom of floating weightlessly in a limpid, *eau de nil* sea, plunging into an **ice-cold pool**, soaking tired limbs in a **hot, steamy bath**, or rinsing prickly sea-salty skin under a gushing, freshwater hose – every one of these is a sensual experience. Happily, as a reflection of the current mood and the trend for ritual and a more **natural approach to life**, bathing is considered much more than a basic hygienic necessity (I shiver at the thought of the arctic school showers and dank bathrooms of my childhood). No longer is the bathroom just a clinical space or a cramped, avocado-hued nightmare.

My ideal bathroom combines efficient **plumbing** with simplicity and natural **textures** – wood, stone, terra-cotta, rough loofahs, soft cotton, and **scented soaps** and lotions. It is a visually calm, warm retreat, just like the **blue ceramic-tiled bathroom and walk-in shower** that belongs to English food writer Alastair Hendy (see this page and opposite). While also being **practical and easy-to-clean,** this bathing haven, filled during the day with soft, muted light from the skylight above, is a joy to use at any time.

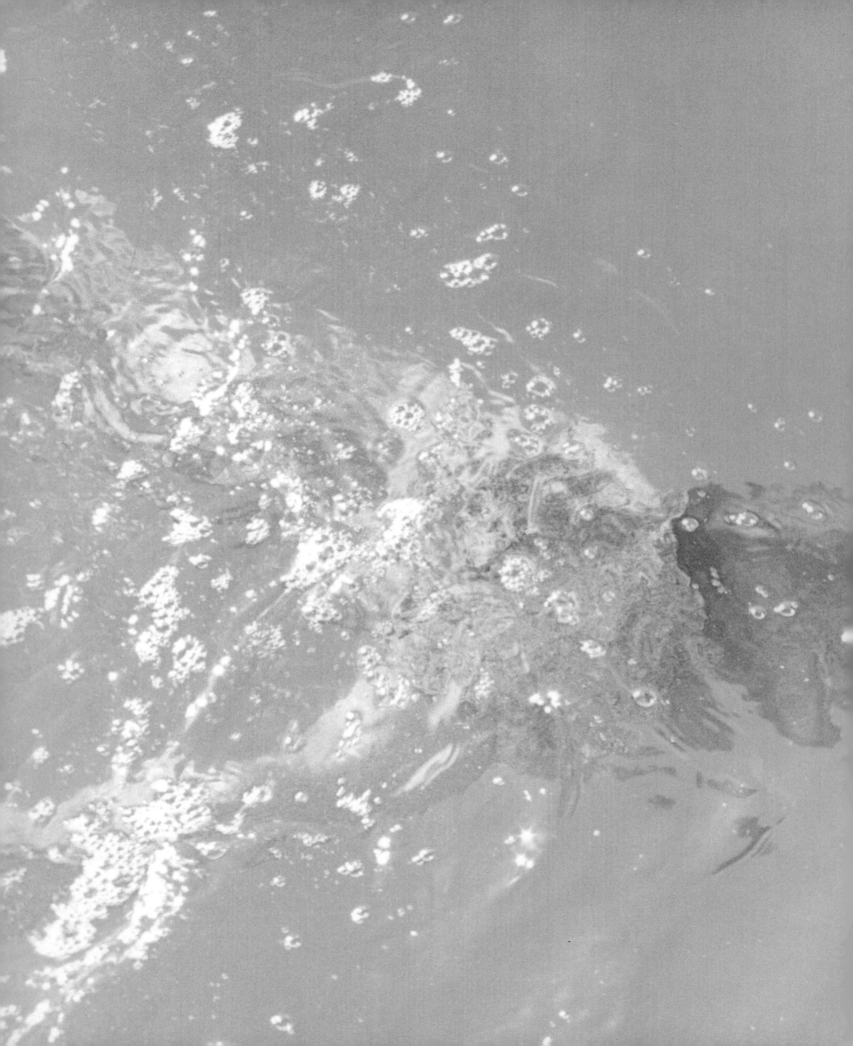

Plain tiling, useful for its waterproofing and hygienic qualities, has long been standard issue in institutional and public swimming pools. Despite their clinical associations, I love the simplicity of **gleaming white tiles** and purchased them cheaply in huge quantities to line the walls and sides of the bathtubs in the three simple bathrooms in our Spanish house (see the guest bathroom, this page and opposite). White tiles are **light-reflecting** and make the room feel **airy and spacious**; they are deliciously cool during the long, hot summer in Spain.

I think **natural textures** can help to counteract the bleak look that is a danger with such a large expanse of whiteness – try **terra-cotta flooring**, made warmer with underfloor heating, crisp white cotton towels, fresh flowers, the odd piece of old, painted shelving, or a woven basket for laundry.

Wood is a texture perfectly suited to the bathroom environment: wooden floors are warm to the touch, and wood-paneled walls and bathtubs look natural whether painted in white eggshell, as in my bathroom in London (see this page and opposite), or left as **sealed pine planks** and battened to the walls, as in the cozy **cabin-style** bathroom (see p.237) in the windswept and romantic Scottish castle belonging to Lachie and Annie Stewart. Paneling walls and boxing-in bathtubs is a useful way to hide ugly plumbing, and it can also be used to create cupboards and storage space for potions and lotions.

The **clean and functional** look of a simple bathroom is also determined by its fixtures. I find that standard **plain white ceramic** basins and toilets, and enameled steel bathtubs (that can be boxed in) are more stylish and functional than flashy marble bathtubs with glitzy gold-trimmed faucets, or other over-the-top, celebrity-status-symbol plumbing. Plain bathroom fixtures are available from good home improvement centers or bathroom stores.

Recycled or **reclaimed** 19th- or early 20th-century **bathroom equipment** can be found in reclamation yards; such fixtures are **utilitarian** and tend to be solidly made. A pair of old-fashioned Victorian brass faucets, an old sink on a pedestal, or a huge hotel-style shower head can add interesting detail to the plainest bathroom interior, whether it is contemporary in mood or more **traditional** like the bathroom, right, and the bathroom in my previous house (pp.234–235), both in restored Georgian row houses in London's Spitalfields area. I miss the old **cast-iron, roll-top bathtub** that we found in a salvage yard that needed six men to carry it upstairs. It sat rather regally on a wooden plinth, and I remember many blissful hours spent soaking in its **deep and curvaceous** proportions while looking out onto the Dickensian rooftops. Note that old faucets may need new washers, and may not deliver such an efficient water flow as modern ones. You will probably need to re-enamel most period cast-iron bathtubs.

Planners have established minimum bathroom dimensions, but it's important to create a bathroom that suits your **individual needs**. Existing plumbing arrangements can be determining features. It is usually the case that a **family** desires a **larger space for bathing** than a one-person household. In our home, everyone piles into the bathroom for a chat, or to sit down or just to read. If space is at a premium, a **small walk-in shower room** might be all that is practicable. However, if equipped with an efficient shower, lined with beautiful tiles, and decked with **slatted teak**, it can be as sensual a washing retreat as a bigger bathroom.

White is an obvious and practical **color** for the bathroom, useful because of its **light-enhancing** qualities, but **blues** and **greens** inspired by the **sea** and **sky** are also great for creating **serene** bathing retreats. The cool blue tiles in Alastair Hendy's bath and shower room (see pp.220–221) show the use of color to perfection.

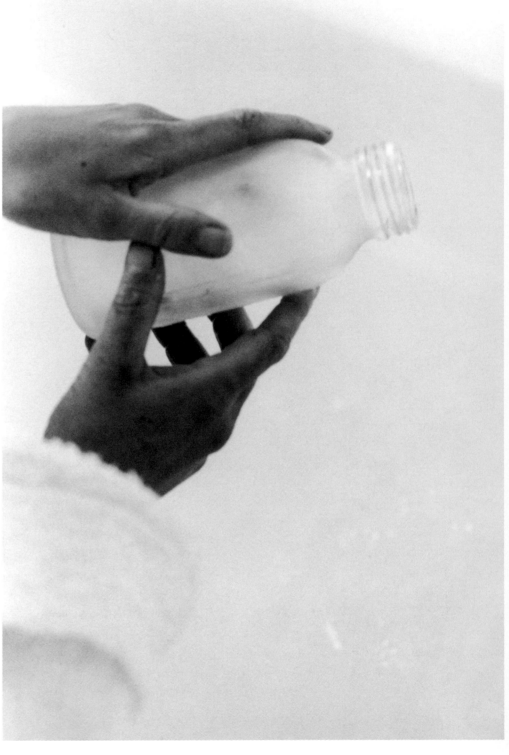

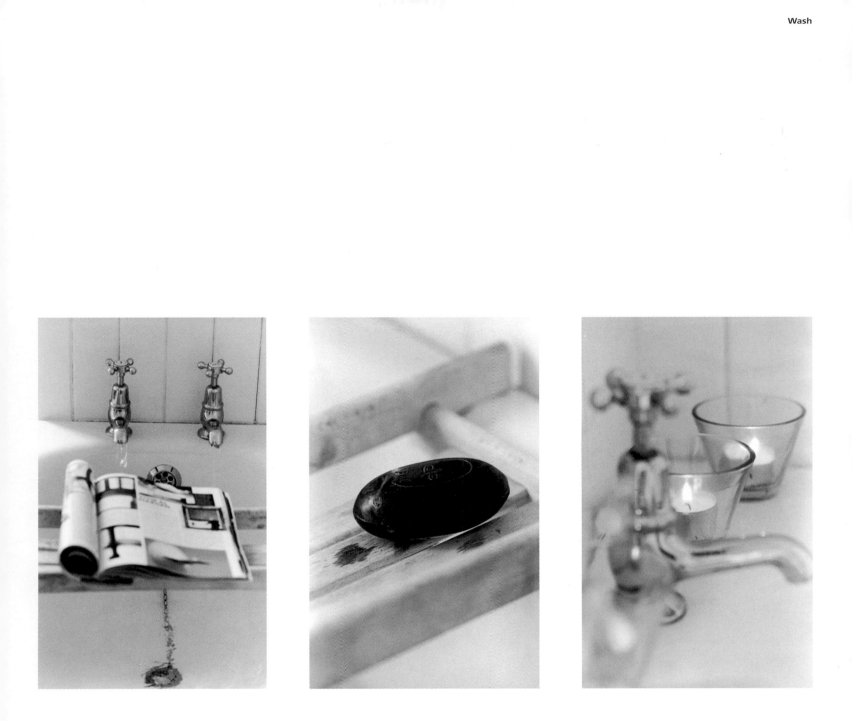

Having a bath   I am a complete **bath addict** and couldn't imagine a day without taking at least one **hot, steamy soak** in the tub. The ritual begins when I put in the plug and turn the hot faucet to release a gush of water. This signals the suspension of domestic duties for as long as I can wangle. I pour in some spicy **orange cologne** to scent the water and swish it about. When the water is just below the overflow drain, I ease myself into its inviting depths and submerge the day's tensions and **relax body and mind**. There I lie – contrary to sensible advice – for at least half an hour, warming up the water from time to time. I might read a **glossy magazine**, or light **candles** if there's no one else at home. **Wrapping** myself in **a warm towel** and heading for bed is the ideal way to round off the experience.

The **sensual bathroom** needs to be warm and draft free, especially in winter, and it must have a plentiful supply of **hot running water**.

A **light and airy** space is a **healthy** environment. A dank, dark bathroom will not produce an invigorating or rejuvenating experience. Don't worry about creating lots of steam – it's all part of enjoying the sensual aspects of bathing, but open the window afterward to aid the airing process.

When taking a bath note that **hot** water **relaxes muscles** and **relieves stiffness** but it also expands blood vessels. A long, hot bath (over 105°F) is not generally a good idea since it tends to be exhausting, and it dries out the skin by drawing out natural oils.

After a bath or shower, be inspired by the sauna ritual, which culminates in jumping into **ice-cold water** or snow, and finish off with a shower of cold water; or sponge cold water over your body to **stimulate** the circulation, close pores, tone, and **invigorate**.

Use **natural** soaps and lotions, and **flower water** such as lavender or rose to splash on and energize skin after a bath, and almond oil for moisturizing dry skin. Basic **mud** face packs are good **skin cleansers** and can be applied while enjoying a long, relaxing soak. **Olive oil** is a great natural conditioner: massage a tablespoon into damp hair and leave for half an hour then rinse out.

Good-quality **soaps** that soften the skin contain fats and oils, rather than harsh artificial detergents. Look for **palm-oil** soap – mild, creamy, and good for the face and dry or sensitive skin; **almond-meal** soap – a good body or face scrub; **oatmeal** soap - an old-fashioned skin cleanser, which is soothing to irritated skin; and **rosemary** soap – slightly astringent and good for oily skin.

Use a few drops of natural fragrant **essential oil** in the bath and choose a particular scent to suit your mood – lavender, melissa, and ylang ylang are **soothing**, while rosemary, lemon grass, and grapefruit are **uplifting and invigorating**.

Your bathroom gear should also include a **loofah** mitt or **rough linen towel** to tone and exfoliate skin, and a good long-handled **scrubbing brush** for backs.

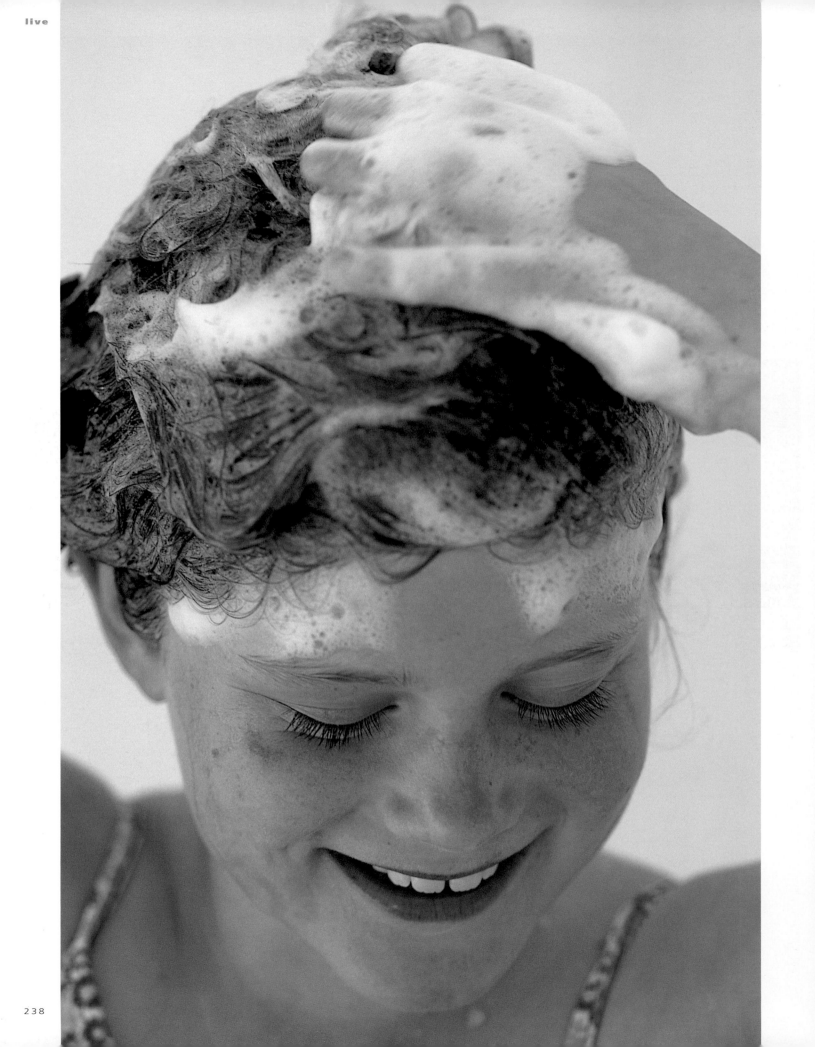

Wash basics   Years ago, on a grueling overland trip from England to Morocco, I know that I only survived the weeks of heat and cramped living conditions in the knowledge that there'd be a reviving shower at the end of each day. When traveling today, I equip myself with a basic wash kit of cotton towel, toothbrush, toothpaste, and cologne. At home, essential bathroom fixtures include durable surfaces and wipe-down flooring.

Essential bathroom fixtures, whether on the move or staying at home, include lashings of hot water on demand, practical and durable washable surfaces and accessories, ceramic sinks, wipe-down flooring, and towels in linen and cotton textures.

Sleep Make the bedroom an oasis away from the demands of everyday domestic life.

Choose a good firm mattress for your bed and snuggle up with crisp cotton sheets and warm woolen

blankets, or the lightest of light-and-cozy goose down comforters. Get a good night's sleep in a

ventilated room, and tuck a cotton bag filled with sleep-inducing dried lavender under your pillow.

Nowadays, we live in a 24-hour society where **sleep** is an increasingly prized commodity. Phone calls at all hours, small children crying in the night, and early rising for work all chip away at the eight hours or so of restoring slumber that is essential to keep us in good mental and physical health. It's no wonder that half the population are supposed to suffer from some form of sleep deprivation.

The bedroom, therefore, should be a **retreat** and a **calm oasis** away from daily demands – **beds** should be nests of **soft pillows**, **crunchy linens**, and **warm blankets**. Light and airy spaces with good ventilation are also essential bedroom ingredients. At night, sleep with the heating turned down or off altogether – if it's too high, it's drying to the skin and makes the air stuffy. Leave a **window open** enough to let in a **cool breeze**.

To make your bedroom a comfort zone, it's worth investing in the best bed linen you can afford – crisp, cotton sheets, light goose down comforters, and wool blankets. Outlaw the television and listen to the radio instead – it's much more relaxing for the brain and calming to the soul. If space is not at a premium, introduce a small couch or armchair for extra seating or for feeding a baby at night.

If you have children, buy a big bed with a good mattress so that everyone can snuggle up together to eat jammy toast and read the papers on weekends.

Paint bedroom walls in light-reflecting white or calming, soft lilacs or greens. A vibrantly painted bedroom is not the most restful environment to sleep in, but I do find that **shots of bright color** work well in a white scheme; for example, in my Spanish bedroom (see pp.242–243), the **orange cotton** throw, **pink-checked**, **floaty**, **muslin** curtain, and **crimson roses fresh from the garden** seem to heighten and intensify the bright light and airiness, especially in the summer.

Basic window treatments for bedrooms include **simple blinds** and looped or tie-on curtains; internal or external **wooden shutters** are also useful for blocking out early morning light, which may disturb light sleepers, or for keeping a bedroom cool and shady during the heat of the day.

Even if a bed is used for only one night by an **overnight guest** who snuggles into a comforter or a sleeping bag, it should be **comfortable and functional**. Although a feature of Japanese sleeping arrangements for centuries, roll-up, cotton-padded futon mattresses are the new, laid-back sleeping idea for cool urbanites; they **create flexible sleeping** when space is limited, such as in a cramped studio or small apartment, and, being inexpensive, are accessible for students and others on tight budgets. This type of bedding **needs very little effort** and can be rolled up during the day and used as a seating surface when not in use as a bed. A traditional folding bed with a mattress on a metal frame is another cheap, **temporary sleeping solution**; it provides a firm surface and, being raised, is particularly suitable for elderly guests who may not be eager to rough it on the floor.

A divan bed with a mattress and a box spring is a **traditional bed shape** that can be used in any bedroom as a **basic sleeping** surface and then covered with layers of bedding as desired. In the lilac bedroom (see p.256), a plain double divan has been dressed in simple white bed linen to create an inviting, completely pared-down sleeping idea. A single divan is a good idea for creating **extra sleeping space** in a small area; pushed against a wall and covered with throws and cushions to function as a sofa for daytime use, it can be turned back into a full-fledged bed with sheets, pillows, blankets, and a comforter at night.

I think that understated **wooden bed frames** are honest and **functional shapes**. They look neat and have a **visual lightness**. Old metal-framed twin beds painted in a soft, powdery blue eggshell paint and made up with **cozy flannel sheets and pillowcases** and checked wool blankets look stylish as well as homey (see opposite). Basic metal beds or old brass bedsteads – better than new brass, which looks too flashy – also have a similar feel.

making a comforter cover   As a cheaper alternative to buying a premade cover, buy white cotton sheeting by the yard and dye it the **color** of your choice. Although dyeing in the washing machine is easier, results are unpredictable since it is difficult to work out how much dye to use. **Hand dyeing** in the bathtub is more reliable. Dyeing can also revive an old, unpatterned comforter cover. After dyeing, cut the material to size and finish. Simple ties, buttonholes, or Velcro fastenings can be added to the open end.

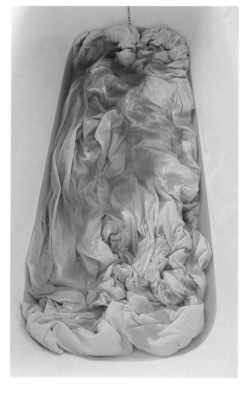

1 Assemble the materials: 15 ft of white cotton sheeting to fit a large bed (87 x 157 in) (prewash the material to remove fabric sizing); pair of rubber gloves; bucket; old wooden or plastic spoon; dye; salt; fixative; 1 yard of 1-in-wide heavy-duty Velcro strip.

2 Weigh the fabric to assess how much dye is needed. One box or tube of standard dye is sufficient to dye 2.2 lb dry weight of fabric. You will also need to add table salt and soda ash dye fixer (with some dyes this may not be necessary; check the instructions on the packet).

3 Mix the dye ingredients in a bucket following the instructions on the package and pour into the bathtub. Add the fabric, keeping it fully submerged. Move the fabric around to ensure an even finish. When the dyeing time is complete, rinse the material and wash and dry it.

4 Cut the fabric in half to make two equal lengths. Overlock or zigzag stitch the raw edges, place the two pieces together, then sew three sides together ⅜ in from the edge. Fold back the edges of the open side and stitch a 2 in hem. Cut the Velcro strip into 10 in pieces and stitch them at regular intervals along the open edge of the cover (making sure that the two halves meet when the fabric is closed together). Turn the finished comforter cover the right way around and press. The cover is now ready to be put onto a comforter (see right). Wash separately the first time you use it.

Childrens' bedrooms demand their own set of priorities: a large enough space to accommodate **beds**, **toys**, **books**, **and a desk or table**, and floor space to sprawl around on.

Space-saving **bunk beds** are a great idea for housing several children in one room. Build-it-yourself versions in pine are cheap and stocked by most large furniture stores; they can be **painted** in white, blue, or your child's favorite color. There are also raised beds that have a **built-in workspace** below with a ladder to reach the bed above; these are good for squeezing into the smallest room. Junk shops and salvage yards are good hunting grounds for old-fashioned metal beds from hospitals and school dormitories, which are generally robust and neat in proportion (see p.248).

If you have to give in to lurid cartoon prints for walls, curtains, and comforter covers, it isn't the end of the world; however, **comforters and sheets in stripes**, **checks**, **or plain colors** (see the homemade, dyed comforter cover on p.252) are more appealing as far as most adults are concerned.

When **children have to share a room**, it's important that they each have **individual closet space**. I chose floor-to-ceiling built-in closets along the length of one wall in my children's room; divided into three sections – one for each child – the closets house child-height hanging space for clothes, and shelving, with more shelves higher up for toys and games that are less frequently needed (which are reached by a lightweight, folding, aluminum ladder).

It is good to encourage individual creative talents by allowing children **wall space for their artwork** (see my children's room in our London apartment, p.252), together with a working surface, such as a wooden trestle table (also in my children's bedroom, see p.253), which is like the one in our office space. We have put a piano in the children's bedroom to encourage practicing. Although my children spend most of their time in the main living area, it is always good to know that they can retreat to **the sanctuary of their bedroom** if they want to – a relief for the parents, too.

To maintain a sense of calm in your sleeping oasis, keep bedroom clutter to a minimum by stowing away your clothes and linen. **Built-in closets** (see right) are the neatest solution. At the most basic level, you can simply curtain off an alcove and install some shelves and a hanging rail. Small **nightstands** and chests of drawers (see left) can accommodate small pieces of clothing and other bedroom paraphernalia, such as bedside reading matter. Be inventive and **recycle furniture** designed for other purposes; for example, in one bedroom a **1960s dining room hutch** has been given a new lease on life as a storage space to hold socks and underwear (see p.257). Owners of large shoe collections might find it tidy to stow them away in plain boxes under the bed; this is also a useful idea for keeping sweaters, blankets, and other bulky items hidden when they are not in use.

Making a chair slipcover   Every bedroom needs a chair, and even the most basic folding chair can be transformed by dressing it in a removable cover. A neutral cotton or linen fabric will soften the edges of the bedroom environment and add to the feeling of calm and repose. To achieve a really fresh, clean look, the bottom edge of the cover can be defined with a band of contrasting color trimming; blue always goes well with neutrals. This simple shape can be made quickly and easily on a sewing machine, even for those inexperienced at sewing.

1 Measure the chair to calculate fabric requirements. For the length of fabric, add the depth of the seat to twice the height of the back plus an extra 4 in. The width of material is the chair width plus 1 in. For our chair, the seat depth was 13 in, back height 14 in, and width 17 in so the piece of fabric required was 45 x 18 in. When cut to size, overlock or zigzag stitch the raw edges. You will need the same length of trim as the skirt length (see Step 3).

2 Place the fabric on the chair so that the seat edge is overlapped by about ⅜ in on three sides and the extra length hangs down at the back. Pin the edges together at either side of the seat back, noting with a pin or dressmaker's chalk the point where the seat meets the back of the chair. Take the fabric off the chair and sew two vertical seams where you have pinned. This makes the main part of the slip that covers the back and seat of the chair.

3 To make the skirt, you need to cut a strip of fabric that in length is twice the depth of the seat plus the width plus ¾ in, and 4 in wide. For our chair, the strip was 43¾ x 4 in. Overlock or zigzag stitch the raw edges. Turn a ⅜-in hem along the length on one side only, then do the same for the short ends. Put the cover back onto the chair, still inside out, and pin the skirt into place, leaving a ⅜-in seam. Make sure that all the hems and seams are facing outward.

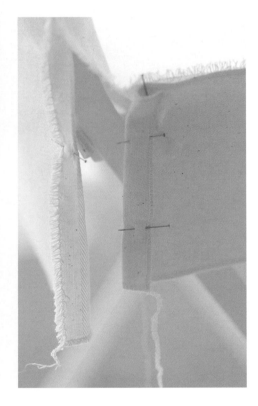

4 Remove the cover and sew where you have just pinned. Hem the back edge of the cover so that it is the same length as the skirt using a ⅜-in hem. When all the edges are hemmed, turn the cover the right way around and you can apply the trim. Simply place your chosen ribbon or trim about ⅜ in from the bottom of the side and front edges of the cover, pin, and sew using thread in a matching color. Press to flatten the trim, and slip onto the chair (see right).

Tactile, **natural fabrics** are the most **luxurious** bedroom textures; wear nothing at all between the sheets or loose cotton pajamas, a big, white T-shirt, or a simple cotton nightgown – beautiful, embroidered Victorian nightgowns can be picked up quite cheaply. When you clamber out of bed in the morning, wrap up in a deliciously soft, oversized **cotton robe**. Warm your feet with **woolen slippers** or thick bedsocks when the temperature drops.

Soft cotton **rugs** are welcome underfoot when you are springing out of bed on a cold morning; if they are not too large, they can be cleaned in a washing machine.

Classic cream **wool blankets** with a satin trim, which are central to traditional English bedroom decor, are warm and sensual in the contemporary bedroom. **Slipcovers** soften the edges of bedroom chairs and can be easily made to disguise a folding chair (see pp.260–261). I like creamy **cotton**

or **linen** fabrics, which can also be used for **blinds** or **simple curtains** to create a unifying effect through the room.

Washed **antique** bedlinens are soft and have a lovely worn, faded quality that can add to the serenity of a bedroom environment. I have mounds of old, white cotton sheets and pillowcases handed down through the family, and I am a collector of old **pretty quilts** with delicate **floral patterns**. One of my favorites is the 18th-century, lavender-striped quilt that covers the white cotton linen and blankets on my box bed – painted a deliciously soft and soporific green eggshell – in our London apartment (see opposite).

If money were no object, I think we should all sleep only in **linen sheets**; spun and woven from flax, linen doesn't retain moisture like cotton and has a cooling effect that makes it ideal for the summer. Two sets of fine linen sheets used alternately can easily last twenty-five years.

directory

Paint

Fabric

Flooring

Eat

Work

Garden

Rest

Play

Wash

Sleep

Paint

white

cream and yellow

terra-cotta

green

blue

pink

Paint data

Paint is one of the **simplest and most effective ways** to transform our living space and the objects in it. How we paint our homes is intrinsic to establishing who we are, what we feel, and what we aspire to. Scientists have known for years that **different colors trigger** different **emotional responses**: children paint with black to express unhappiness; **white is uplifting**; **red is exciting and eyecatching** (traffic lights worldwide are red); **yellows and oranges are optimistic**; **blue is cool and calming**; and **green** is at the center of the color spectrum and represents **balance**.

The choice of colors and textures today has never been so wide and confusing. Don't get stressed looking for shades that have to be exactly right. Paint samples on cards are unlikely to match exactly with the real stuff on the walls as color *in situ* is affected by wall texture, the amount of light in a room, and the color of surrounding floors and furniture.

Be true to your individual needs. A decade or so ago, when I restored our early Georgian house in Spitalfields, London, there was pressure from traditionalists to use **authentic colors**, most of which were dull and somber. Being housebound with babies and in need of light and airy surroundings, I did not want my house to be gloomy and depressing. Ignoring the "tut tuts" of the conservationist brigade, I stuck to my gut feelings and painted the paneled rooms in **matte eggshell country creams**, **whites**, **and greens**. The resulting look was **fresh and modern** but not at all out of place in its historic context.

Be aware of the effects that different colors have on our **perception of space**: **warm colors**, such as **deep creams**, **yellows**, and **terra-cottas**, **advance** and make a room appear smaller and cozier; **cool colors**, such as **white**, **slate gray**, **and blues recede** and have the opposite effect, enlarging the room and making it feel light and airy.

Think about the colors that you like and see in your immediate **environment**; color doesn't always travel – seductive hot Mediterranean pinks, blues, and yellows that look beautiful in bright sunshine can fall flat in the cool northern light.

Many different **colors and contrasts** throughout a house or in one room are unharmonious and can be stressful. I now live very happily with **calming white wraparound color** in our London flat and our house in Spain. To prevent the whole look from being too clinical, I have introduced **shots of brilliant color** by adding throws, **cushions**, painted pots, and **jugs of bright flowers**.

Textures

For walls and ceilings, a water-based paint, such as **emulsion**, is best. An **oil-based eggshell**, with mid-to-low sheen, is good for protection against moisture; I use it on woodwork and for painting furniture. **Water-based eggshell** – a more environmentally friendly eggshell – provides a tough washable surface for interiors, although it's not so good for surfaces that take a lot of wear and tear, such as shelves or worktops. **Exterior masonry paint** is a water-based paint for exterior cement, stone, and brickwork. **Floor paint** is oil-based with an eggshell finish and can be used for wood and concrete floors. **Flat oil paint** used on wood, plaster, and metal is a good traditional finish for period interiors. **Limewash** is a traditional matte-textured paint based on chalk and water and colored with artists' pigments – limewashed houses in white, blue, green, and terra-cotta are typical in Mediterranean countries such as Greece and Spain. Its high alkalinity – it was once used to disinfect hospitals – can cause problems, and users are advised to wear gloves and goggles when mixing it up and painting with it.

Eco-notes

There is an increase in environmentally friendly paint formulas, and products are now made with fewer solvents, fungicides, chemical preservatives, and toxic volatile organic compounds (VOCs) that contribute to low-level pollution. **Natural paints** contain **organic, renewable, and biodegradable ingredients** such as orange-peel oil or binder derived from resin that is harvested in a non-destructive, sustainable way from the dammar tree, which grows in tropical rainforests. **Traditional distemper** or **casein paint** (based on a milk-derived protein) and limewash are also less destructive to the environment. **Recycle**, and take care to dispose of unwanted paint in an ecologically responsible manner. Countless half-finished paint cans are thrown away with the household trash only to end up contaminating landfills, or unwanted paint is poured down the drain to pollute water supplies. To remove the last dregs in a can, pour onto absorbent paper and allow it to dry. **Dry paint** can be disposed of with the household garbage. Look at recycling centers to find a source for steel paint cans; contact your local municipal board to dispose of liquid paint.

white

the huge variety of white paints available allows me to experiment with tones and textures for painting walls, floors, and furniture

1

2

3

4

5

6

1 **clay emulsion**
A water-based paint that is perfect for calm, understated neutral walls in any interior.

2 **chalk emulsion**
Easy to apply, this creates a light, modern, and unifying effect if used throughout a house or apartment.

3 **neutral eggshell**
The durable finish of this paint adds practicality as well as style to a basic chain-store pine kitchen table.

4 **paper eggshell**
This has an easy-to-clean finish that is ideal for wooden shelves or cupboard doors.

5 **Queen Anne's lace floor paint**
Heavy-duty paint that is good for wooden floorboards.

6 **weathered white eggshell**
Eco-friendly water-based eggshell is used to transform a battered side table from a market (see opposite).

7

8

9

7 **pebble eggshell**
An oil-based paint that gives a matte covering suitable for wood paneling or tongue-and-groove lined walls.

8 **canvas exterior eggshell**
A more durable paint that is ideal for painting junk garden tables and chairs.

9 **ice-cream emulsion**
For customizing flower pots, which can then be filled with plants for indoor use.

cream and yellow

I find inspiration for creams and yellows from sunburned fields, sunflowers, straw, and sandy beaches

1   **caramel eggshell**
Could be used as a wood-effect paint to revamp a plain wooden lamp base.

2   **beeswax eggshell**
A country color that I used to good effect in the hall and stairways of our 18th-century house in London.

3   **sand emulsion**
For a warm covering that would suit a south-facing family room with blue-checked fabrics.

4   **toffee eggshell**
Gives a warm sheen and a durable finish to woodwork and paneling in a period house.

5   **butter eggshell**
A tough paint in creamy yellow to jazz up a wooden crate for colorful kitchen storage (see opposite).

6   **honey eggshell**
Cream paint with a hint of warmth to liven up plain kitchen cupboards.

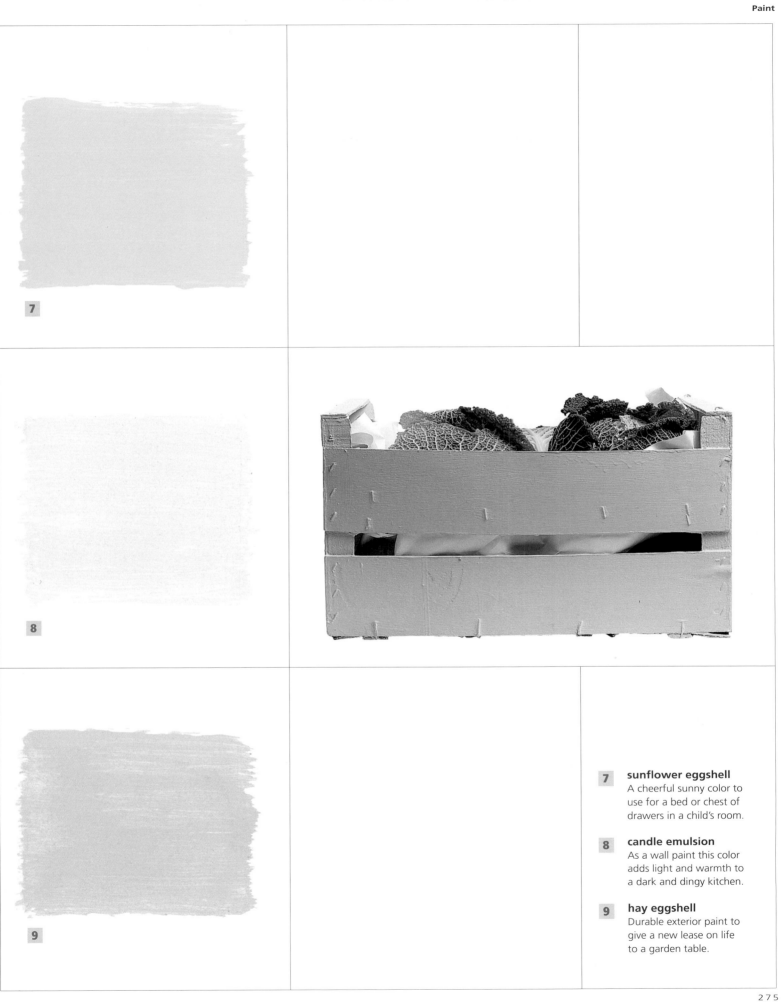

7 **sunflower eggshell**
A cheerful sunny color to use for a bed or chest of drawers in a child's room.

8 **candle emulsion**
As a wall paint this color adds light and warmth to a dark and dingy kitchen.

9 **hay eggshell**
Durable exterior paint to give a new lease on life to a garden table.

terra-cotta

good old-fashioned earthy colors for use in kitchens, gardens, and on exterior walls

1

2

3

4

5

6

1 **flowerpot emulsion**
A rich, clay color for the walls to give wamth and intimacy to a small room.

2 **earthenware eggshell**
Just the thing for disguising cheap plastic flowerpots as the real item, and it makes them sturdier too.

3 **pumpkin eggshell**
Brighten up and protect garden pots with earthy paint and place on a white patio for a Spanish look.

4 **brick exterior eggshell**
Paint a garden shed in this natural shade that will blend beautifully with garden hues.

5 **chestnut eggshell**
A paler terra-cotta that looks good on a side table placed in a room with whites and neutrals (see opposite).

6 **pantile eggshell**
A pink-toned paint that is used to best effect in small doses, for example to unify a display of cheap wooden photograph frames.

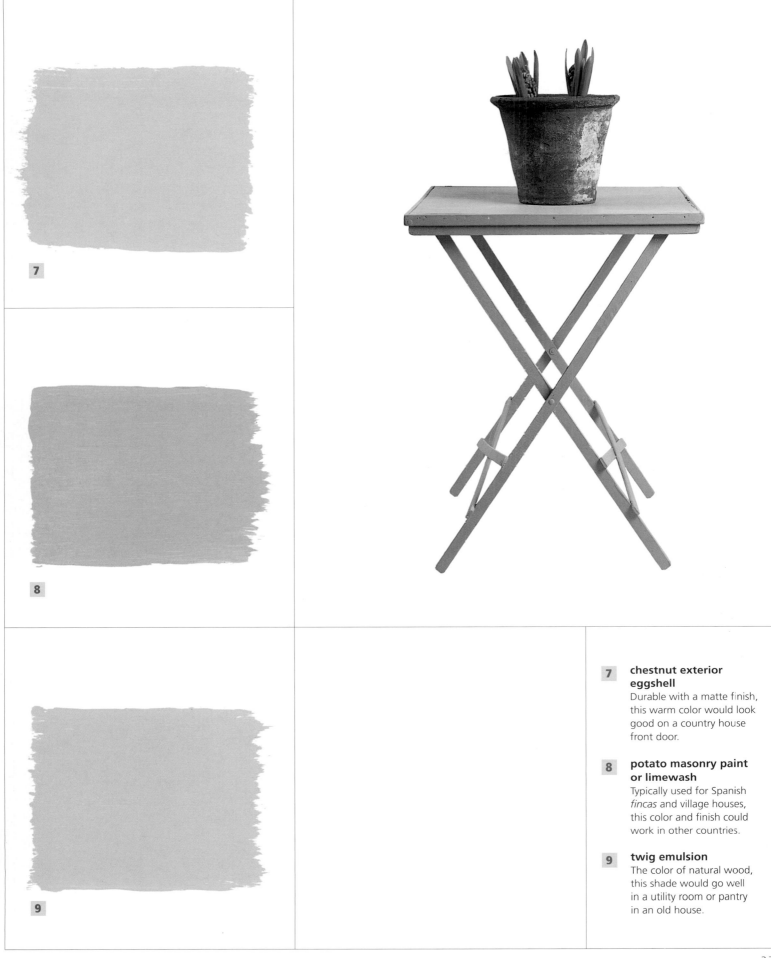

7

7 chestnut exterior eggshell
Durable with a matte finish, this warm color would look good on a country house front door.

8 potato masonry paint or limewash
Typically used for Spanish *fincas* and village houses, this color and finish could work in other countries.

9 twig emulsion
The color of natural wood, this shade would go well in a utility room or pantry in an old house.

green

garden green shades that can be used inside and out

1   **fig leaf emulsion**
A bold, bright color that will uplift a living room.

2   **lime green emulsion**
To perk up a pot for interior display (see opposite).

3   **asparagus eggshell**
A subtle shade for junk garden chairs and tables.

4   **apple eggshell**
Gives a flat covering that complements Georgian wood paneling.

5   **grass exterior eggshell**
This would be suitable for a country cottage front door.

6   **broad bean emulsion**
A matte finish that lifts the appearance of a garden trellis; it may wash off in the rain but can be repainted yearly.

7
white cabbage emulsion
For a change from white
on den walls; looks good
with lavender and lime-
green accessories.

8
mint emulsion
Conveys a breezy seaside
feel when painted on walls
in a kitchen or bathroom.

9
lettuce eggshell
For the wooden frame of a
folding chair; add a cream
canvas cover for outside use.

blue

my favorite blues come
from observations of sea,
sky, and swimming pool

1

2

1 **beach hut eggshell**
An ideal summery color
to paint patio and garden
tables and chairs.

2 **pale denim eggshell**
A lively shade to brighten
up a set of wooden kitchen
drawers (see opposite).

3 **wave eggshell**
For shelving and cabinets;
provides contrast in a white
painted bathroom.

4 **pool exterior eggshell**
If you don't want your
garden shed to fade into its
surroundings, try painting it
this delicious blue.

5 **sea eggshell**
A calming color that is good
for wooden bunkbeds in the
children's bedroom.

6 **cloud emulsion**
For coolness without the chill
factor; team with crisp white
bed linen in the bedroom.

3

4

5

6

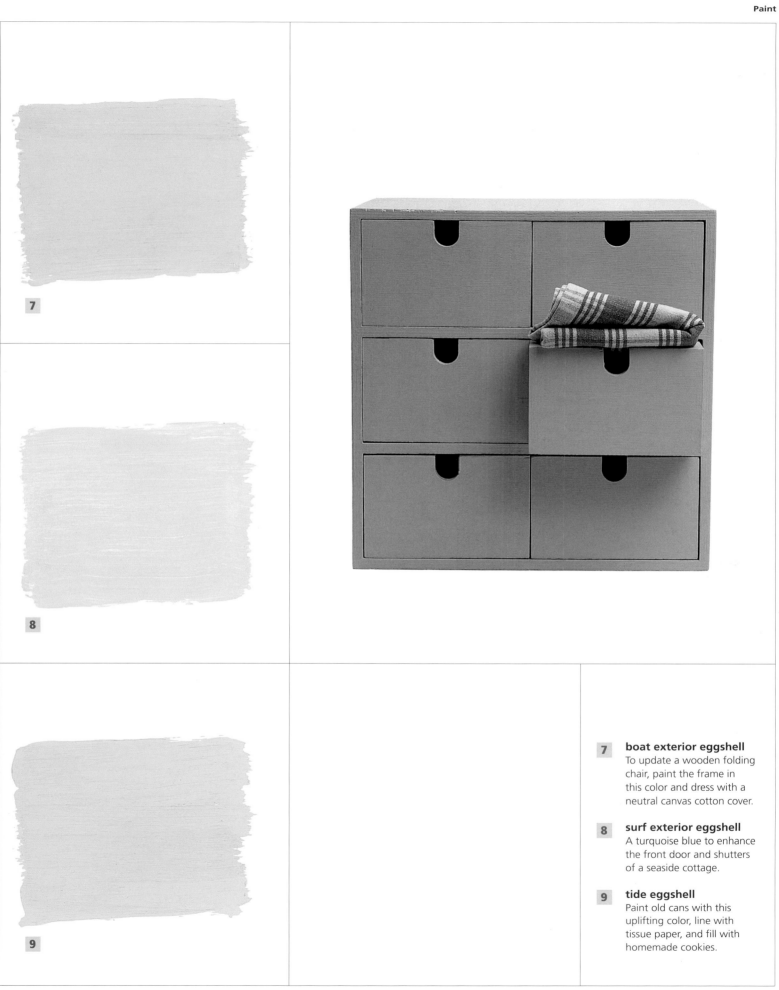

7 **boat exterior eggshell**
To update a wooden folding chair, paint the frame in this color and dress with a neutral canvas cotton cover.

8 **surf exterior eggshell**
A turquoise blue to enhance the front door and shutters of a seaside cottage.

9 **tide eggshell**
Paint old cans with this uplifting color, line with tissue paper, and fill with homemade cookies.

pink

shocking and pale pinks, mauves, and lilacs from garden borders brimming with foxgloves, lavender, and other flowers are reinterpreted in the home

1

2

1 **fuschia eggshell**
Great for jazzing up old food cans for use as kitchen or workroom containers (see opposite).

2 **rose emulsion**
A pretty shade to paint on a young girl's bedroom walls.

3 **hyacinth emulsion**
A warm color suitable for family room walls that looks especially good with green.

4 **pale lavender eggshell**
Painted wooden frames in this color will complement children's drawings.

5 **petal exterior masonry paint or limewash**
For the outside walls of a country cottage.

6 **lilac emulsion**
A pretty bedroom in this pale hue would be further enhanced by floral bed linen.

3

4

5

6

7

8

9

7 tulip eggshell
A good color with a matte finish to update an old chest of drawers or cupboard in a feminine room.

8 bud eggshell
Brighten up patio flowerpots with a lick of pastel paint.

9 foxglove emulsion
For a version of white with just a hint of pink, use on walls for warmth and light.

Fabric

neutral fabrics

plain colors

checks and stripes

floral fabrics

Fabric data

Natural fabrics are sensual and tactile. **Linen sheets are deliciously smooth** on the skin; **floaty muslin curtains** catch the breeze on a searing hot day; **wool is beautifully soft and durable**, and makes tough, upholstered surfaces – snuggle up with warm woolly throws in checks or plain colors, or sprawl outside on a soft picnic blanket.

It's not necessary to lay out large sums of money for good quality and great colors. Try **craft stores** or the discount fabric outlets at a shopping center near you for **basic blue-and-white ticking**, cotton, and strong canvas. There are also **wholesale companies** that sell **muslin**, cotton, **canvas**, and **other basic fabrics** for theater backdrops, artists' studios, and other commercial outlets, that will sell small quantities to individuals. I buy durable cotton for loose covers and bright muslin for children's dress-up clothes from a local wholesaler. Toweling normally supplied to hospitals and schools comes by the thick roll to make up into cushions, loose covers, and simple table runners. It is also worth scouring the fabric departments of **large department stores** for **cheap silk**, **plastic-coated cotton**, **ticking**, and **muslin**, especially when things are on sale.

Cotton

The white downy fibrous balls that enclose the seeds of the cotton plant are woven into cloth and thread of various weights and weaves: **canvas** – unbleached cotton cloth; I use the heaviest weights for loose covers; **chintz** – printed, and usually glazed, cotton; tiny traditional floral prints are my favorites; **drill** – coarse, twilled (with a diagonal weave) cotton; **denim** – extremely durable, twilled cotton, usually dyed indigo; **duck or canvas** – strong, untwilled cotton; good for garden chairs, awnings, and heavy-duty laundry bags; **gingham** – checked cotton cloth, usually of one color on a white background; comes in many different sizes of check; **muslin** – loosely woven, very fine, cotton fabric; makes floaty curtains; **ticking** – stout twilled cotton, closely woven in one-color stripes on a cream or white background, traditionally used for covering mattresses; makes good chair covers and curtains; also pretty when old and faded; **voile** – a thin semitransparent material; good for fine curtains or blinds.

Linen

A durable material with many uses that is derived from **flax** – a blue-flowered plant also cultivated for its seeds (linseed). There are many different weights of linen ranging from **cambric** – fine white linen used for handkerchiefs – to heavyweight upholstery quality. Linen sheets must be one of life's great luxuries. There are other textural and tough linen-type fabrics cultivated from plants: **hemp** – a herbaceous plant from India used mainly for rope; **jute** – plant fiber from Bangladesh used for sacking, carpeting, and mats; **burlap** – strong coarse cloth made from hemp or jute; it was fashionable in the 1960s for covering walls; now useful for bags and bulletin boards; **sackcloth** – coarse fabric woven from flax or hemp; **canvas –** strong unbleached cloth of hemp or flax.

Silk

Fine, soft thread harvested from the cocoons of specially raised silkworms that feed on a diet of mulberry leaves, silk is warm and luxurious to wear. No longer prohibitively costly, silk comes in many different weights and qualities to suit requirements: **velvet** – luxurious, closely woven fabric with a thick short pile on one side; **dupion** – heavy silk with a textured weave; **tsar** – cloth with a linen-look weave; **saraburi** – heavy, flat-look, Thai silk; **parachute silk** – very lightweight silk for making billowy curtains.

Wool

Hair from sheep, alpaca, and goat that is spun into yarn for knitting or weaving. Wool is warm in winter, cool in summer, water-resistant on the outside, and absorbent on the inside. It is woven into many different textures: **flannel** – woven woolen fabric, usually without a nap; **alpaca** – luxuriously soft fabric made from the long, woolly hair of the alpaca llama; **cashmere** – fine, soft, but expensive, wool from the Kashmir goat; if you can afford it, it's worth the investment of at least one throw; **mohair** – fine, hairy yarn from the angora goat; makes great shawls and beautifully warm throws; **felt** – matted, woolen material that is non-fraying and easy to cut; comes in a great range of colors for bulletin boards, chair pads, and children's art projects.

neutral fabrics

I choose bone, cream, stone, and other earth colors for rooms with natural textures

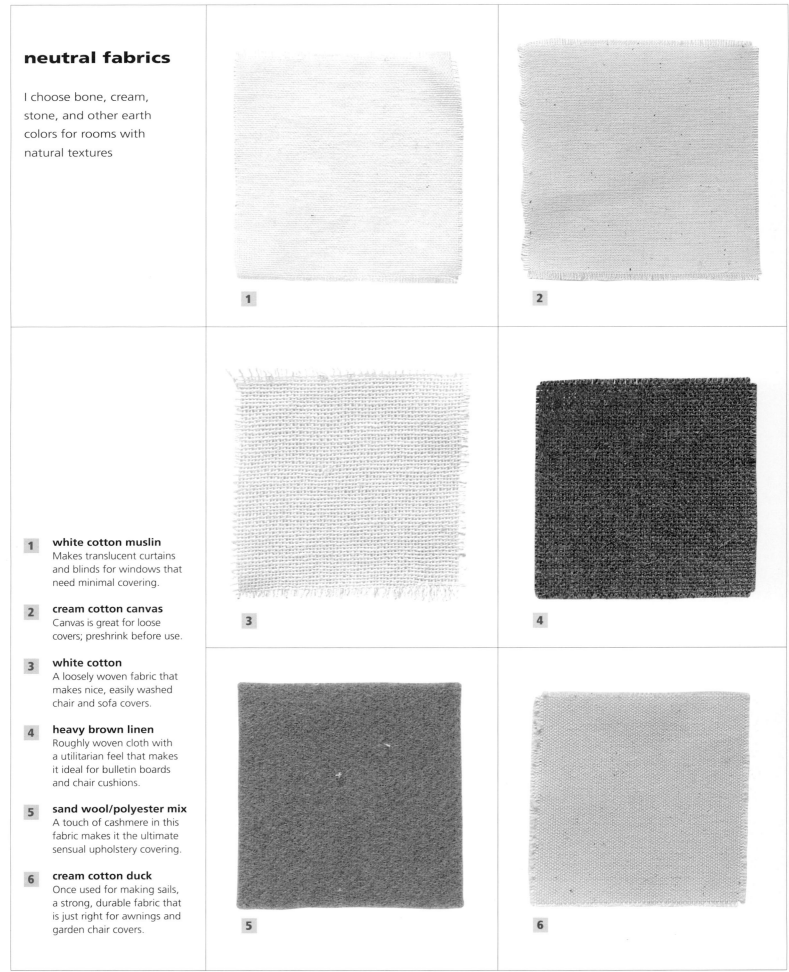

1 **white cotton muslin**
Makes translucent curtains and blinds for windows that need minimal covering.

2 **cream cotton canvas**
Canvas is great for loose covers; preshrink before use.

3 **white cotton**
A loosely woven fabric that makes nice, easily washed chair and sofa covers.

4 **heavy brown linen**
Roughly woven cloth with a utilitarian feel that makes it ideal for bulletin boards and chair cushions.

5 **sand wool/polyester mix**
A touch of cashmere in this fabric makes it the ultimate sensual upholstery covering.

6 **cream cotton duck**
Once used for making sails, a strong, durable fabric that is just right for awnings and garden chair covers.

7

7 earth-brown silk muslin
Ideal for a simple blind or lightweight bed throw.

8 cream wool mix
A luxurious upholstery fabric that should be restricted to child-free zones.

9 stone-brown jute
Sackcloth for fashioning into lightweight curtains, bags, and cushions.

10 fine white linen
A light weave for napkins, tablecloths, and bed linen.

11 medium-brown linen
A midweight texture suitable for roman blinds and bed covers.

12 egg-white ribbed cotton
To make a beautiful set of chair slipcovers.

plain colors

use fabrics in strong
shades of green, blue,
and pink to bring color
details into the house

1 blue wool mix
Use to cover an armchair to
brighten up a neutral room.

2 bright pink cotton drill
Durable fabric suitable for a
roller blind, roman blind, or a
simple curtain.

3 pink cotton muslin
Perfect for lightweight floaty
curtains that introduce a
splash of color.

4 spring green felt
For covering bulletin boards
and making handmade
Christmas stockings.

5 sky blue wool
Durable, soft, and
warm upholstery covering
to curl up on.

6 pale violet cotton muslin
Ideal for stitching up flower
and herb bags for scented
drawers and gifts.

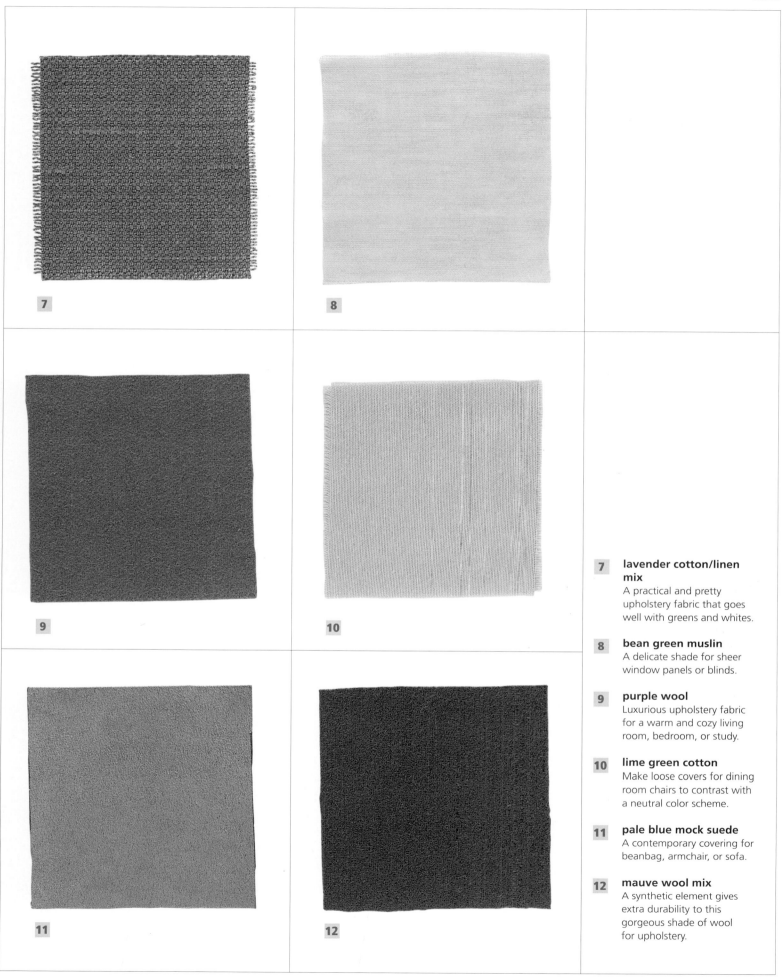

7 **lavender cotton/linen mix**
A practical and pretty upholstery fabric that goes well with greens and whites.

8 **bean green muslin**
A delicate shade for sheer window panels or blinds.

9 **purple wool**
Luxurious upholstery fabric for a warm and cozy living room, bedroom, or study.

10 **lime green cotton**
Make loose covers for dining room chairs to contrast with a neutral color scheme.

11 **pale blue mock suede**
A contemporary covering for beanbag, armchair, or sofa.

12 **mauve wool mix**
A synthetic element gives extra durability to this gorgeous shade of wool for upholstery.

checks and stripes

I like the simplicity, timeless style, and sense of order found in these patterns

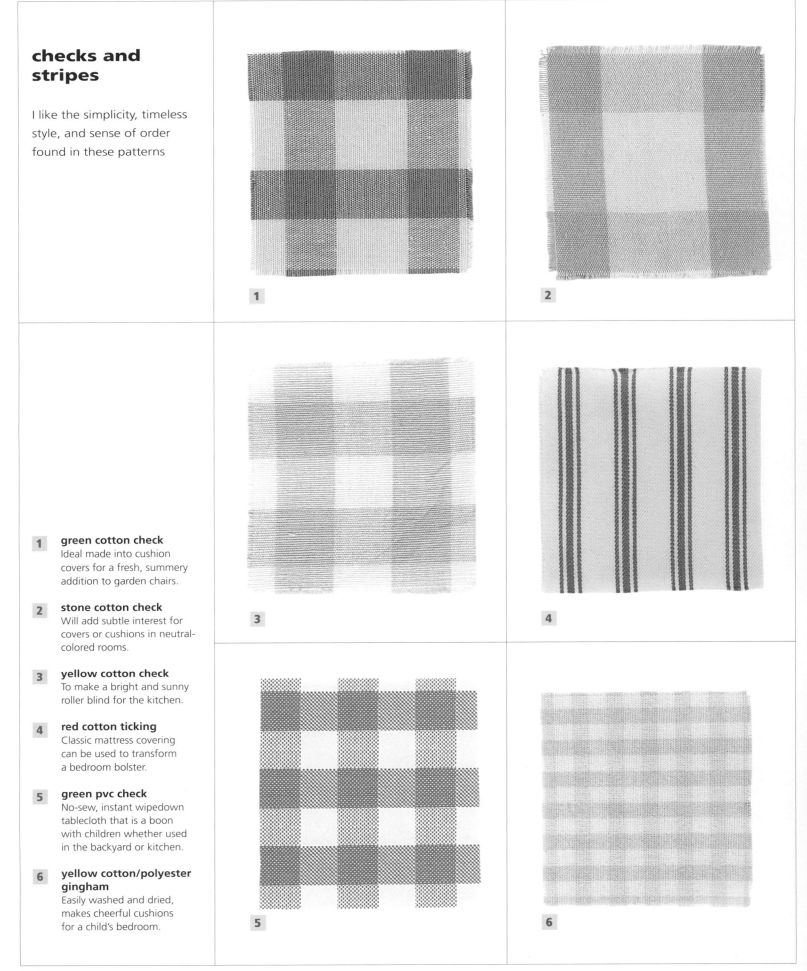

1 **green cotton check**
Ideal made into cushion covers for a fresh, summery addition to garden chairs.

2 **stone cotton check**
Will add subtle interest for covers or cushions in neutral-colored rooms.

3 **yellow cotton check**
To make a bright and sunny roller blind for the kitchen.

4 **red cotton ticking**
Classic mattress covering can be used to transform a bedroom bolster.

5 **green pvc check**
No-sew, instant wipedown tablecloth that is a boon with children whether used in the backyard or kitchen.

6 **yellow cotton/polyester gingham**
Easily washed and dried, makes cheerful cushions for a child's bedroom.

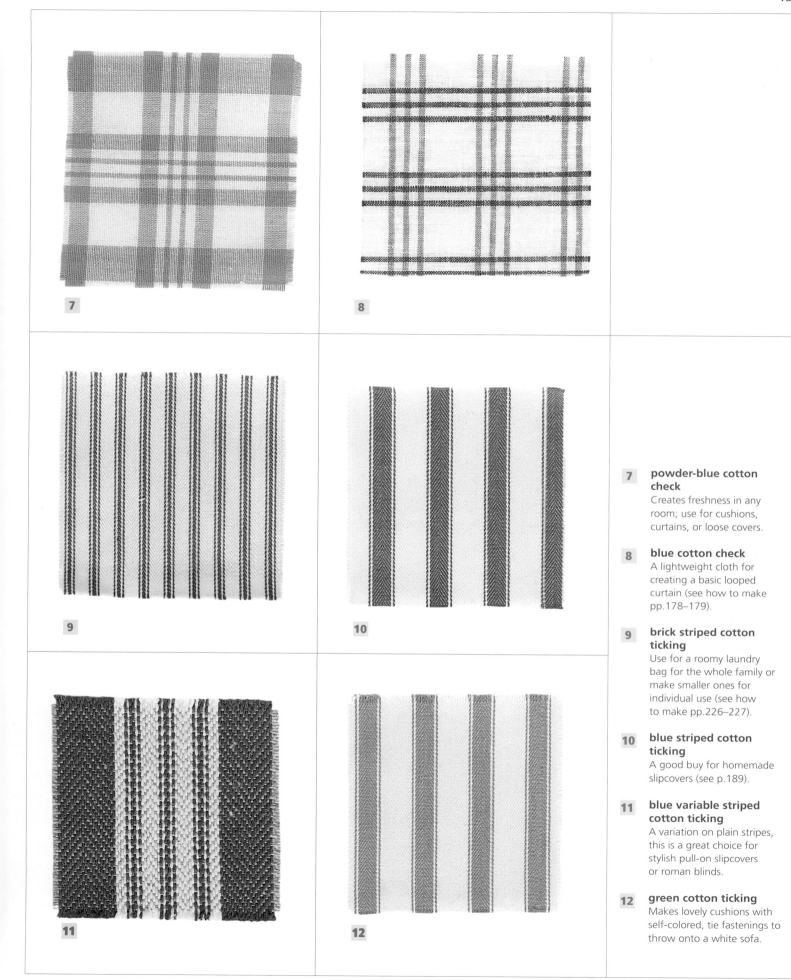

7 **powder-blue cotton check**
Creates freshness in any room; use for cushions, curtains, or loose covers.

8 **blue cotton check**
A lightweight cloth for creating a basic looped curtain (see how to make pp.178–179).

9 **brick striped cotton ticking**
Use for a roomy laundry bag for the whole family or make smaller ones for individual use (see how to make pp.226–227).

10 **blue striped cotton ticking**
A good buy for homemade slipcovers (see p.189).

11 **blue variable striped cotton ticking**
A variation on plain stripes, this is a great choice for stylish pull-on slipcovers or roman blinds.

12 **green cotton ticking**
Makes lovely cushions with self-colored, tie fastenings to throw onto a white sofa.

floral fabrics

cotton prints with spriggy
buds and blooms for floral
interest around the house

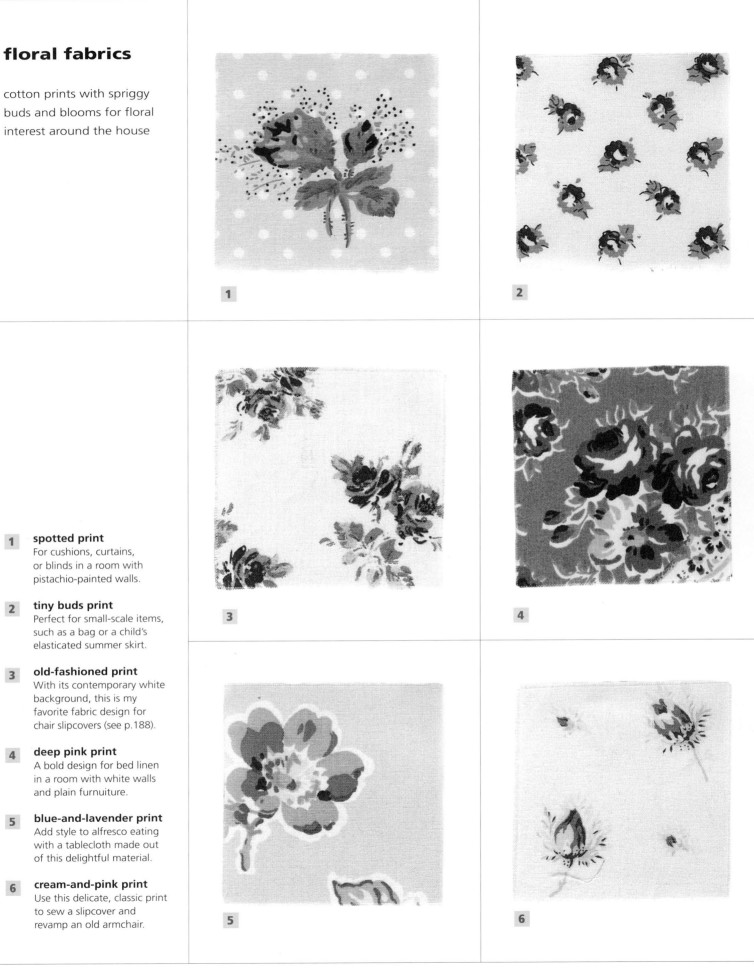

1 **spotted print**
For cushions, curtains,
or blinds in a room with
pistachio-painted walls.

2 **tiny buds print**
Perfect for small-scale items,
such as a bag or a child's
elasticated summer skirt.

3 **old-fashioned print**
With its contemporary white
background, this is my
favorite fabric design for
chair slipcovers (see p.188).

4 **deep pink print**
A bold design for bed linen
in a room with white walls
and plain furnuiture.

5 **blue-and-lavender print**
Add style to alfresco eating
with a tablecloth made out
of this delightful material.

6 **cream-and-pink print**
Use this delicate, classic print
to sew a slipcover and
revamp an old armchair.

7

8

9

10

11

12

7 rosy sprig print
The subtlety of the pattern allows abundant use in the bedroom for sheets, curtains, and matching chair cover.

8 border print
A striking design with a defined edge – perfect for roller or roman blinds.

9 buds-and-hearts print
This print's strong pink background and bold design cries out for a room with a neutral color scheme.

10 crisp multicolored print
A timeless design to use for cushions; combine with an old, faded quilt throw for a stronger floral look.

11 buds-and-roses print
Use this fine lawn for scented lavender bags, pillowcases, children's kerchiefs, or bags (see p.51).

12 retro rose print
A 1950s-style pattern suitable for an ironing board cover or a laundry bag (see how to make pp.226–227).

Flooring

hard flooring

soft flooring

hard flooring

wood, cork, rubber, terra-
cotta, and stone floor
surfaces to suit individual
needs and budgets

1 **reclaimed oak boards**
These are nicely worn,
textured, and durable;
alternatively, use new
oak sealed with a matte
varnish for a paler, more
modern look that will
weather with age.

2 **waxed pine boards**
Unbeatable basic, practical,
and affordable flooring; sand
and scrub with soap for a
Scandinavian look, or apply
paint or lime paste.

3 **hardwood parquet**
Reminiscent of polished
floors in Parisian apartments,
this floor covering works
well in modern and period
homes alike.

4 **cork tile**
A 1970s revival that is also
ecological – cork is harvested
from the same tree every nine
years. Insulating and warm,
cork can be used in hallways,
workrooms, and playrooms.

5 **rubber tiles**
6 Modern, warm, and
easy-to-clean flooring for
7 most areas; comes in many
colors, including white.

1

3

4

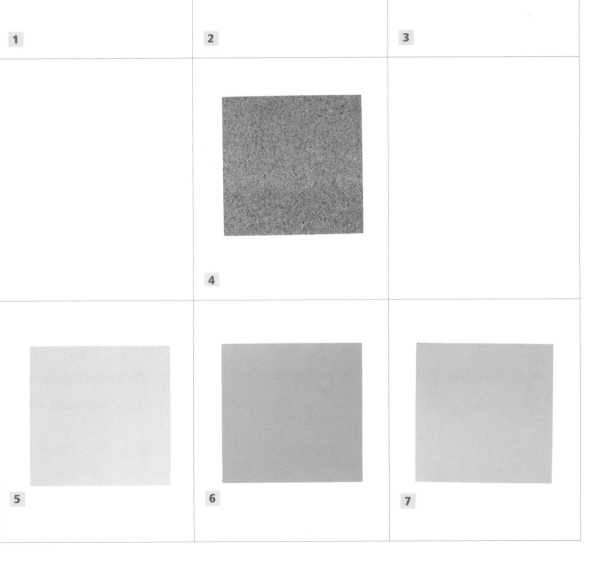

5

6

7

8

9

10

11

8

8 terra-cotta tile
In Spain, I have terra-cotta tiles throughout the house bought cheaply from the local contractors' supplier; they are sealed with linseed oil for a flat, unglossy finish.

9 limestone tiles
10 Natural and durable, limestone comes in a range
11 of colors and looks modern and streamlined in the kitchen and sun room.

soft flooring

tactile surfaces underfoot
add warmth and texture

1 **mat in seagrass squares**
A relic from the 1960s
(I grew up with them) that
has seen a revival with
the current trend for more
natural-looking floors.

2 **herringbone coir**
A rough-textured covering
derived from coconut husks.
Useful in heavily trafficked
areas such as stairs and halls.

3 **basketweave seagrass**
Grown in salt marshes, this
fiber looks good woven into
large mats bordered with
neutral or contrast-colored
cotton webbing.

4 **bouclé sisal**
A tough, lustrous fiber
from East Africa; being
soft on bare feet, it is a
good choice for bedrooms.

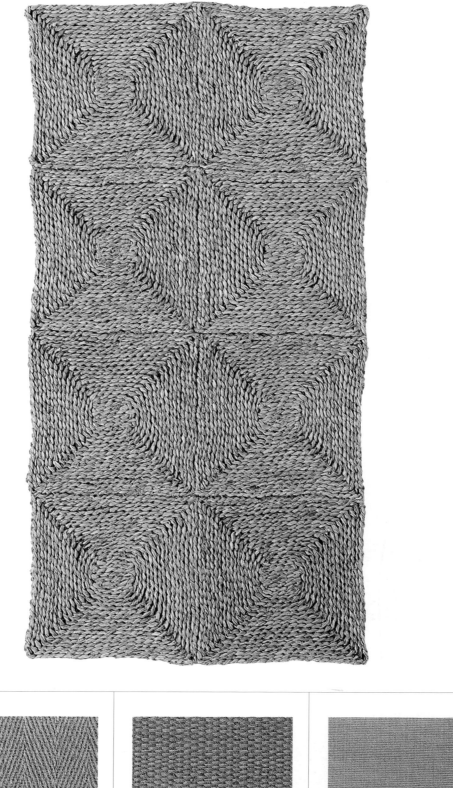

1

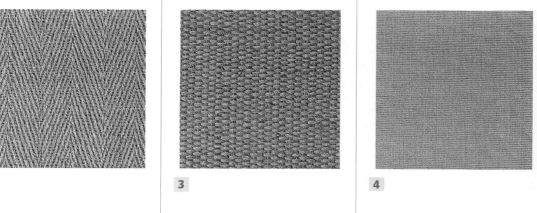

2

3

4

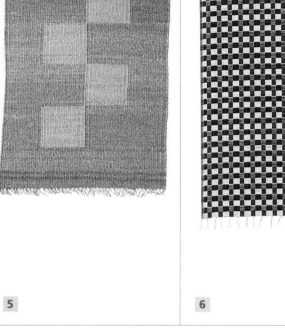

5

6

7

8

5 **fine seagrass rug**
Practical and softer than
some seagrass (see 1 and 3),
this is ideal as a hearth rug.

6 **woven plastic mat**
A tough, washable mat
from Africa that makes
perfect sense in kitchens
and bathrooms.

7 **cream rag rug**
Made from old pieces of
fabric, this softly textured
rug looks great on painted or
bare scrubbed floorboards.

8 **cotton check rug**
I have several of these
rugs in different colors
bought from chain stores;
immensely practical, they
can be rejuvenated in the
washing machine.

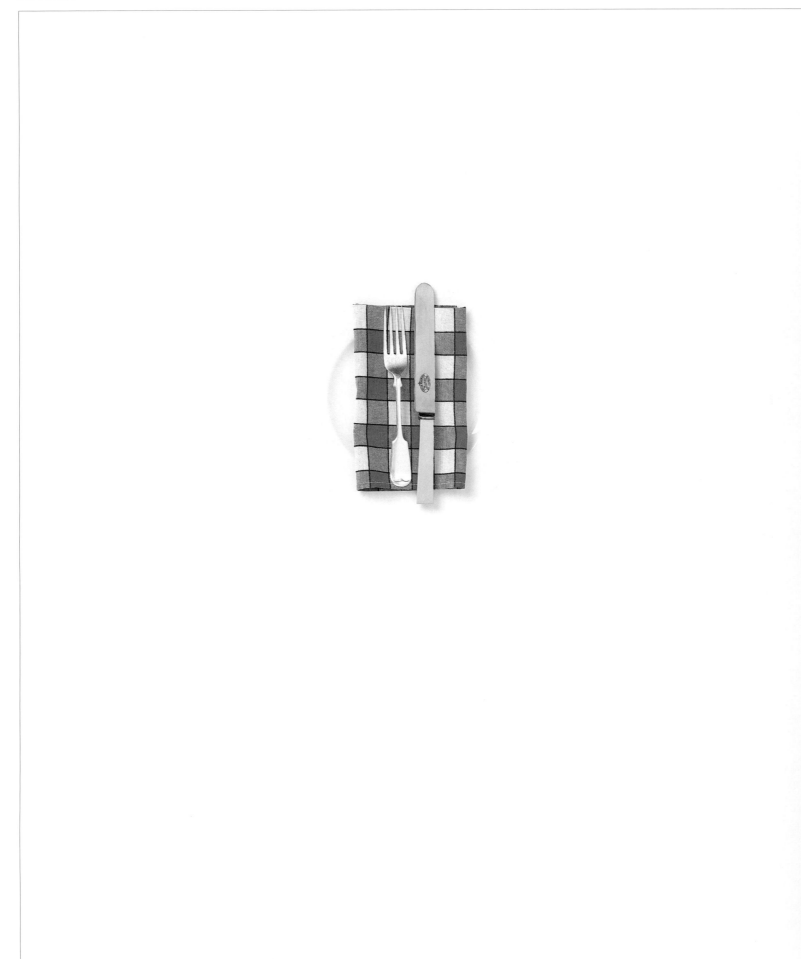

Eat

kitchen tools

food cupboard

kitchen storage

functional tableware

basic china and linen

tables

picnic

kitchen tools

basic gear for routine kitchen and cooking activities

1 **wooden spoon**
I have a collection picked up very cheaply from hardware stores all over the world. Useful for stirring stews, fools, and soups, a wooden spoon is simple, functional, and satisfying to hold.

2 **mixing bowl**
Cream-colored ceramic mixing bowls have been around for years. I use them for making sponge desserts, mixing chocolate cakes, as salad bowls, and even for planting spring bulbs.

3 **sharp knife**
I find that a small, good-quality stainless steel knife is invaluable for chopping herbs, garlic, fruit for jam, and slicing bread, cake, or oranges for school lunches.

4 **balloon whisk**
This style of whisk is good for small-scale cooking jobs such as whipping cream, mayonnaise, and salad dressing (my favorite is made of olive oil, lemon juice, Dijon mustard, and garlic).

5 **metal colander**
Mine hangs strategically above the sink and I like the ritual of rinsing dirt-covered potatoes and watching the water drain through the holes. Metal is more durable than plastic and can cope with greater heat.

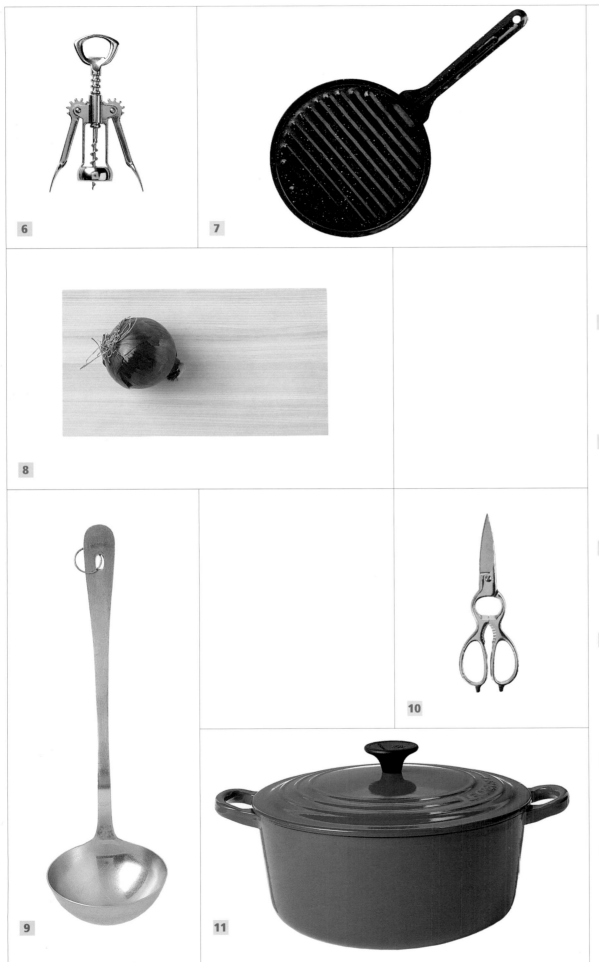

6   **lever-type corkscrew**
The easiest corkscrew to use – once screwed into the cork, minimal effort is required to lever it out. Panic breaks out in my household when it's mislaid, so I advise keeping it in a safe place.

7   **metal griddle pan**
A cheap find from a Spanish market, it produces perfectly seared swordfish or tuna steaks (marinated in olive oil, freshly chopped parsley, garlic, and lemon juice).

8   **wooden chopping board**
I have several boards in different sizes for different uses. Keep color-coded plastic boards that are used only for raw meat and fish.

9   **stainless steel ladle**
Indispensable for stirring jams and marmalades, and dishing up homemade soups in the winter – leek and potato, Jerusalem artichoke, chicken and vegetable, mushroom, and chestnut.

10   **kitchen scissors**
These have endless uses; they are particularly handy for topping and tailing beans, cutting up squid, or gutting sardines and mackerel.

11   **blue, oval enameled cast-iron casserole**
A heavy-based pan is ideal for slowly cooking juicy stews of chicken, pork, or rabbit with tomatoes and rosemary – my favorite.

food cupboard

edible essentials for my kitchen. See also pantry-stocking ingredients on p.102

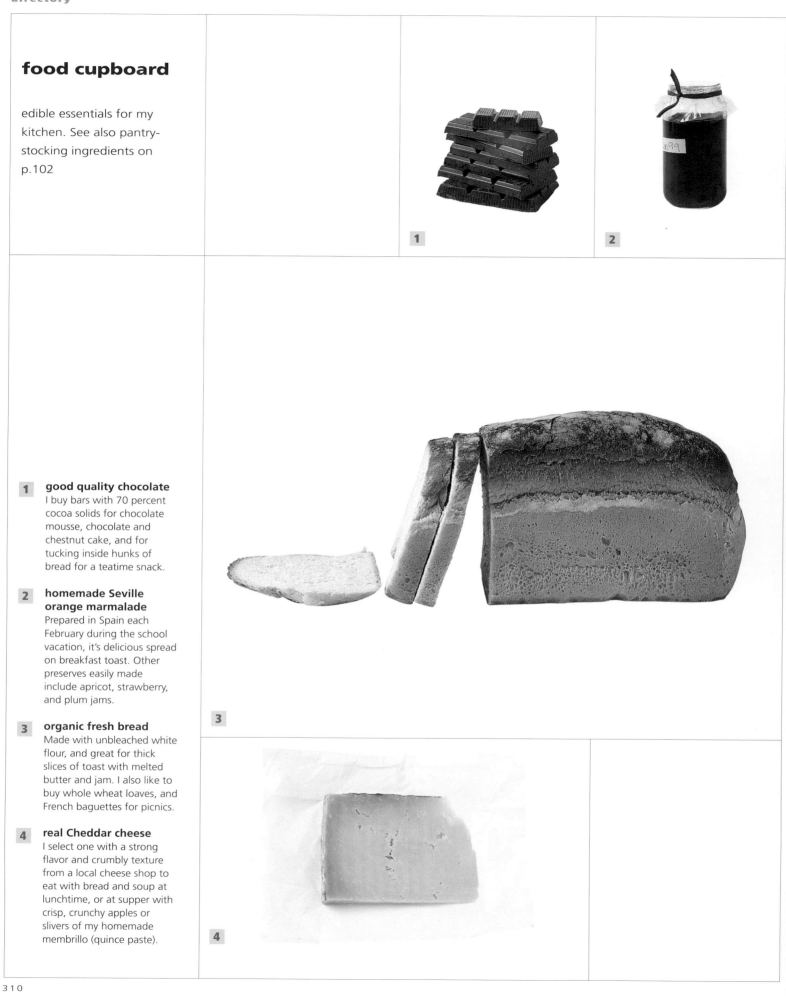

1

2

3

4

1 **good quality chocolate**
I buy bars with 70 percent cocoa solids for chocolate mousse, chocolate and chestnut cake, and for tucking inside hunks of bread for a teatime snack.

2 **homemade Seville orange marmalade**
Prepared in Spain each February during the school vacation, it's delicious spread on breakfast toast. Other preserves easily made include apricot, strawberry, and plum jams.

3 **organic fresh bread**
Made with unbleached white flour, and great for thick slices of toast with melted butter and jam. I also like to buy whole wheat loaves, and French baguettes for picnics.

4 **real Cheddar cheese**
I select one with a strong flavor and crumbly texture from a local cheese shop to eat with bread and soup at lunchtime, or at supper with crisp, crunchy apples or slivers of my homemade membrillo (quince paste).

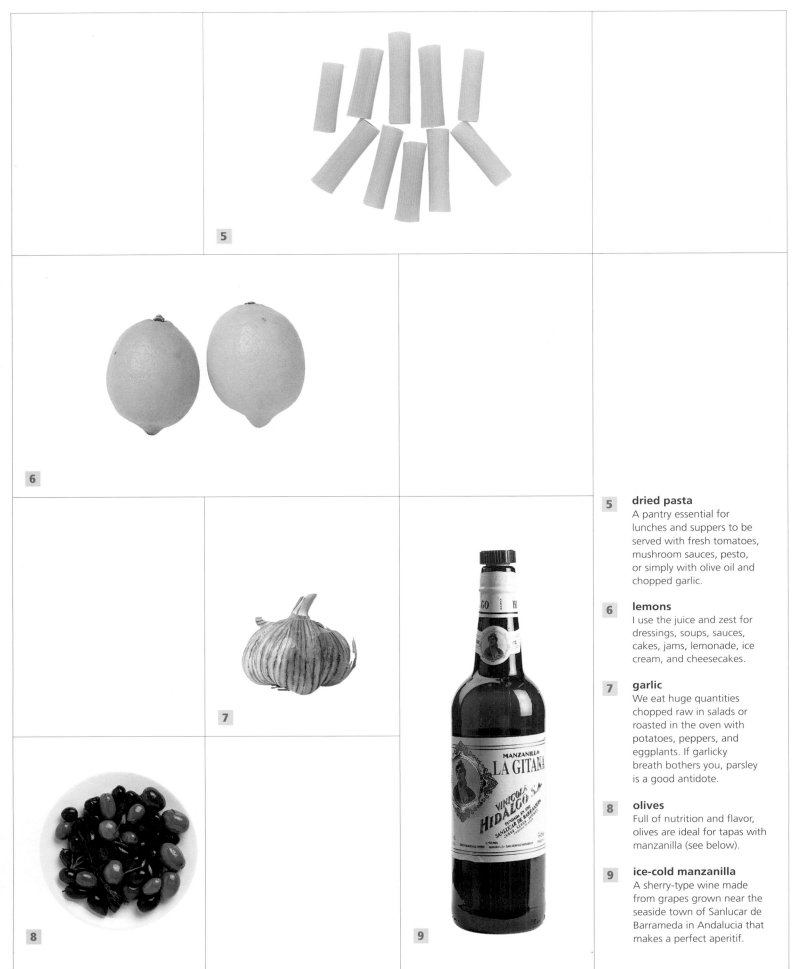

5 **dried pasta**
A pantry essential for lunches and suppers to be served with fresh tomatoes, mushroom sauces, pesto, or simply with olive oil and chopped garlic.

6 **lemons**
I use the juice and zest for dressings, soups, sauces, cakes, jams, lemonade, ice cream, and cheesecakes.

7 **garlic**
We eat huge quantities chopped raw in salads or roasted in the oven with potatoes, peppers, and eggplants. If garlicky breath bothers you, parsley is a good antidote.

8 **olives**
Full of nutrition and flavor, olives are ideal for tapas with manzanilla (see below).

9 **ice-cold manzanilla**
A sherry-type wine made from grapes grown near the seaside town of Sanlucar de Barrameda in Andalucia that makes a perfect aperitif.

kitchen storage

functional ideas for storing food, cutlery, china, linen, and other kitchen items

1 **mesh food net**
A useful device for covering cooked meat before it is put in the refrigerator, or for protecting plates of cheese from flies and wasps.

2 **plastic cart**
A portable idea for storing vegetables, linen, and other kitchen paraphernalia.

3 **1950s Bakelite® cutlery tray**
Found in a market stall and bought for its pea-green color.

4 **1950s enameled stacking tin**
A junk shop find, I store cake in the bottom part and layers of cookies above. A modern version in stainless steel is available.

5 **stainless steel container**
With a plastic lid – a simple camping-style idea for packed lunches, picnics, and general food storage.

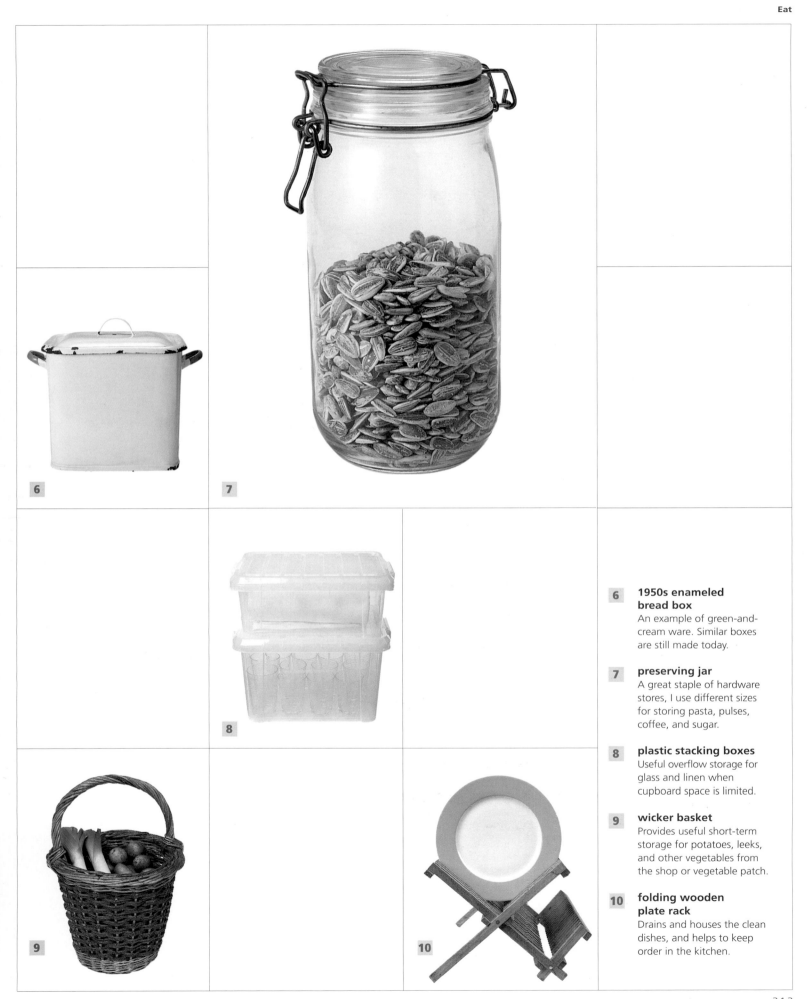

6

7

8

9

10

6 **1950s enameled bread box**
An example of green-and-cream ware. Similar boxes are still made today.

7 **preserving jar**
A great staple of hardware stores, I use different sizes for storing pasta, pulses, coffee, and sugar.

8 **plastic stacking boxes**
Useful overflow storage for glass and linen when cupboard space is limited.

9 **wicker basket**
Provides useful short-term storage for potatoes, leeks, and other vegetables from the shop or vegetable patch.

10 **folding wooden plate rack**
Drains and houses the clean dishes, and helps to keep order in the kitchen.

functional tableware

ideas borrowed from utilitarian cafés and institutional canteens

1 white-handled stainless steel cutlery
Bistro-style cutlery that goes in the dishwasher.

2 stainless steel cutlery
Solid, formal cutlery that can be buffed up with a linen dish towel for a gleaming shine.

3 robust glass
Unbreakable glassware available in a range of sizes and shapes for orange juice, water, or any other drink.

4 espresso maker
I have a small two-cup size for weekdays and a large eight-cup model for large numbers on weekends.

5
6 salt and pepper shakers
A plain and simple idea borrowed from café tables.

7   1930s ice cream bowl
Perfect for portions of home-made ice cream, served sundae style with a delicious cookie; equally good for raspberry fool.

8   robust tumbler
Hard to break, this vessel is perfect for breakfast milk, lunchtime lemonade, or a cool beer in the evening.

9   sugar shaker
Another sturdy café detail that keeps the sugar dry and away from little hands.

10   silver fork and bone-handled knife
Buy beautiful cutlery secondhand, to team with a crisp white cotton cloth and napkins.

11   simple wine glass
Can be bought cheaply in boxes of twelve from kitchen shops or department stores.

12   glass water pitcher
As used in cafeterias. Buy from hardware stores.

basic china and linen

plain white china and linen,
with a splash of blue,
for everyday eating and
special occasions

1 **white mug**
Easy to replace and looks
good in my white kitchen.

2 **white dinner plate**
I buy this classic design in
bone china during the sales
at department stores.

3 **pale blue-and-white
striped table linen**
For a fresh feel to your
dining area. Always iron
linen when damp.

4 **white mug edged in
dark blue**
To complement your plain
white crockery.

5 **plastic checked cloth**
Easily wiped down, this is
the ultimate practical table
covering for everyday use. I
buy it by the yard from a
hardware store.

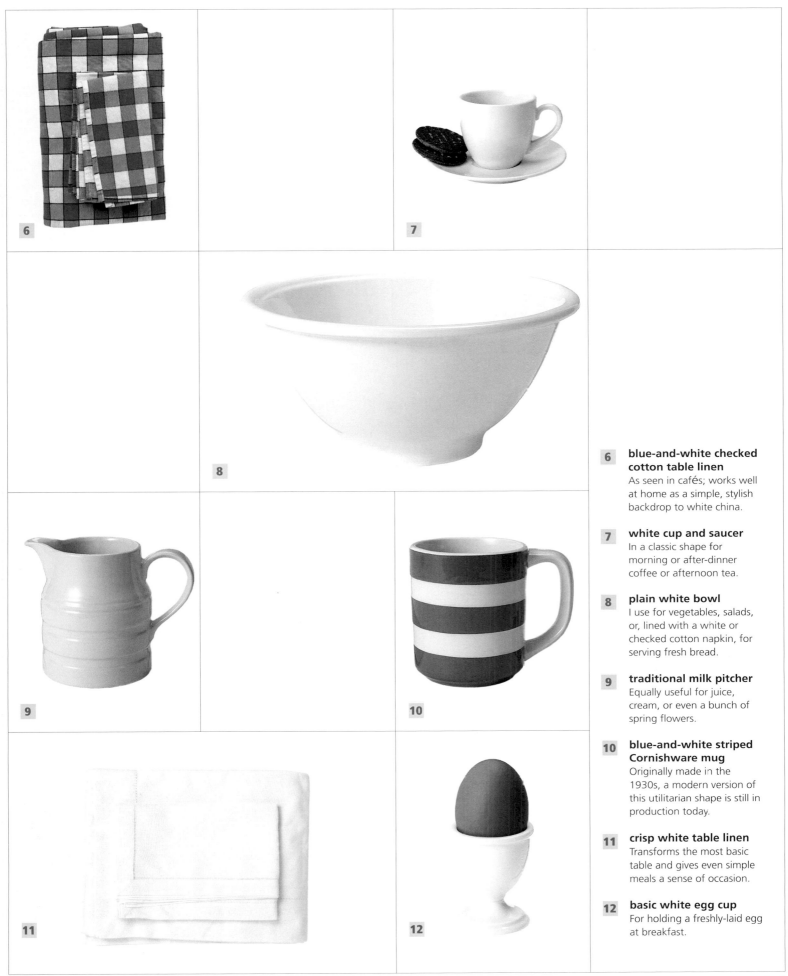

6 blue-and-white checked cotton table linen
As seen in cafés; works well at home as a simple, stylish backdrop to white china.

7 white cup and saucer
In a classic shape for morning or after-dinner coffee or afternoon tea.

8 plain white bowl
I use for vegetables, salads, or, lined with a white or checked cotton napkin, for serving fresh bread.

9 traditional milk pitcher
Equally useful for juice, cream, or even a bunch of spring flowers.

10 blue-and-white striped Cornishware mug
Originally made in the 1930s, a modern version of this utilitarian shape is still in production today.

11 crisp white table linen
Transforms the most basic table and gives even simple meals a sense of occasion.

12 basic white egg cup
For holding a freshly-laid egg at breakfast.

tables

multifunctional surfaces
on which to prepare food,
eat, and work

1

2

3

4

1 secondhand oak desk
Doubles as a dining table,
here laid with white plates,
simple glasses, cutlery, and a
single potted hyacinth.

**2 lightweight folding
metal table**
Easily carried, this table is
really useful for picnics and
other outdoor eating ideas.

3 folding wooden table
A simple, small, slatted table
painted in white eggshell has
an endless number of uses
around the house.

4 pine kitchen table
Used for food preparation,
family meals, and as a
surface for my children to
work on.

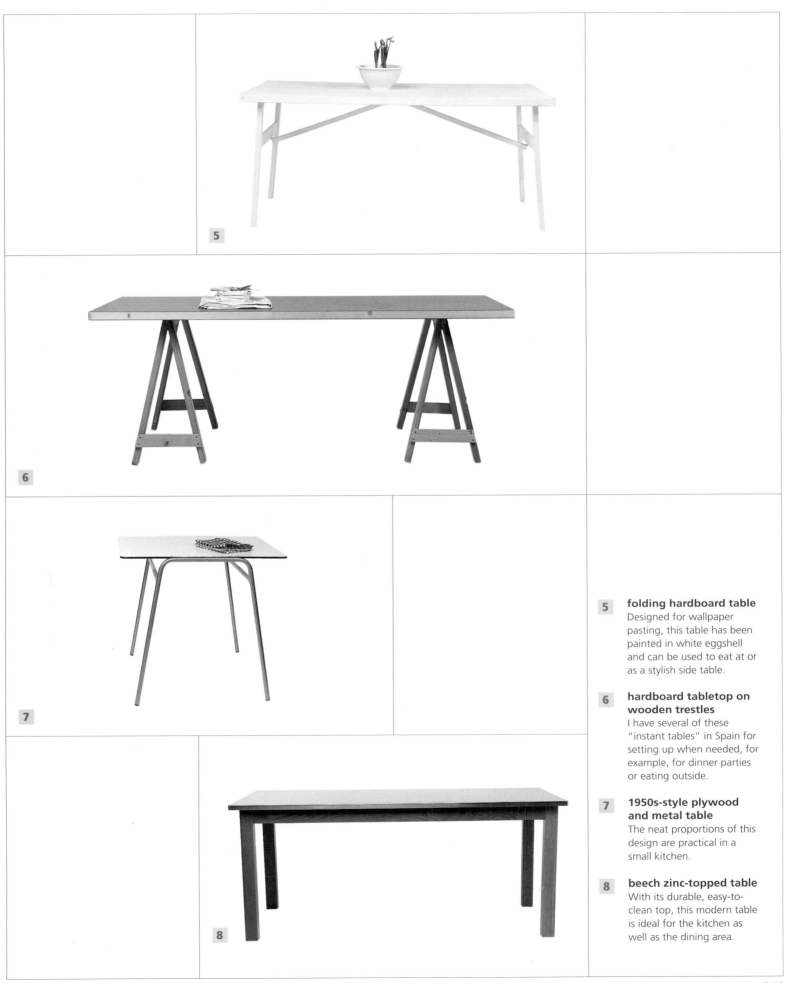

5 folding hardboard table
Designed for wallpaper pasting, this table has been painted in white eggshell and can be used to eat at or as a stylish side table.

6 hardboard tabletop on wooden trestles
I have several of these "instant tables" in Spain for setting up when needed, for example, for dinner parties or eating outside.

7 1950s-style plywood and metal table
The neat proportions of this design are practical in a small kitchen.

8 beech zinc-topped table
With its durable, easy-to-clean top, this modern table is ideal for the kitchen as well as the dining area.

picnic

just add ice-cold wine, good cheese, and some bread to the items shown here for a perfect picnic

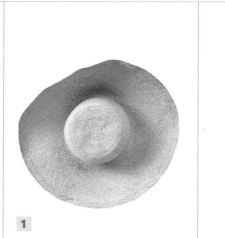

1

2

3

1 **floppy straw sunhat**
A wide-brimmed hat is essential for beach picnics or whenever shade is minimal.

2 **small camping kettle**
To boil water for coffee or tea on a campfire or camp stove.

3 **Spanish grass basket**
My favorite picnic basket – generally stuffed with a rug, sunscreen, a corkscrew, and a good book.

4 **portable barbecue**
Big enough for frankfurters or skewered chicken, and easily carried to the beach or countryside picnic area.

5 **refreezable water packs**
I keep loads in the freezer, and use to pack around food in the picnic basket, or place in a cooler or bag to keep food and drinks cool in high summer.

4

5

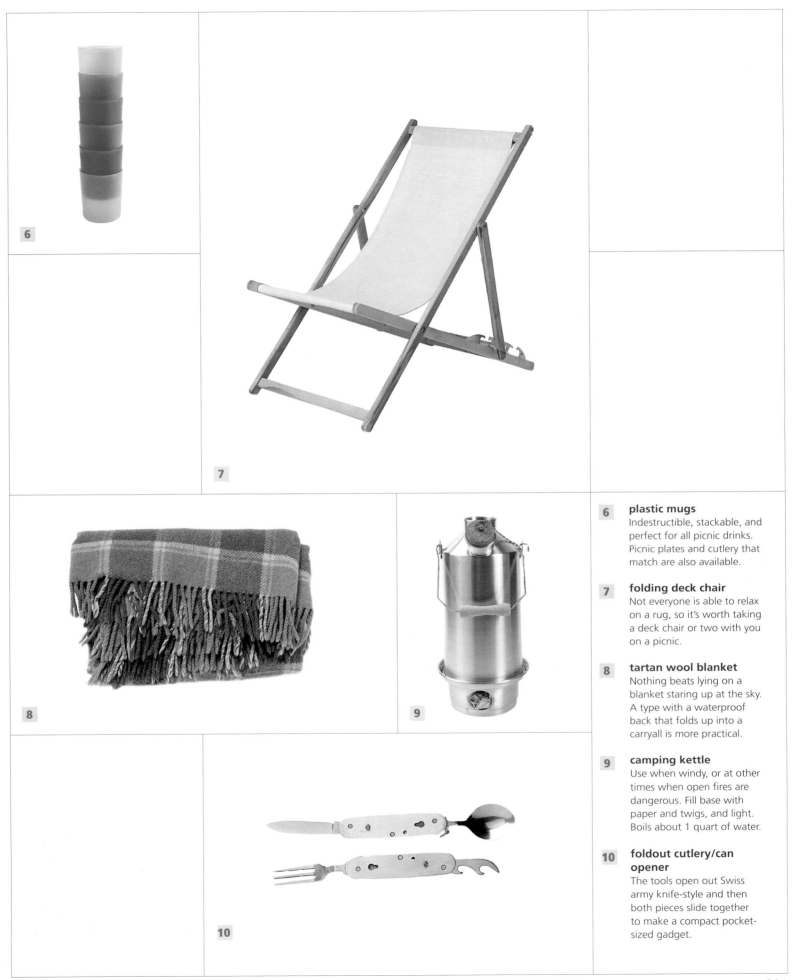

6 plastic mugs
Indestructible, stackable, and perfect for all picnic drinks. Picnic plates and cutlery that match are also available.

7 folding deck chair
Not everyone is able to relax on a rug, so it's worth taking a deck chair or two with you on a picnic.

8 tartan wool blanket
Nothing beats lying on a blanket staring up at the sky. A type with a waterproof back that folds up into a carryall is more practical.

9 camping kettle
Use when windy, or at other times when open fires are dangerous. Fill base with paper and twigs, and light. Boils about 1 quart of water.

10 foldout cutlery/can opener
The tools open out Swiss army knife-style and then both pieces slide together to make a compact pocket-sized gadget.

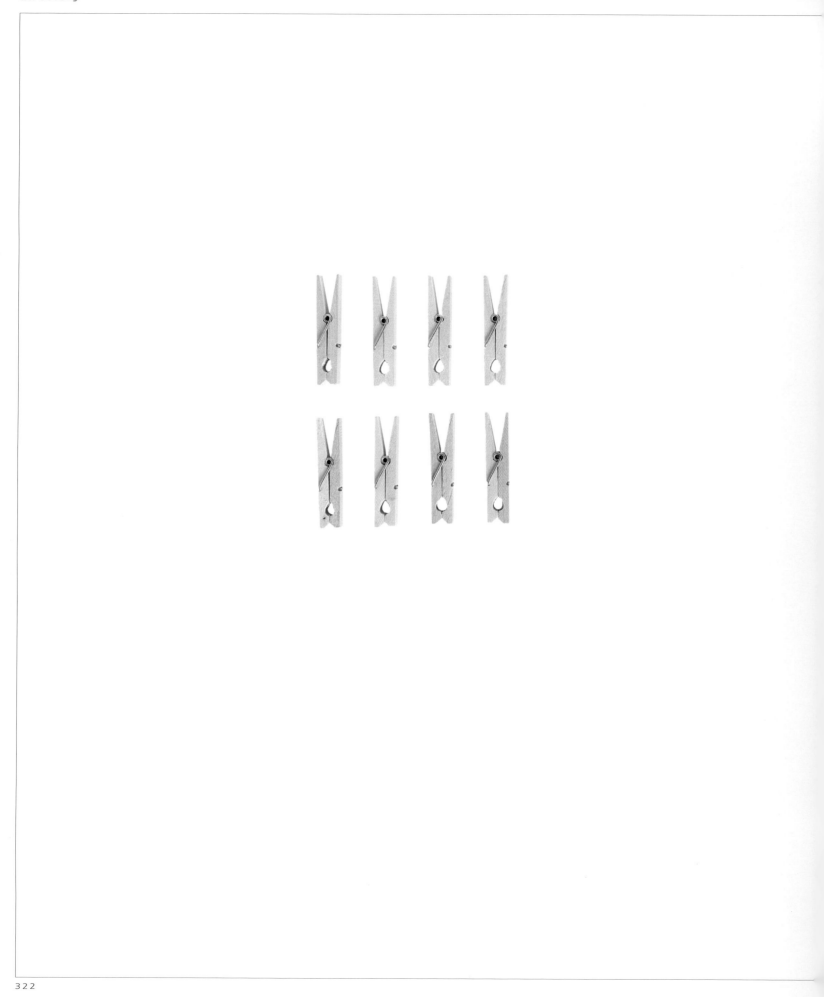

Work

household

eco-friendly

storage

seating

Work data

In the new millennium, housewives/mothers/workers do not expect to be domestic saints – we realized long ago that the odds are stacked against us.

Consider one of my typical domestic scenarios – squealing children, a hamster with a gungy eye that needs to be rushed to the vet, a broken dishwasher, pasta sauce boiling and bubbling, and a work deadline to be met – all to be dealt with before I allow myself a pampering trip to the swimming pool.

Efficiency

I have found that the following **solutions** help to keep imminent insanity at bay: **domestic cleaner –** when I am working, Sandra takes the strain off me by washing last night's dishes and cleaning up the bomb site that is the childrens' room; **laundry baskets** – I have one for dirty clothes, one for things to be ironed, and one for ironed laundry that is ready to be put away; **clothes rack** – good for small spaces, and a neat, eco-friendly way of drying laundry; **damp mop and duster –** for whizzing around the apartment and cleaning up dust and dirt efficiently; **linen tea towels** – the only way to dry glasses; **take the weight off your feet –** some people I know do the ironing while sitting down; **notebook** – for copious lists; **computer** with email facility, **and mobile phone** – indispensable items; **anglepoise desk lamps –** for spotlighting work tasks on gloomy days and at night; **open shelving** forms my desk, with filing boxes for all work cuttings and research material; **office filing cabinets** – painted white for all personal filing; **big bulletin board –** for displaying all the family's social commitments.

Eco-office

Help to take the pressure off the environment by being eco-conscious around the house: **use recycled paper** and write notes on both sides; keep a pile of scrap paper and ultimately recycle; **recycle old computer equipment**, and printer, fax, and photocopier toner cartridges can be sent to developing countries; **save envelopes** for reuse; **stop junk mail** by contacting companies and having your name removed from their mailing lists.

Eco-household

Buy household cleaning products with only natural botanical and mineral ingredients, with no petrochemical detergents, phosphates, optical brighteners, bleaches, synthetic perfumes, or colorings; **buy recycled** toilet paper and kitchen towels; **choose products with reusable packaging**, for example, jelly jars and ice-cream cartons can be used for storage around the house, and glass bottles can be reused up to 100 times; take newspapers, glass and plastic bottles, jars, and aluminium cans to recycling centers; **recycle old clothes** and take them to a charity shop; those not good enough to sell can be recycled to make blankets; **use cloth diapers** since disposable ones make up 4 percent of household waste; new styles have velcro fasteners and snaps, and some have biodegradable liners that can be flushed down the toilet; **use cooler wash temperatures** and only place full loads in the washing machine (the average washing cycle uses 25 gallons of water, and a full load uses less water than two half loads), and let clothes dry naturally; **replace washers** in dripping faucets – one dripping faucet could waste 23 gallons of water in one week; **insulate** the attic and insulate the hot water heater and pipes to save heat and money; **boil only as much water** as you need in the kettle; **cool water** kept in the fridge is more refreshing and you don't have to let the faucet run for ages to get a cold drink; **install a water meter** to monitor how much water you use; **turn down the heating** thermostat by 2°F or use one hour less heating a day to cut household CO_2 emissions by 5–10 percent; **salt** will soak up fruit juice, urine, and red wine – pour a large mugful onto the spill, leave for several hours to absorb, and vacuum or shake out; **borax** (an alkaline mineral salt) loosens dirt and grease and works as an antiseptic; add 1 tablespoon of borax to 1.5 gallons of water to soak stained clothes and linens, and use half a cup in a bucket of hot water for kitchen cleaning; **a vinegar-and-water solution** can be used for cleaning the toilet; **castor oil** conditions leather boots, saddles, and bags; **citric acid** (found in lemon juice) removes hard-water limescale from the bathtub and toilet, and cleans brass; **a moth deterrent** can be made by putting lavender, cloves, cinnamon, black pepper, and orris root in a muslin bag and placing among clothes; **baking powder** (sodium bicarbonate) removes stains from china, glass, tiles, and the fridge (use as a paste mixed with water); **washing soda** (sodium carbonate) is useful for cleaning and clearing drains; **beeswax polish** is sold in blocks and can be bought from hardware stores; to make the polish, scrape or grate 1 oz beeswax into 5 fl oz turpentine and leave to dissolve for several days; shake before using and wear gloves when applying; **to restore whiteness** to white cotton socks and other small, white items boil for 5 minutes in water containing a slice of lemon.

household

basic equipment for an
efficient home

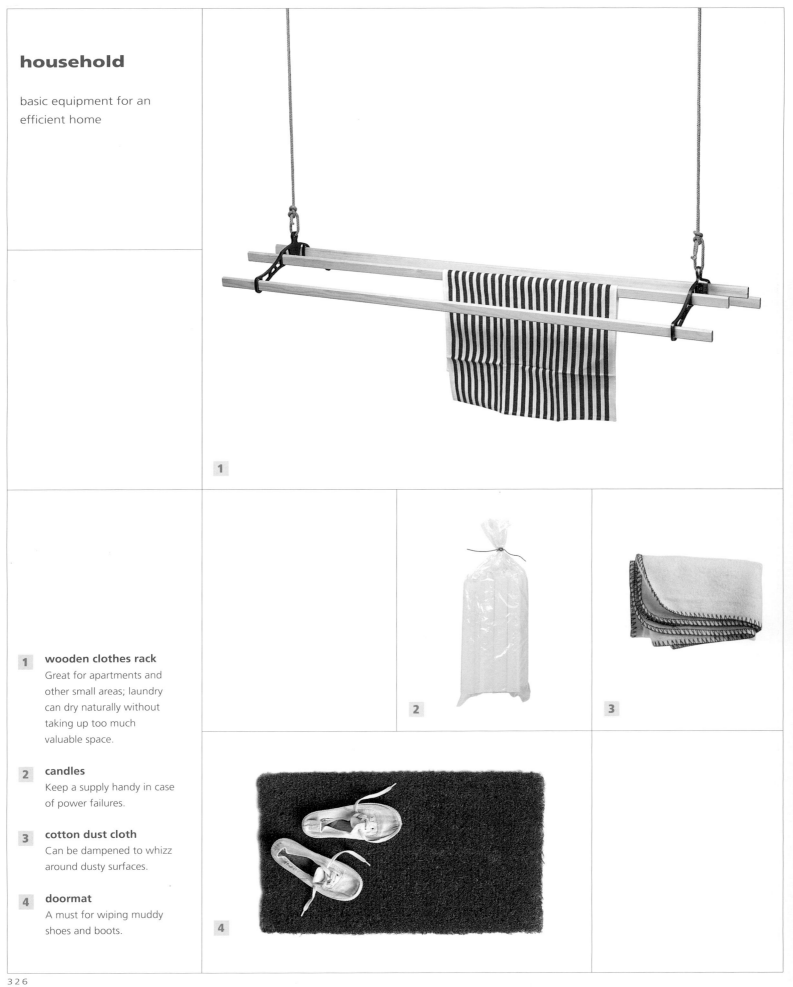

1 **wooden clothes rack**
Great for apartments and
other small areas; laundry
can dry naturally without
taking up too much
valuable space.

2 **candles**
Keep a supply handy in case
of power failures.

3 **cotton dust cloth**
Can be dampened to whizz
around dusty surfaces.

4 **doormat**
A must for wiping muddy
shoes and boots.

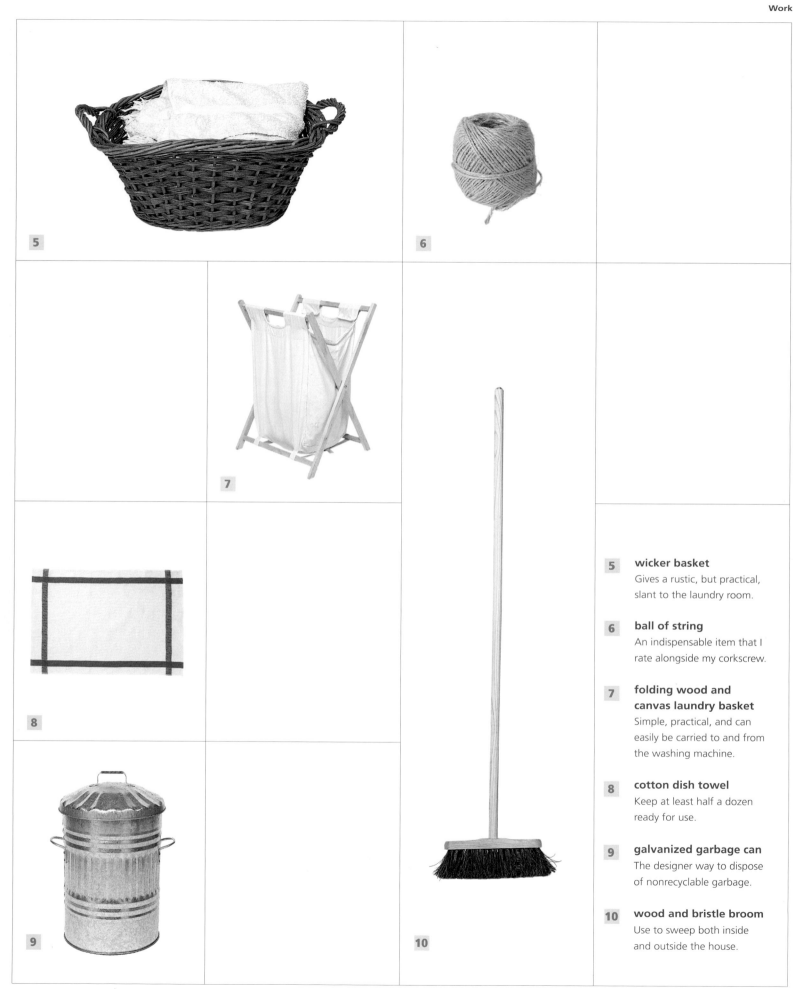

5 wicker basket
Gives a rustic, but practical, slant to the laundry room.

6 ball of string
An indispensable item that I rate alongside my corkscrew.

7 folding wood and canvas laundry basket
Simple, practical, and can easily be carried to and from the washing machine.

8 cotton dish towel
Keep at least half a dozen ready for use.

9 galvanized garbage can
The designer way to dispose of nonrecyclable garbage.

10 wood and bristle broom
Use to sweep both inside and outside the house.

eco-friendly

recycled, resourceful, and
energy-saving ideas

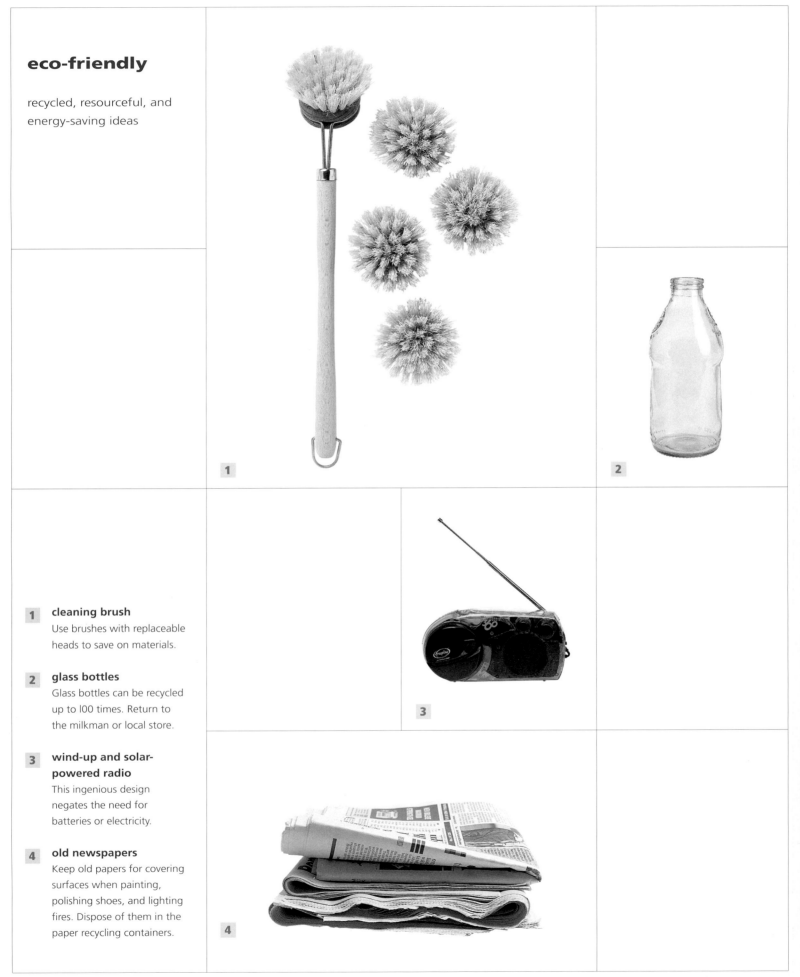

1

2

3

4

1 cleaning brush
Use brushes with replaceable
heads to save on materials.

2 glass bottles
Glass bottles can be recycled
up to l00 times. Return to
the milkman or local store.

**3 wind-up and solar-
powered radio**
This ingenious design
negates the need for
batteries or electricity.

4 old newspapers
Keep old papers for covering
surfaces when painting,
polishing shoes, and lighting
fires. Dispose of them in the
paper recycling containers.

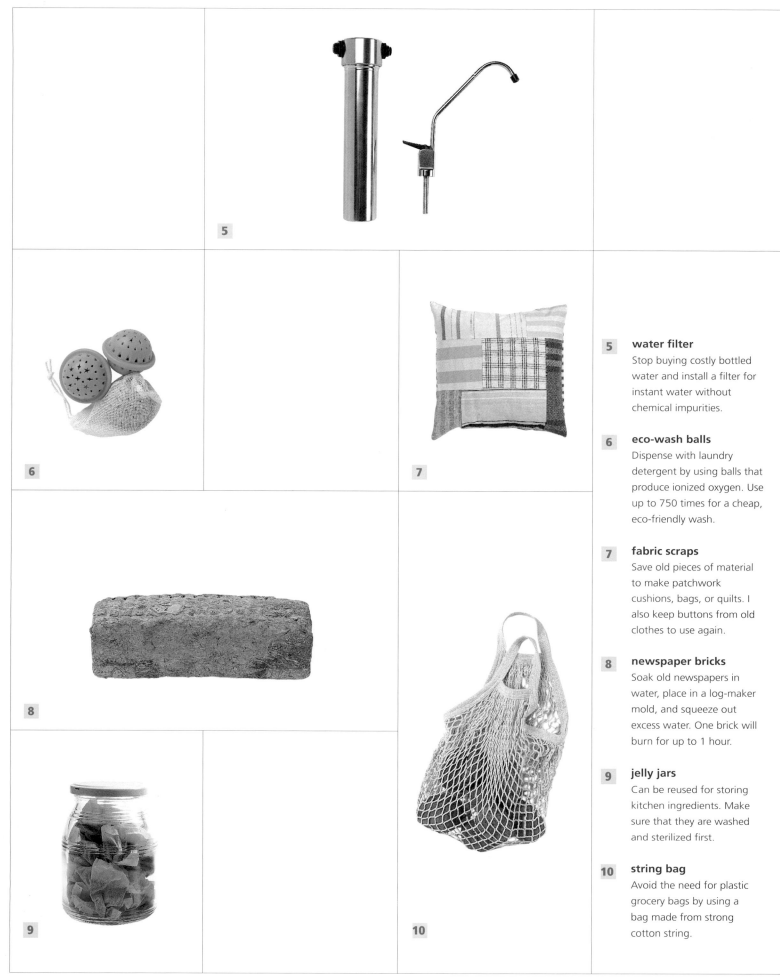

5 **water filter**
Stop buying costly bottled water and install a filter for instant water without chemical impurities.

6 **eco-wash balls**
Dispense with laundry detergent by using balls that produce ionized oxygen. Use up to 750 times for a cheap, eco-friendly wash.

7 **fabric scraps**
Save old pieces of material to make patchwork cushions, bags, or quilts. I also keep buttons from old clothes to use again.

8 **newspaper bricks**
Soak old newspapers in water, place in a log-maker mold, and squeeze out excess water. One brick will burn for up to 1 hour.

9 **jelly jars**
Can be reused for storing kitchen ingredients. Make sure that they are washed and sterilized first.

10 **string bag**
Avoid the need for plastic grocery bags by using a bag made from strong cotton string.

.storage

multifunctional crates,
baskets, and shelves

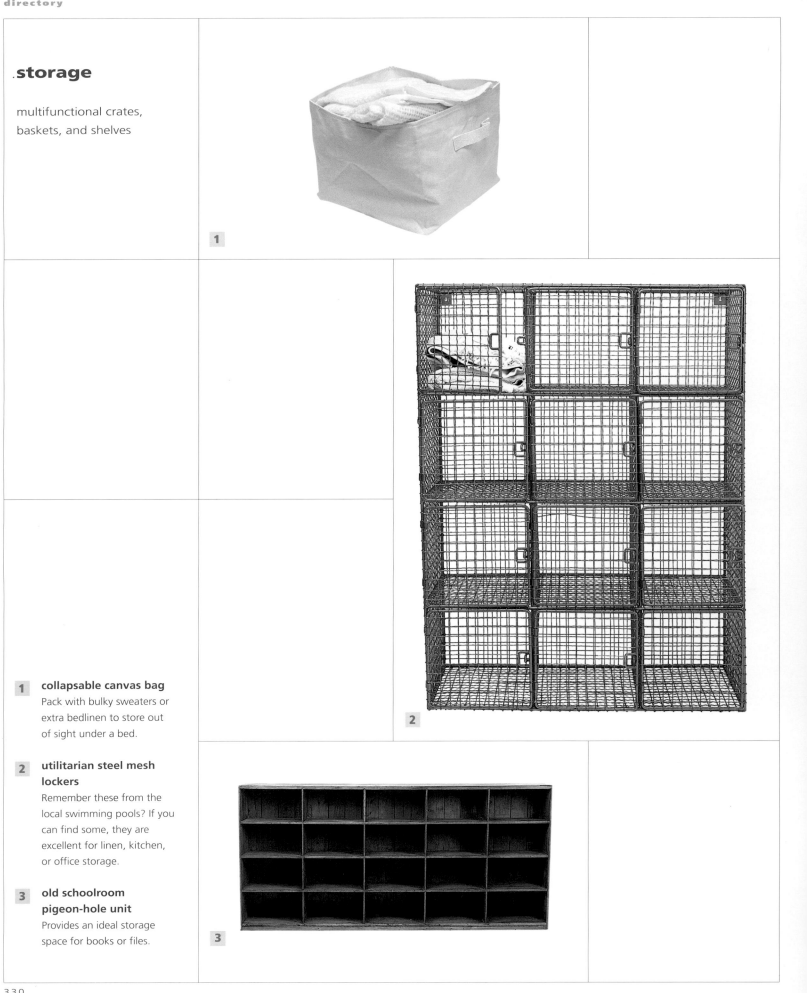

1

2

1 collapsable canvas bag
Pack with bulky sweaters or
extra bedlinen to store out
of sight under a bed.

**2 utilitarian steel mesh
lockers**
Remember these from the
local swimming pools? If you
can find some, they are
excellent for linen, kitchen,
or office storage.

**3 old schoolroom
pigeon-hole unit**
Provides an ideal storage
space for books or files.

3

4

woven grass baskets
These stackable containers can be used to hold sewing tools and fabrics.

5

rattan baskets
Rigid, lidded containers that can be used in the bedroom, kitchen, playroom, or office.

6

recycled pulpboard shelves
Flat-pack, lightweight, and compact shelving that is perfect for a home office.

7

l9th-century wooden cupboard with shelves
An old-fashioned storage solution for kitchenware, books, or linens. Paint white for a contemporary look.

8

recycled flat-pack cardboard drawers
The perfect desk caddy, this chest is ideal for storing pens and other stationery items.

9

plastic crates
Light, stackable boxes that can be hidden away in a cupboard with their contents labeled for easy accessibility.

seating

flexible shapes for all
around the house

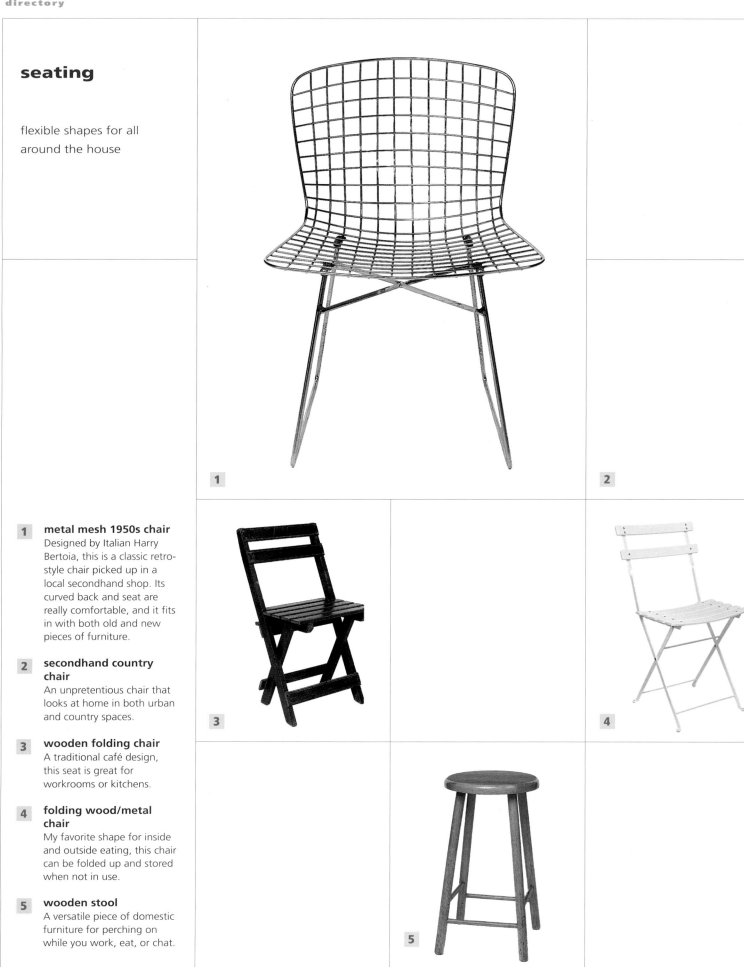

1 metal mesh 1950s chair
Designed by Italian Harry
Bertoia, this is a classic retro-
style chair picked up in a
local secondhand shop. Its
curved back and seat are
really comfortable, and it fits
in with both old and new
pieces of furniture.

2 secondhand country
chair
An unpretentious chair that
looks at home in both urban
and country spaces.

3 wooden folding chair
A traditional café design,
this seat is great for
workrooms or kitchens.

4 folding wood/metal
chair
My favorite shape for inside
and outside eating, this chair
can be folded up and stored
when not in use.

5 wooden stool
A versatile piece of domestic
furniture for perching on
while you work, eat, or chat.

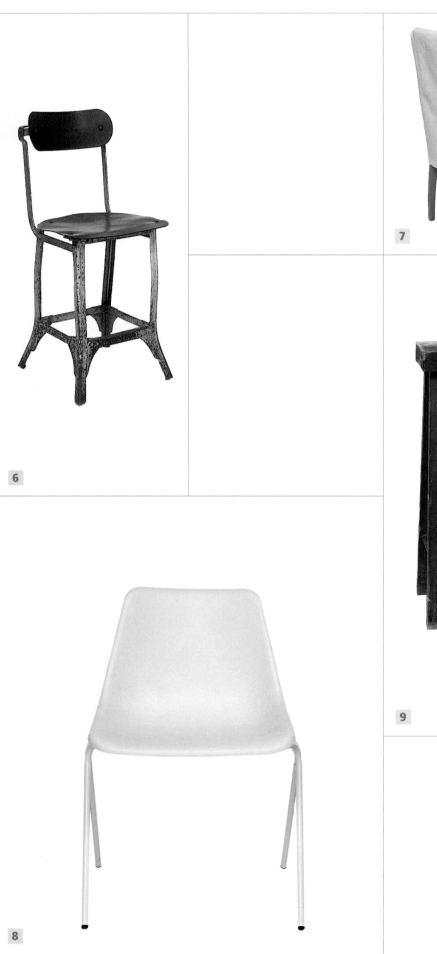

6

7

9

8

6 **metal factory chair**
A utilitarian chair from an old wool mill that would work well as a work or dining chair.

7 **basic upholstered chair**
For a dining table. Its simple cotton cover can be thrown into the washing machine whenever necessary.

8 **stacking plastic chair**
Clean, practical, colorful, and modern, this is an update of the classic 1960s design by Robin Day – loved by schools and other institutions.

9 **old stool**
Probably originating from an old factory or warehouse, this solid oak stool was a bargain from a secondhand shop.

Garden

garden tools

organic produce

pure style flowers

container ideas

Garden data

Gardens are our own little eco-systems, where we can grow nutritious produce and maintain a balance with nature by using organic gardening methods. Making compost from vegetable peelings, eggshells, and even old teabags is an ecological and resourceful way to make the most of household garbage. It is tempting to use chemical fertilizers that promise rapid rates of growth, but in the long term they can damage the soil structure and their residues are passed into the human body. Equally, chemical pest control can be so effective that it wipes out all bugs in the garden, including useful ones.

Compost

The main source of soil fertility in the organic garden should be recycled organic materials, such as compost and well-rotted manure. Buy **organic compost** and growbags or, better still, make your own **compost heap** using organic household waste. Buy or construct **a compost bin** – ideally made of wire, or plank fencing with ventilation holes; choose or make the largest you can fit into a corner of your garden and place it on earth not concrete. **Keep a bucket** for all organic kitchen waste – fruit and vegetable peelings, tomato skins, eggshells, bread, cereals, tea bags, coffee grounds, and non-animal leftovers; although cooked meat and fish flesh decomposes nicely, it is best avoided as it attracts rats, foxes, and hungry dogs; **dampen** cardboard and newspaper to speed up decomposition before adding to the heap; **use organic material** from outside the garden, for example leaf mold from the park or woods; seaweed from a trip to the beach; leaf sweepings from the street (organic gardeners soon develop an eye for possible compost material); **add different textures** to the heap – woody, grassy, leafy – in alternating layers; **turn the heap** two or three times to add air and generate aerobic activity (that is, activate the oxygen-loving microbes to break down the organic matter); **add nitrogen** in the form of fishmeal to encourage the rotting process further: the compost needs to be very hot for continued decomposition and while young green growth contains enough nitrogen to achieve this heat, dry matter, such as straw, does not; the heat kills most seeds, which is why you don't see tomato plants, apple tree saplings, or even weeds growing out of compost heaps. Once built, cover the heap with a layer of earth and a lid to retain the heat and speed up the rotting process. **Fresh compost can be applied** directly to the soil or dug in according to the garden's needs and the time of year. **Depending on the season** and the weather, a heap 5 ft high will take between three and six months to rot down. The complete cycle from food to decomposition and back to food can take as little as two years.

Fertilizers

Overdressing with nitrates and other **artificial fertilizers** leads to soil debility with the result that plants lose their strength. Where supplies of compost are insufficient or there are major deficiencies in the soil, use one or more of the following **organic fertilizers**: bonemeal, which is a slow-release form of organic phosphate that promotes strong root growth; fish, blood, and bone, which contains slow-release nitrogen and phosphate for steady growth and a strong root system; gypsum, a conditioner for heavy clay soils; potash for healthy tomatoes and fruit. Also, **rotate vegetable crops** (that is, don't grow the same crop on the same ground for two years running) to keep the soil from becoming depleted of nourishment, which may necessitate the use of chemical fertilizers. **Synthetic pesticides** can do long-term damage since they upset the natural balance of pests and predators; this negative aspect is often overlooked because of the temporary benefits the chemicals produce; in addition, they are toxic to other insects, plants, and humans. **Natural pesticides** include insecticidal soap, which is a liquid soap that kills aphids by dissolving the wax layer on their skins so they dry up and die, and derris with tropical plant derivatives, which kills caterpillars, aphids, trips, and sawfly (don't forget that these insecticides may also kill beneficial insects so use as sparingly as possible).

Pest control

Many plants have chemical defenses against pests and disease; by growing them in strategic places or by mixing them with other crops, plant damage can be minimized. For example, **onions** have a fungicidal effect and can be usefully grown between strawberry plants to discourage disease and planted next to carrots to deter carrot fly; **French marigolds** repel a variety of vegetable pests, and interplanted with cabbages and tomatoes **encourage** pollinators and predators; wild flowers attract pollinating bees, which improve fruit yields. **Variety** is the key to attracting wildlife and keeping down pests, so don't grow too many plants of the same type close together. **Barriers, traps, and repellents** are all means of keeping pests at bay that don't harm other insects, animals, and humans; for example, bird-scaring tape that hums in the breeze; a good old-fashioned scarecrow; slug and snail tape that repels intruders with a small electric charge; reusable mesh sheet that prevents larger insects from reaching the plants. **Biological pest control** uses one living organism to control another, with no danger to humans, pets, and beneficial insects, such as the mite that feeds on the red spider mite, and the tiny parasitic wasp that lays its eggs in young whitefly.

garden tools

I use an assortment of
modern and well-
seasoned old implements
in the garden

1 old hoe and pitchfork
Ideal tools for weeding,
digging, and preparing the
ground for planting.

2 twig broom
For sweeping leaves from
grass and stone surfaces.

3 fine sieve
For removing stones from
soil and rinsing earth off
freshly picked cucumbers
and other garden produce.

4 enameled watering can
A small can is easy to carry
and practical for container
plants. Use a hose for
general garden watering.

5 cast aluminum tools
Easy-to-clean, compact
shapes that can be stored
neatly with other garden
gear (from left: weeder, fork,
trowel, bulb planter).

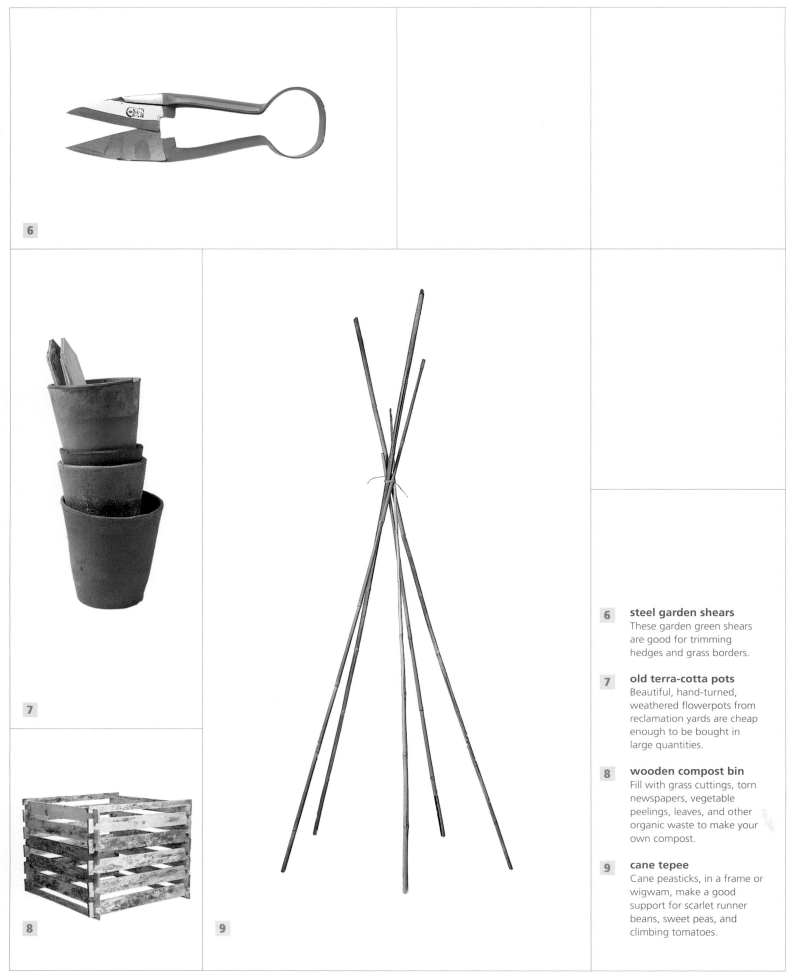

6 steel garden shears
These garden green shears are good for trimming hedges and grass borders.

7 old terra-cotta pots
Beautiful, hand-turned, weathered flowerpots from reclamation yards are cheap enough to be bought in large quantities.

8 wooden compost bin
Fill with grass cuttings, torn newspapers, vegetable peelings, leaves, and other organic waste to make your own compost.

9 cane tepee
Cane peasticks, in a frame or wigwam, make a good support for scarlet runner beans, sweet peas, and climbing tomatoes.

organic produce

fruits, vegetables, and herbs from the garden, vegetable plot, and window box

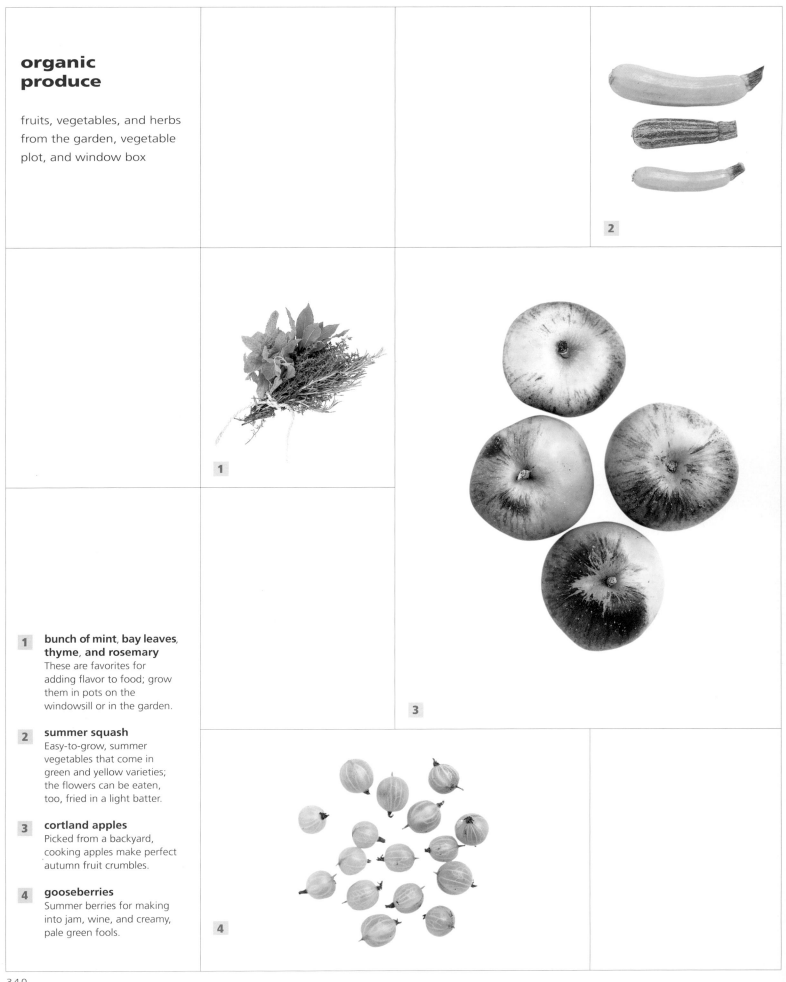

1. **bunch of mint, bay leaves, thyme, and rosemary**
   These are favorites for adding flavor to food; grow them in pots on the windowsill or in the garden.

2. **summer squash**
   Easy-to-grow, summer vegetables that come in green and yellow varieties; the flowers can be eaten, too, fried in a light batter.

3. **cortland apples**
   Picked from a backyard, cooking apples make perfect autumn fruit crumbles.

4. **gooseberries**
   Summer berries for making into jam, wine, and creamy, pale green fools.

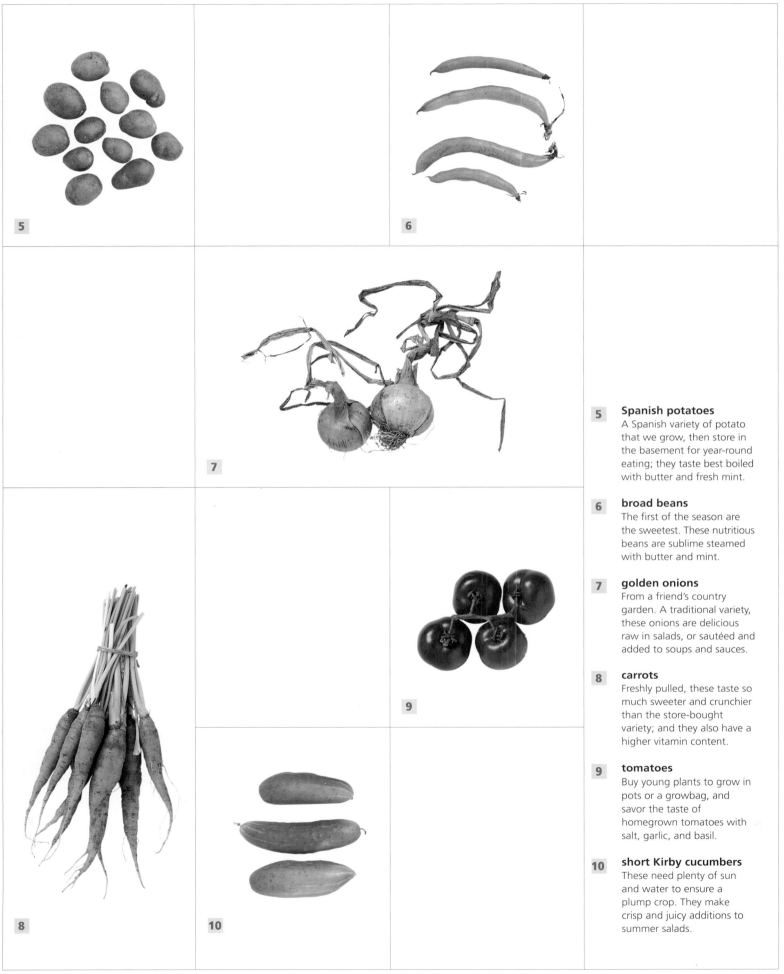

5 **Spanish potatoes**
A Spanish variety of potato that we grow, then store in the basement for year-round eating; they taste best boiled with butter and fresh mint.

6 **broad beans**
The first of the season are the sweetest. These nutritious beans are sublime steamed with butter and mint.

7 **golden onions**
From a friend's country garden. A traditional variety, these onions are delicious raw in salads, or sautéed and added to soups and sauces.

8 **carrots**
Freshly pulled, these taste so much sweeter and crunchier than the store-bought variety; and they also have a higher vitamin content.

9 **tomatoes**
Buy young plants to grow in pots or a growbag, and savor the taste of homegrown tomatoes with salt, garlic, and basil.

10 **short Kirby cucumbers**
These need plenty of sun and water to ensure a plump crop. They make crisp and juicy additions to summer salads.

pure style flowers

grow your own flowers or visit a flower stall for buds and blooms to give color, scent, and life to the home

1 **allium**
Pink, fluffy balls on tall stems look good in metal buckets. From the onion family, they also come in purple, blue, and white.

2 **narcissus**
Buy in bunches for subtle color and a heady, fragrant scent, or grow from bulbs in the garden or inside in pots.

3 **peony**
To bring back childhood memories of pink peony blooms soaked in summer rain, I buy or pick a few blowsy heads for the table.

4 **amaryllis**
This is fast growing, especially if placed in a warm room. I buy the white variety of this voluptuous flower, which I plant in old terra-cotta pots.

5 **sunflower**
Easy to grow, sunflowers make dramatic borders, especially the giant variety with platelike heads. In Spain, we dry the seeds and nibble them as tapas.

6 **hyacinth**
I grow this heavenly scented flower indoors from forced bulbs and outside in warmer weather in pots on the patios in Spain. Hyacinths come in pink, white, and a deep, purply-blue – probably my favorite.

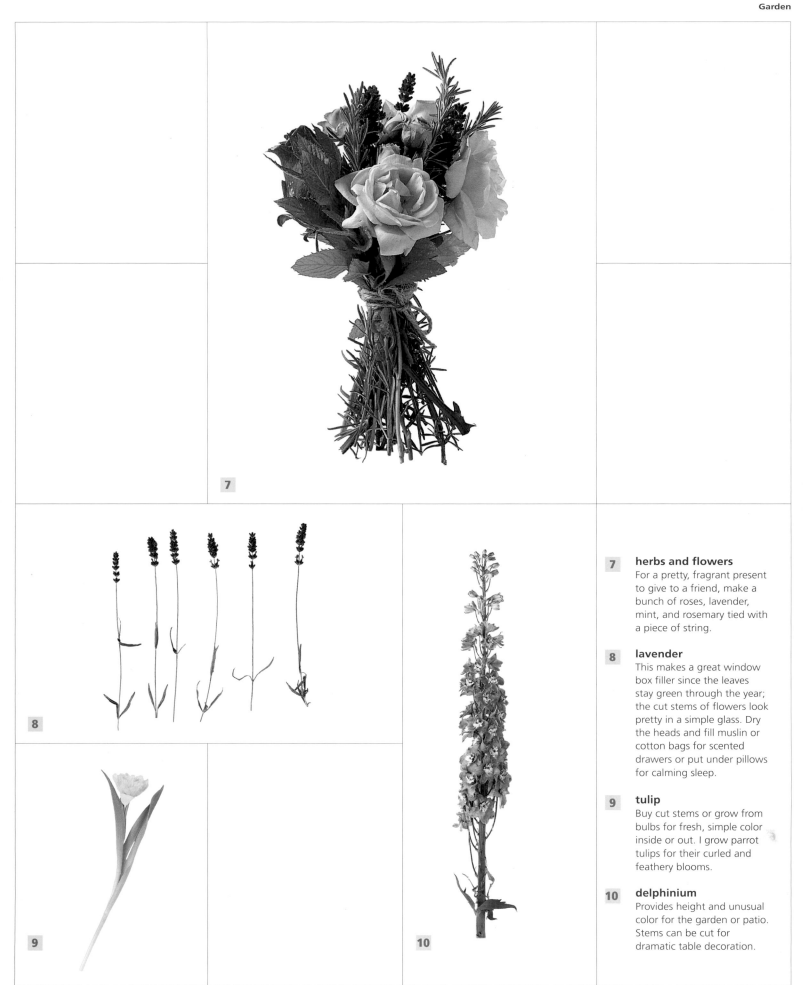

7

7 **herbs and flowers**
For a pretty, fragrant present to give to a friend, make a bunch of roses, lavender, mint, and rosemary tied with a piece of string.

8 **lavender**
This makes a great window box filler since the leaves stay green through the year; the cut stems of flowers look pretty in a simple glass. Dry the heads and fill muslin or cotton bags for scented drawers or put under pillows for calming sleep.

9 **tulip**
Buy cut stems or grow from bulbs for fresh, simple color inside or out. I grow parrot tulips for their curled and feathery blooms.

10 **delphinium**
Provides height and unusual color for the garden or patio. Stems can be cut for dramatic table decoration.

8

9

10

container ideas

flowerpots, boxes, and
buckets for patios, yards,
and balconies

1

2

3

4

5

1   wooden window box
Painted in greeny-blue and
planted with lavender, this
will bring crisp color to an
urban yard or balcony.

2   old terra-cotta flowerpot
A small pot is good for
nurturing a single bulb. Add
a handful of springy moss to
soften the look and give a
green and earthy effect.

3   galvanized steel bucket
A sturdy, utilitarian container
for a miniature olive tree,
and other plants suitable for
topiary, such as lavender,
rosemary, and shrubs.

**4   galvanized steel
window box**
Fill a metal box with daisies
for a fresh, modern look.

5   modern terra-cotta pot
Plant foxgloves in small
flowerpots and place in a
row along a wall to bring
instant, long-lasting color to
your garden.

6 old tin can
Recycle cans to make pots
for flowers and herbs;
puncture the bottoms with
holes for drainage before
filling with soil and planting.

7 natural window box
A cedarwood container that
will weather and look more
beautiful and textured with
age; plant with rosemary (as
here) or lavender for an
earthy, organic look.

8 painted flowerpots
Paint small pots in different
shades of green and plant
with lemon verbena, thyme,
and other scented herbs.

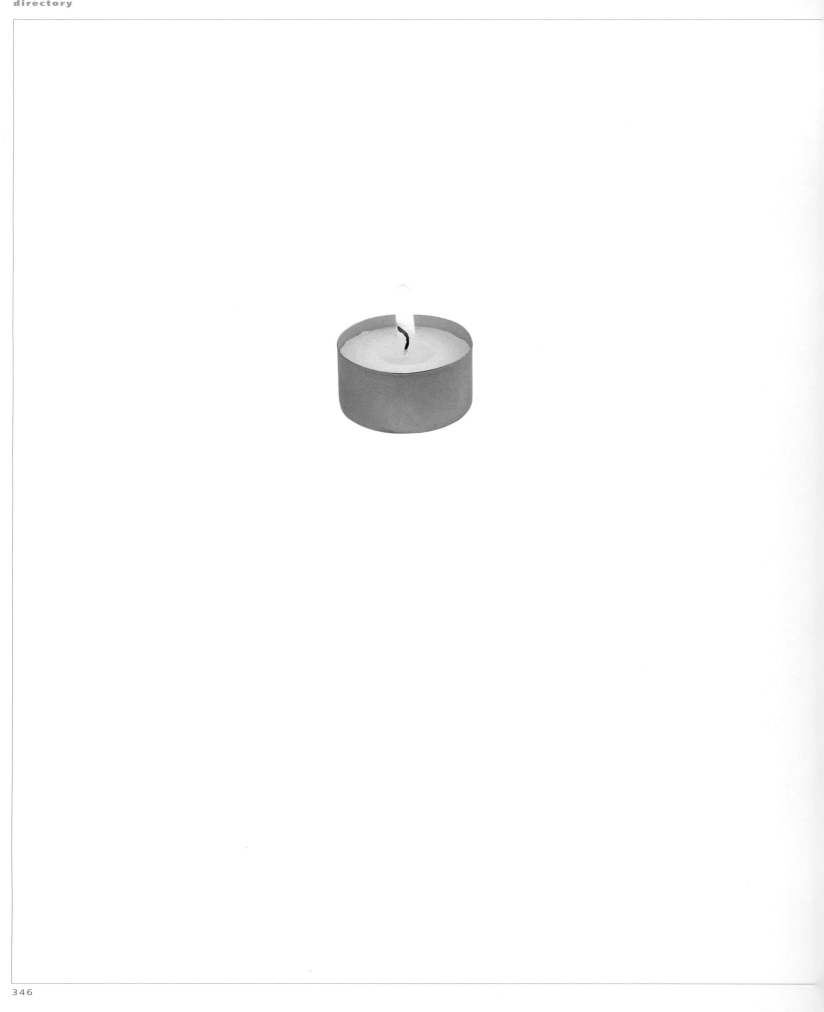

Rest

seating

fireside accessories

electric lighting

scent

natural lighting

Rest data

For many of us, too much time is taken up with work, either responding to the demands of emails, faxes, and phone calls, worrying about office politics, or simply wondering how to make ends meet. It's no wonder that stress-related illnesses are on the increase. We need to remember that taking time off to relax is vital for our mental and physical well-being.

Our homes should be refuges from the hurly-burly outside, and we owe it to ourselves to make them as welcoming and as calming as we can. Make time to read a book, to lie back and think about nothing in particular, or stretch out on the sofa to snooze. Rooms to rest in should be peaceful (except for the occasional cathartic burst of opera or loud rock music), with soft comfortable textures. I made sure that one end of our open-plan living space in our London apartment feels snug and homey, with comfy chairs and a sofa large enough for us all to flop onto and watch a scary, Saturday night thriller.

Seating

Choose the biggest sofa you can afford. **A good sofa** should have a solid hardwood frame, with a sprung base and back – the springs are padded with layers of cotton wadding, wool felt, and hair; cheap sofas are foam-filled, and not as durable. **Measure** before you buy, and not just the space you have available for the sofa – measure the height and width of the front door, and look at narrow corridors, tight corners, and stairs to make sure your sofa can reach its destination. **Cushions** come in different fillings: **feathers** – deliciously soft and cozy, they mold to your shape as you sink in and need plumping up every day to maintain their shape; **feathers and fiber** – less giving than pure feathers but also less expensive; plump up as for feather-only cushions; **quallofil-foam** – soft and springy, and cheaper, but don't mold to your shape and, therefore, less comfortable. Don't expose sofas directly to **heat sources –** radiators or strong sunlight can cause warping. Sitting on **sofa arms** weakens the structure, so avoid at all costs. **Rotate seat and back cushions** weekly to even out wear and fading. To **plump up a cushion,** hold it up in the air, punch from all sides, and finally drop it on the floor to let air filter slowly back into it.

Summer ideas

In the heat of the summer, **airy rooms** should be shuttered during the day to keep out the sun and opened only when the heat has died down later. The **scent of flowers** intensifies in the evening – I have pitchers of tuberose and jasmine in Spain. **Make foam-filled cushions** with tough, removable canvas covers to flop onto for the grass, terrace, or by a swimming pool; when damp, remove covers and dry out. **Wear cool, loose clothing** – linen is best, followed by cotton. **Drink lots of water –** the body quickly dehydrates in the heat, which leads to headaches and irritability. **Put up a makeshift awning** for cool, shady picnics on the beach or at the park (see pp.170–171); choose a dark canvas and secure with rope and old-fashioned tent pegs; it is especially important for babies and small children to be kept out of the sun, and they will need hats and high-protection sun screen as well. At the end of the day, **hang strings of lanterns** outside or scatter tealights across a mantelpiece for glowing, flickering light.

Winter ideas

To create warmth and homeyness in the bleaker months, **use natural textures**, such as a woven grass log basket, rough natural matting, wool rugs, and layer sofas in warm, woolly throws and blankets; **warm rooms** with underfloor heating, which is less drying and stuffy than central heating; **keep drafts out** with lined curtains. If you have central heating, **aluminum panels** tucked behind radiators help to radiate more heat. **Keep yourself warm** with layers of light clothing – wear cotton or silk next to the skin, followed by wool, or polar fleece; keep your feet warm with thick woolly socks. **Build a blazing fire –** it appeals to our primal instincts for warmth and security; **toast marshmallows** and **roast chestnuts** for comforting winter fuel. For **winter scents**, I burn orange-scented candles to mimic the aromatic peel of oranges and tangerines, and fill bowls with dried lavender and rose petal potpourri for floral notes. **Make soft glowing pools of light** from low-level lamps – avoid horrors like central overhead lights or naked light bulbs; dark walls absorb more light than pale ones so choose wattage accordingly, and whenever possible use low-energy bulbs – they can give the same intensity of light, last longer, and use less energy than ordinary bulbs.

seating

seats of all sizes in my
favorite neutral shades
with comfort, practicality,
and durability being the
key considerations

1

2

1 **old armchair**
Cover in a loose, plain,
white cotton cover to
disguise its origins.

2 **boxy modern sofa**
This creamy yellow sofa
would provide smart seating
in a city loft-style apartment.

3 **1930s secondhand sofa**
A squashy, three-seater
covered in loose white
cotton covers to collapse
into for long afternoon naps.

3

4 simple modern sofa
Low-slung for comfort, a contemporary design that would fit well in any bright and airy living room.

5 Victorian chair
A useful shape for bedrooms and bathrooms, this second-hand chair has been updated with white slipcovers.

6 footstool
In the same style as the sofa (see 4); it can also be used as a coffee table on which to pile books and balance trays of drinks and snacks.

7 Georgian-style two-seater
Bright cushions and a throw offset a compact canvas-covered sofa that is ideal for supplementary seating or to fit into a small space.

8 contemporary sofa
Beautifully streamlined, this dual-function sofa folds down to make a single bed.

fireside accessories

essential equipment for building a blazing fire and other fireside activities

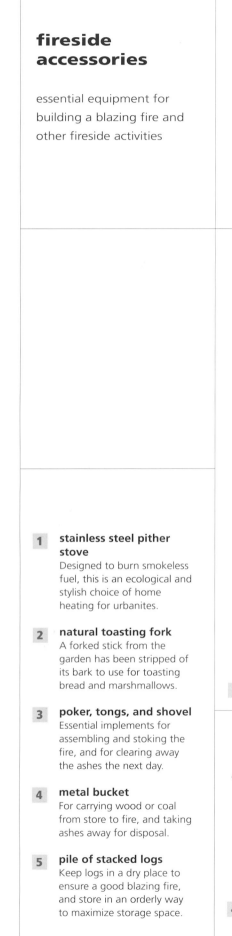

1. **stainless steel pither stove**
   Designed to burn smokeless fuel, this is an ecological and stylish choice of home heating for urbanites.

2. **natural toasting fork**
   A forked stick from the garden has been stripped of its bark to use for toasting bread and marshmallows.

3. **poker, tongs, and shovel**
   Essential implements for assembling and stoking the fire, and for clearing away the ashes the next day.

4. **metal bucket**
   For carrying wood or coal from store to fire, and taking ashes away for disposal.

5. **pile of stacked logs**
   Keep logs in a dry place to ensure a good blazing fire, and store in an orderly way to maximize storage space.

6 **resin-rich firelighters**
For the ecologically inclined, these natural pine firelighters burn well even when wet and release a distinctive resiny, pine fragrance.

7 **chestnut roaster**
Place slit chestnuts in this pan and roast on a log fire for about five minutes. Peel open and eat the delicious sweet and softened nut.

8 **kindling**
Collect and keep a supply of dry sticks and twigs to get a fire going. Pine cones are also good fire starters.

9 **woven grass log basket**
A good, deep shape to hold plenty of logs. This basket is sturdy enough to cope with cumbersome and heavy loads.

10 **small brush**
For sweeping the hearth; a basic tool obtainable from most hardware stores.

scent

for a restful and relaxing
atmosphere, scent your
home with fragrant and
natural aromatics

1

2

3

1 **lavender-scented water**
Imparts a delicious scent
when sprinkled over freshly
ironed bedlinen.

2 **scented candle**
Especially uplifting on a
dark winter's evening – my
favorite smell is tuberose.

3 **dried rose buds**
Impregnated with a rose-
scented oil, these smell
almost fresh and look
beautiful heaped in simple
white bowls.

4 **cedarwood block**
The lovely woody fragrance
permeates storage areas and
has the benefit of being a
natural moth repellent.

5 **incense stick**
Select the perfume of your
choice to uplift your spirits or
as an antidote to cooking
smells in the kitchen.

4

5

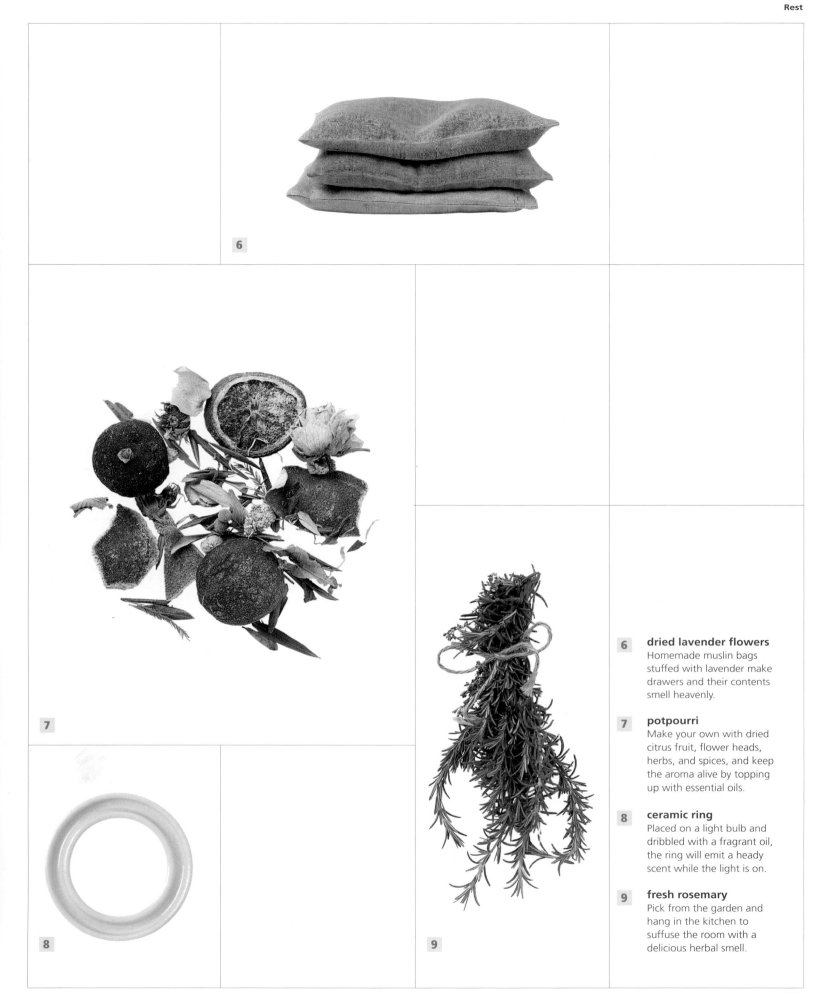

6 dried lavender flowers
Homemade muslin bags stuffed with lavender make drawers and their contents smell heavenly.

7 potpourri
Make your own with dried citrus fruit, flower heads, herbs, and spices, and keep the aroma alive by topping up with essential oils.

8 ceramic ring
Placed on a light bulb and dribbled with a fragrant oil, the ring will emit a heady scent while the light is on.

9 fresh rosemary
Pick from the garden and hang in the kitchen to suffuse the room with a delicious herbal smell.

natural lighting

for romantic evenings turn off the electric lights and burn flickering tealights and cream votives

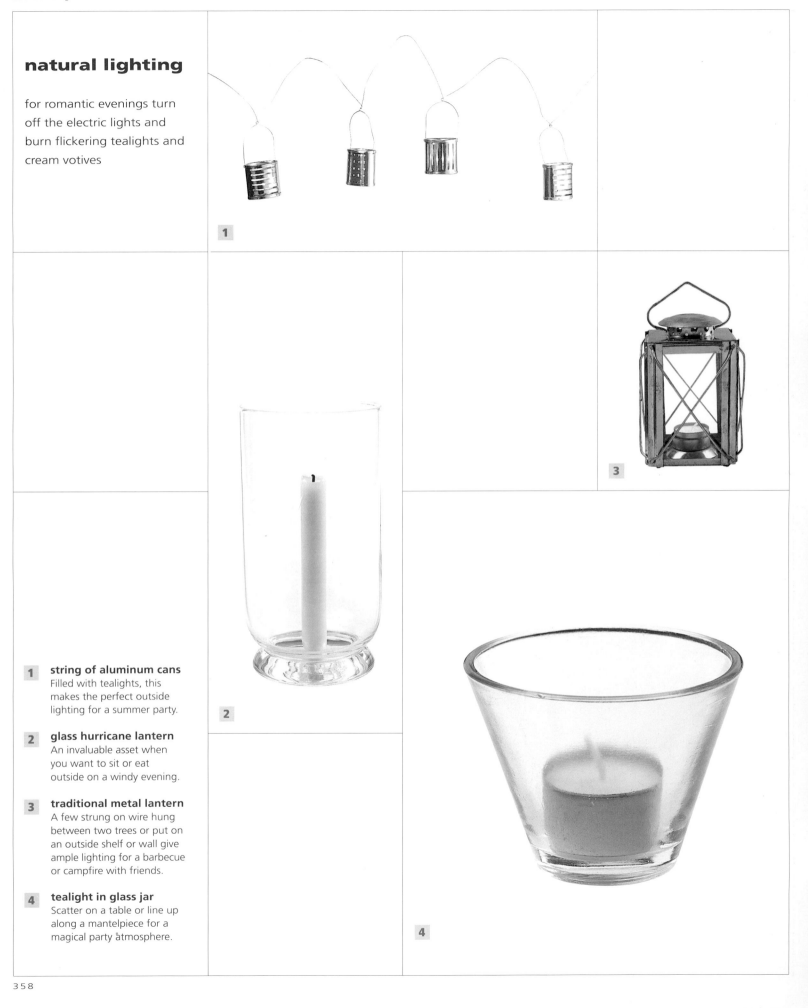

1

2

3

4

1 **string of aluminum cans**
Filled with tealights, this makes the perfect outside lighting for a summer party.

2 **glass hurricane lantern**
An invaluable asset when you want to sit or eat outside on a windy evening.

3 **traditional metal lantern**
A few strung on wire hung between two trees or put on an outside shelf or wall give ample lighting for a barbecue or campfire with friends.

4 **tealight in glass jar**
Scatter on a table or line up along a mantelpiece for a magical party atmosphere.

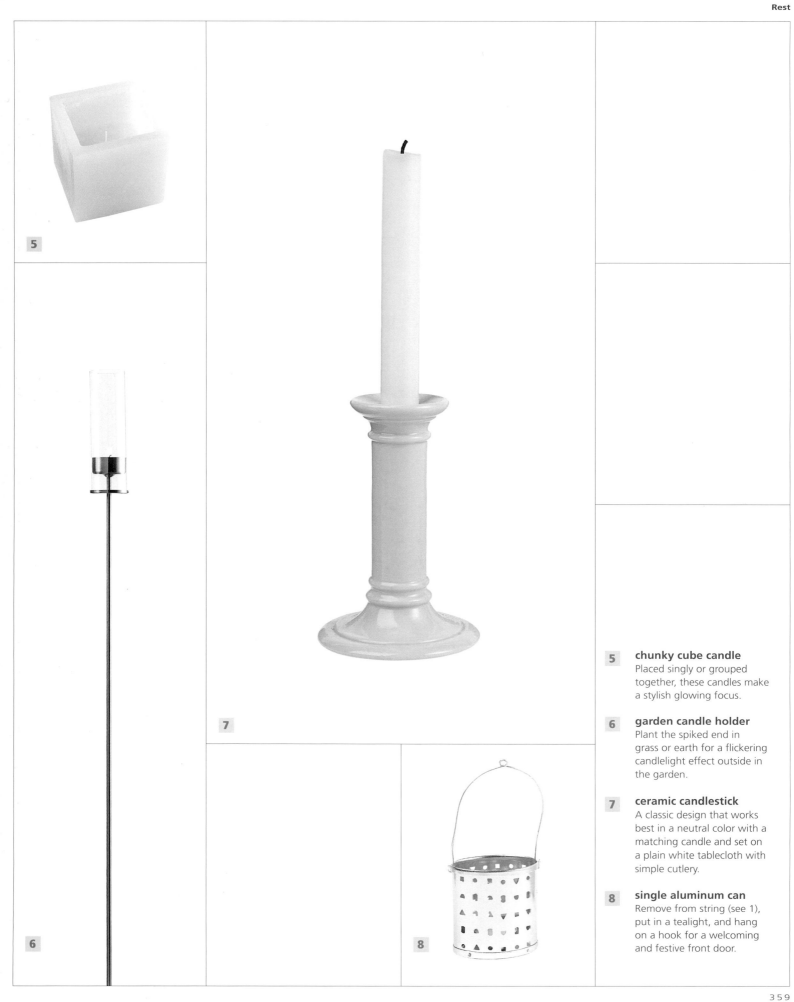

5 **chunky cube candle**
Placed singly or grouped together, these candles make a stylish glowing focus.

6 **garden candle holder**
Plant the spiked end in grass or earth for a flickering candlelight effect outside in the garden.

7 **ceramic candlestick**
A classic design that works best in a neutral color with a matching candle and set on a plain white tablecloth with simple cutlery.

8 **single aluminum can**
Remove from string (see 1), put in a tealight, and hang on a hook for a welcoming and festive front door.

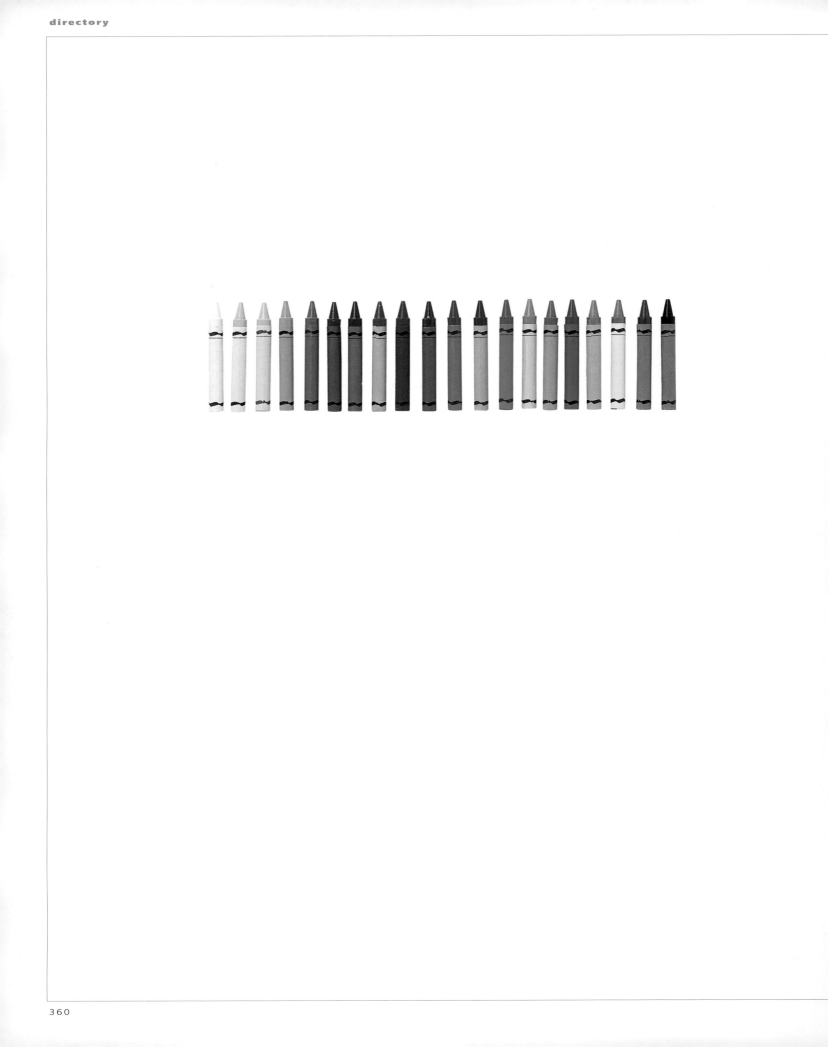

Play

materials

playtime

Play data

There are plenty of things to do at home that will stimulate and inspire children without incurring extra expense. Empty boxes and cartons can make improvised stables, farms, or garages; caves can be made out of blankets and kitchen chairs; old clothes can be recycled for dressing up; sheets of paper and crayons can be used for drawing: all these activities are more likely to develop creativity than manufactured toys that are complete in every detail. If, like me, you were brought up with that marvelous children's television program that showed you how to turn a humble bottle of dishwashing liquid into hundreds of ingenious applications, I am sure you will agree with these old-fashioned sentiments.

Everyday ideas

I keep a supply of paper, felt tip markers, crayons, poster paints, and plain pencils for **painting**, **drawing**, **cutting**, and **gluing**. At Christmas, we make potato print stamps in star or tree shapes, and coat with paint to print our own wrapping paper and Christmas cards. We also make collages using colored paper, fabric, and felt, and cut out chains of dancing dolls or Christmas trees from newspapers (see p.202). At Easter, it's time to get out the poster paints and decorate brown eggs with flowers, stripes, and other spring-like patterns (see pp.206–207). When there are about a dozen we pile them into a basket with straw chicks. I encourage the children to **read** anything – from comics to well-known, contemporary and classic children's authors. Join the local library to borrow books, audio cassettes, and videos. Also, go to secondhand book stores and junk shops for cheap paperbacks. For **dressing up**, we keep a big basket of old clothes, including belts, big pants, grandma's old shirts, and my castoffs; I have made simple capes from muslin and net for princess games, black capes and tights for superhero fun, and outfits out of white sheets for Halloween ghosts. Living for part of the year in Andalucia means that my daughters embrace the tradition of wearing frilly flamenco dresses at fiestas, and these also become important additions to the dressing-up repertoire. As far as **cooking** is concerned, it's good to start them young but always be around to supervise. My children love to make simple cookies, using flour, butter, and sugar, or cupcakes or cookies from mixes; they then decorate them with icing and silver balls – a perfect way to spend a rainy afternoon. Tom, my 11-year-old son, can now rustle up excellent brownies, pancakes, omelettes, and chocolate cake on his own. Try to encourage children to be eclectic in their musical taste and expose them to a variety of different types of **music** – opera, classical, reggae, pop, jazz, country, and folk (my children have learned to appreciate my 1970's heroes, such as Bob Dylan, Neil Young, and Al Green). In addition, if there's an opportunity for your children to learn a musical instrument, make the most of it; start with a basic percussion instrument, such as a tamborine, or a recorder, to avoid discouragement early on.

Parties

The secrets of **successful children's parties** are soda, hot dogs, potato chips, chocolate cake, Madonna blaring in the background, and really good games. The list of party games is infinite, but here are a few of my favorites. **Pass the parcel**: wrap a small prize in layers of newspaper, with a candy or chocolate secreted in every layer (one for every child); sit children in a circle and pass the parcel around. When the music stops, the child holding the parcel removes one layer and takes the candy; this continues until one child opens the final layer and claims the prize. **Pin the tail on the donkey**: draw a donkey on a large piece of paper and cut out a separate tail. Blindfold each child – the goal is to pin the tail in the correct position, so the winner is the child who comes nearest to the correct place. **Musical statues**: the children dance until the music stops and everyone has to freeze; those who move are out. Continue until only one contestant remains – the winner (this is good exercise to wear out over-excited children). **Wrap the mummy**: divide children into two teams, each of which is given a roll of toilet paper; each team wraps a player in the tissue, and the one who uses up the roll first is the winner (a good Halloween game). **Grandmother's footsteps**: one player stands with his or her face to the wall ("grandmother"); the contestants line up and see who can reach the "grandmother" first; when she turns around the children must freeze and if she catches anyone moving they go back to the starting line. **Apple bobbing**: a traditional Halloween game that can be played all year round. Put eight or nine apples in a large bowl of water; children take turns seeing who can grab the most apples with their teeth in a designated time. Although wet and not very hygienic, this game is great fun for participants and onlookers alike. **Potato and spoon race**: each contestant cradles a small potato in a spoon; line up the children and on the order to go, see who can reach the finish line without the potato falling off the spoon. **Sack race**: each child stands in a sack or garbage bag; the winner is the first to jump to the finish line.

Vacations

With the right vacation spot, most children will make their own entertainment, but if a new environment isn't enough (or if the weather is foul), here are some ideas. **Keep a journal** – glue in shells, seaweed, tickets, and postcards; **record a whole day** on a roll of film and write captions for the prints; **make a flicker book**; go to the park, **take a picnic,** and play softball, soccer, or volleyball; have a bonfire or light a disposable barbecue in the backyard and cook hotdogs and other tasty outside grub; **at the beach,** make sandcastles and decorate with shells and seaweed; have sand-drawing competitions; skip stones across the water; run relay races over the sand; fly a kite; learn to body surf (check the currents, don't let your children go out of their depth, and constantly supervise); collect shells to take home and glue on cardboard to make pictures.

materials

let your children show their creativity with crayons, paints, ribbons, and bright tissue paper

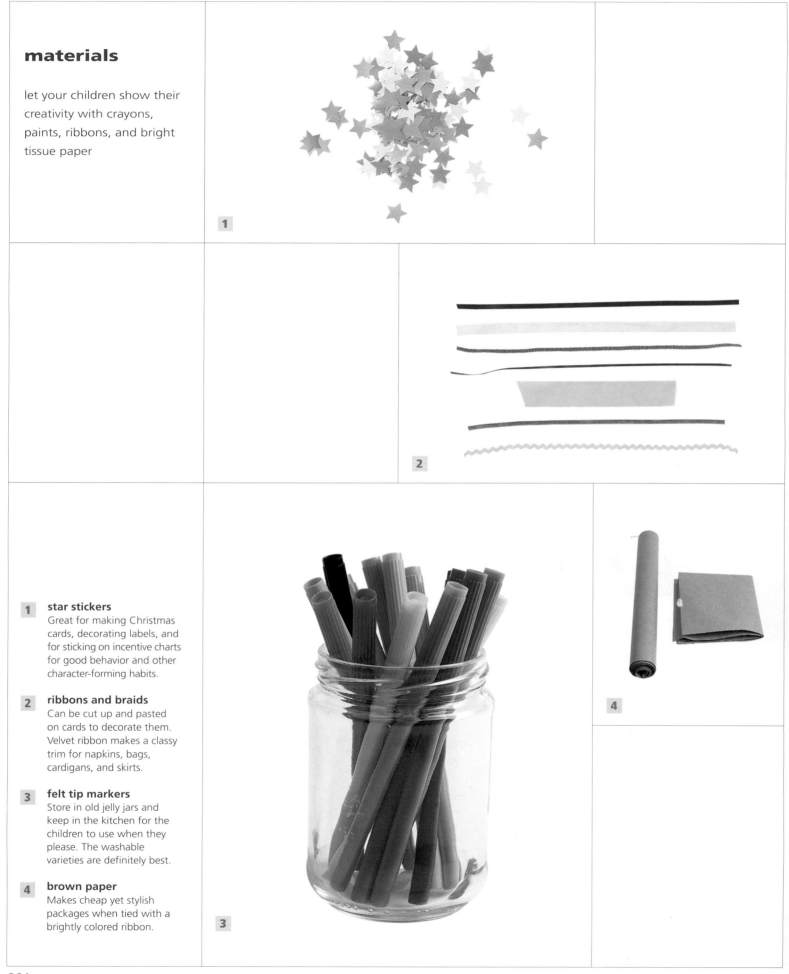

1 **star stickers**
Great for making Christmas cards, decorating labels, and for sticking on incentive charts for good behavior and other character-forming habits.

2 **ribbons and braids**
Can be cut up and pasted on cards to decorate them. Velvet ribbon makes a classy trim for napkins, bags, cardigans, and skirts.

3 **felt tip markers**
Store in old jelly jars and keep in the kitchen for the children to use when they please. The washable varieties are definitely best.

4 **brown paper**
Makes cheap yet stylish packages when tied with a brightly colored ribbon.

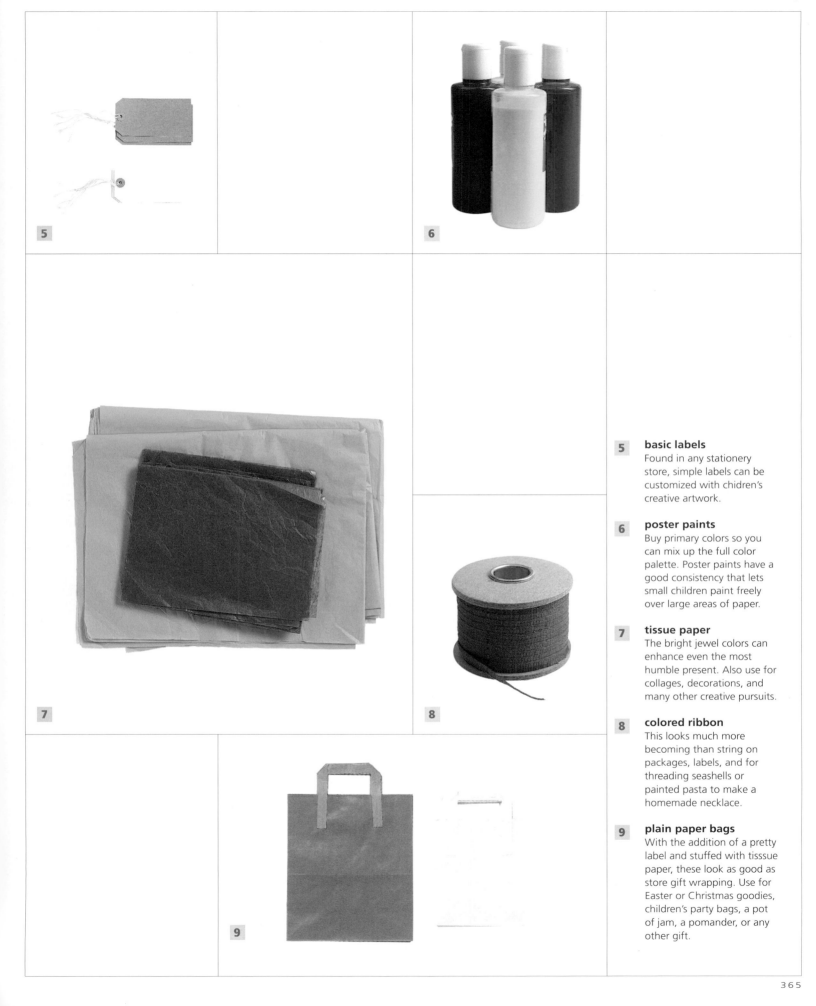

5 **basic labels**
Found in any stationery store, simple labels can be customized with chidren's creative artwork.

6 **poster paints**
Buy primary colors so you can mix up the full color palette. Poster paints have a good consistency that lets small children paint freely over large areas of paper.

7 **tissue paper**
The bright jewel colors can enhance even the most humble present. Also use for collages, decorations, and many other creative pursuits.

8 **colored ribbon**
This looks much more becoming than string on packages, labels, and for threading seashells or painted pasta to make a homemade necklace.

9 **plain paper bags**
With the addition of a pretty label and stuffed with tisssue paper, these look as good as store gift wrapping. Use for Easter or Christmas goodies, children's party bags, a pot of jam, a pomander, or any other gift.

playtime

a selection of ideas to fuel busy young minds and hands and to spark off further imaginative projects

1 **adhesive note paper**
Cut into shapes and stick on paper to make colorful pictures and collages. Hours of fun can be had by anyone old enough to use a pair of blunt children's scissors.

2 **pretty lantern**
Make an original lantern by gluing a hand-decorated label on an old jelly jar and placing a candle inside. Add a string handle.

3 **salt dough**
An easy-to-make modeling material that can be cut into all kinds of shapes. Leave to set, and then paint and decorate.

4 **bucket and shovel**
Making sandcastles at the beach or in a sandbox gives endless pleasure to children and grown-ups alike.

5 **pair of castanets**
Try some music. Castanets can be played alone or along with other instruments.

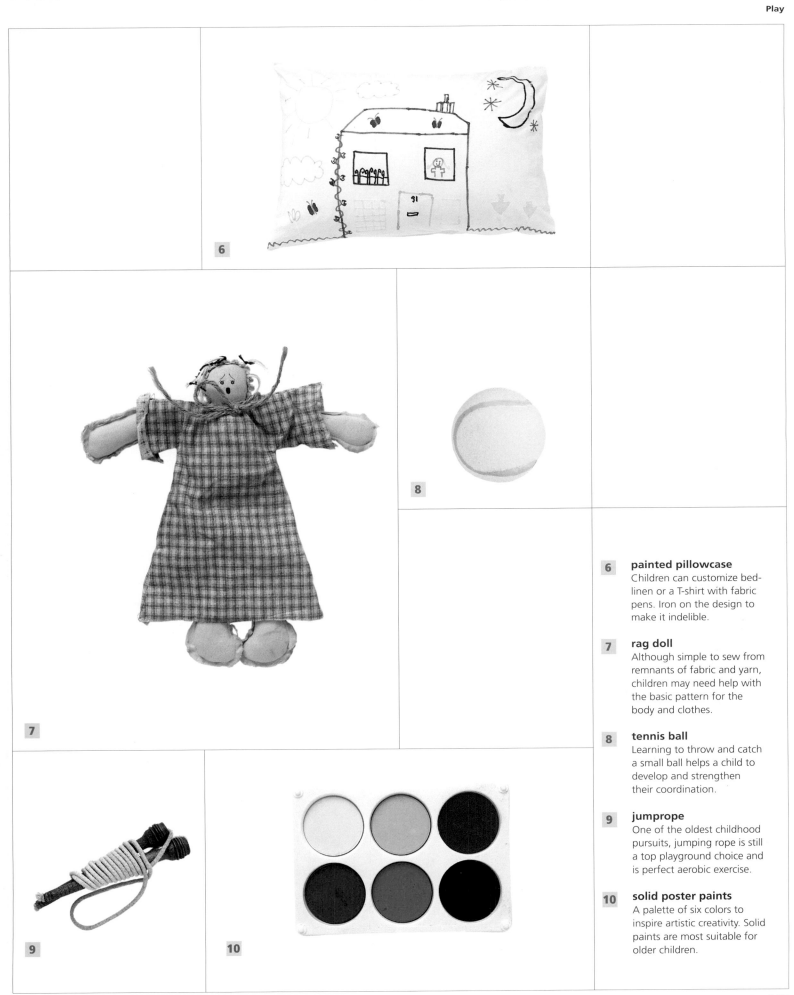

6 painted pillowcase
Children can customize bed-linen or a T-shirt with fabric pens. Iron on the design to make it indelible.

7 rag doll
Although simple to sew from remnants of fabric and yarn, children may need help with the basic pattern for the body and clothes.

8 tennis ball
Learning to throw and catch a small ball helps a child to develop and strengthen their coordination.

9 jumprope
One of the oldest childhood pursuits, jumping rope is still a top playground choice and is perfect aerobic exercise.

10 solid poster paints
A palette of six colors to inspire artistic creativity. Solid paints are most suitable for older children.

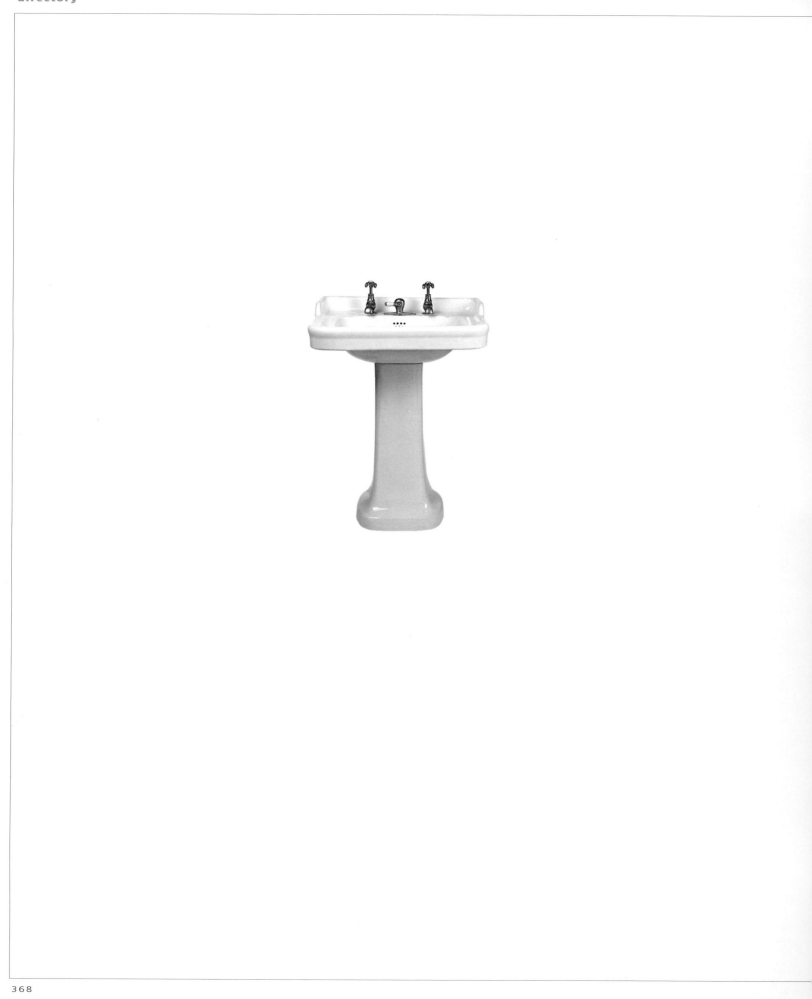

Wash

bathroom fixtures

bathroom accessories

bathroom gear

bathroom linen

Wash data

White ceramic surfaces, natural wood and cotton textures, lashings of hot water, and warm, dry, cotton towels are my key bathroom requirements. Equipping the bathroom and organizing plumbing arrangements can be extremely costly if you go down the route of hi-tech showers, made-to-measure bathtubs, and the latest designer accessories. But if you are prepared to hunt around for basic bath gear in chainstores, reclamation specialists, and home improvement centers you can still create a sensual and comfortable bathroom space.

Bathtubs

Although demanding of water, enameled cast-iron, roll-top bathtubs are durable, heat insulating, and resistant to scratches, cracks, and stains; freestanding on ball-and-claw feet, their deep, curvy proportions provide a luxurious way to take a long hot soak. These bathtubs need sturdy floors to support their own weight, plus the bather, and a bath full of water. **Enameled** steel bathtubs, coated with vitreous enamel and fired to give a hard finish, are strong and durable, relatively cheap, and available from basic home improvement centers; **acrylic** bathtubs are lightweight, easier to install than cast-iron bathtubs, warm to the touch, less slippery than metal, and stain resistant, but they will scratch easily. Both acrylic and enameled steel shapes need a supportive frame, which can be boxed in with tiles or wood; **choose a long bathtub**, as it's much more comfortable for stretching out; **showers in bathtubs** can be contained within a shower curtain – a clear, plastic one is plain and simple; wash and scrub regularly to keep dampness and mold at bay. **Dripping faucets** waste water and create **limescale stains**; replace the washers as soon as possible. To remove **bathtub rings** from an enamel bathtub, fill with hot water and add several cupfuls of sodium carbonate; swill the solution around the bathtub and leave overnight. Next morning, work over the whole bathtub with a stiff cleaning brush. **To remove limescale**, apply a mixture of equal parts of hot vinegar and salt with a toothbrush, and leave until it can be scrubbed off. **Rust marks** can be bleached out with a paste made from salt and lemon juice. Spread the paste over the stain and moisten with more lemon juice for a day or two, then wipe away.

Showers

A shower can be anything from a simple hand set attached to the bathtub faucets to a state-of-the-art walk-in wet room with a generous hi-tech shower head with jets that massage the body, and a drained, sloping floor that serves as a large shower tray. If you are planning such a room, bear in mind that waterproofing a floor needs expert advice. A decent shower depends on an **adequate flow of water** (water pressure varies among areas) and an even water temperature. Conservationists encourage us to take showers instead of baths in order to save water, but water usage can be as great with a shower as with a bath. Depending on the type of fixture and for how long it is used, a quick shower can save the 6.5 gallons needed for a bath, but an eight-minute shower, delivering a therapeutic deluge, uses more water than a bath. To overcome this wastage, some manufacturers make **showers with eco-options** that reduce consumption. Check with the supplier that all shower components – valves, pumps, and the actual shower fixtures – are compatible with each other. To **conceal shower pipes**, the walls need to be at least 3 in thick. Modern thermostatic showers can be encased in period-style bodies, which is ideal if you like old-fashioned, large, rose shower heads.

Flooring

Whatever is used – stone, wood, cork, rubber – it must be sealed or equipped with efficient drainage. Avoid carpet and natural coverings, such as sisal, as they are prone to rot and are difficult to clean. Use soft cotton bath mats to soak up water and warm toes in winter since marble and stone can be slippery and cool underfoot. Hardwoods, such as teak (from sustainable sources), are good for shower floors and bath mats. Ceramic tiles with a matte finish – I favor sea blues and green colors – are practical, together with plain terra-cotta slabs (provided that the floor has adequate support). Consider installing underfloor heating for warm bathroom floors.

Reclamation

Salvage yards sell a variety of utilitarian and functional 19th- and early 20th-century bathtubs, faucets, and other bathroom fixtures; reclamation yards are also a good hunting ground for bathtubs, showers, and fixtures removed from schools, hotels, and other institutions that are being demolished or updated. I think it's particularly worth hunting down and investing in 1930s white ceramic sinks on pedestal bases – they have a pleasing and simple quality. Look also for any lovely old chunky chrome or brass faucets, which can add stylish detailing to even the plainest bathroom.

Ventilation

Working up a warm enveloping steam is all part of the sensual aspect of bathing. On a more practical note, open windows to let out steam and prevent condensation, which will produce black mold that can cause walls, window frames, and floors to rot. If the bathroom is windowless, install an extractor fan.

bathroom fixtures

plain, functional bathtubs and basins, gleaming ceramic surfaces, and gushing hot water are requisites for my bathroom

1

2

1 **early 20th-century cast-iron roll-top bathtub**
A reclaimed bathtub brought right up to date with a re-enameled lining.

2 **modern white ceramic shower tray**
A basic and inexpensive solution for the shower.

3 **1920s French ceramic pedestal basin**
A reclaimed traditional white sink for any style of bathroom.

4 **unglazed ceramic mosaic tiles**
In a shower interior or above a bath these need to be protected with a matte sealer.

5 **early 20th-century nickel shower fixture**
Probably rescued from a grand old hotel, it has a wide head to deliver a good flow of water.

3

4

5

6

7

8

9

6 reclaimed pendant light
Attractive and functional for
basic bathroom lighting.

**7 heated chrome-finished
brass towel rail**
This has a double function in
my bathroom: it warms the
room and dries the towels.

8 enameled steel bathtub
Found in home improvement
centers; box in with tongue-
and-groove wood panels for
a traditional look.

9 reclaimed chrome faucet
A classic, simple shape that
sits well on any basin, old-
fashioned or contemporary.
Always replace the washers
in old faucets.

bathroom accessories

tactile surfaces for bathrooms in wood, metal, and natural fibers

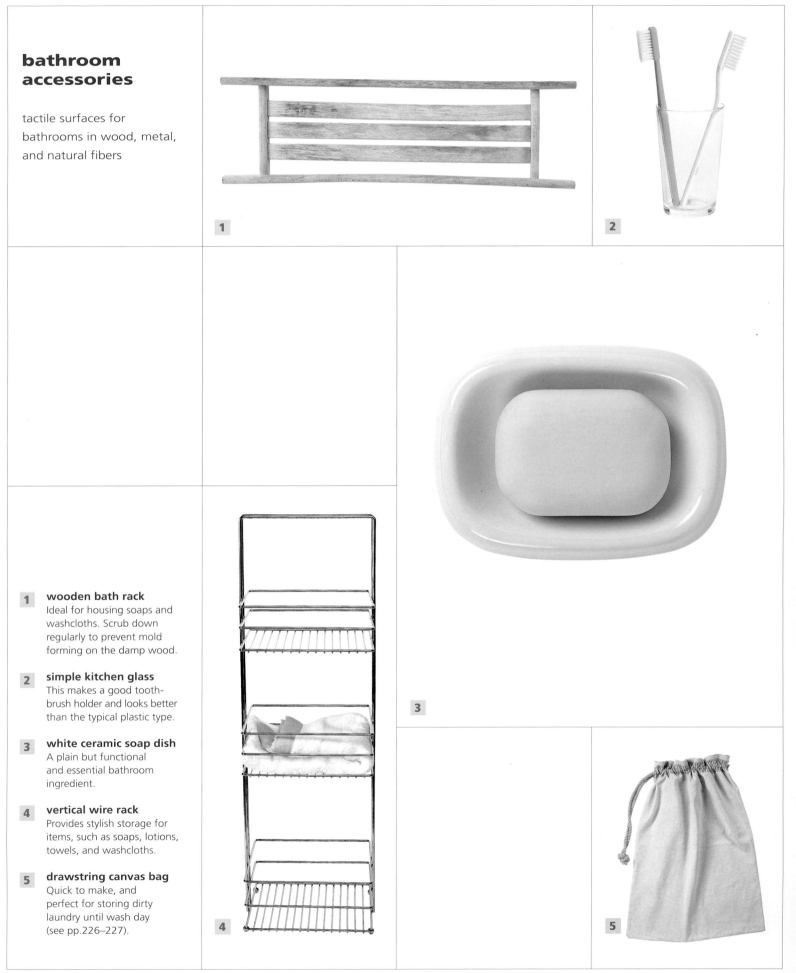

1 **wooden bath rack**
Ideal for housing soaps and washcloths. Scrub down regularly to prevent mold forming on the damp wood.

2 **simple kitchen glass**
This makes a good toothbrush holder and looks better than the typical plastic type.

3 **white ceramic soap dish**
A plain but functional and essential bathroom ingredient.

4 **vertical wire rack**
Provides stylish storage for items, such as soaps, lotions, towels, and washcloths.

5 **drawstring canvas bag**
Quick to make, and perfect for storing dirty laundry until wash day (see pp.226–227).

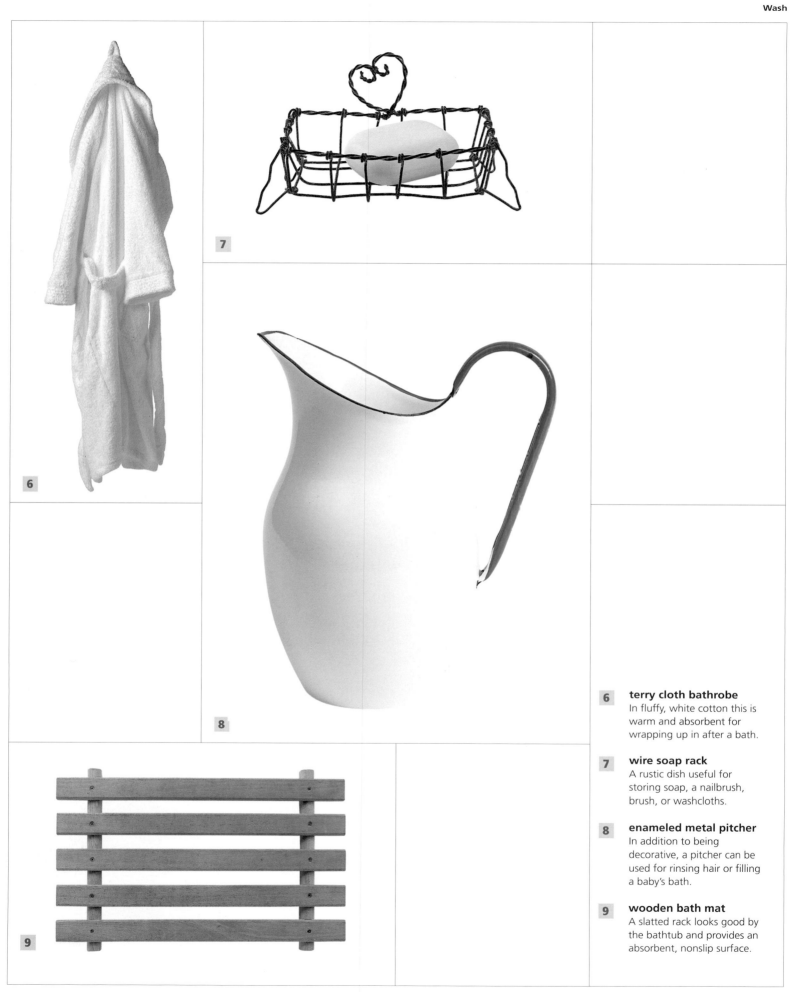

6 **terry cloth bathrobe**
In fluffy, white cotton this is
warm and absorbent for
wrapping up in after a bath.

7 **wire soap rack**
A rustic dish useful for
storing soap, a nailbrush,
brush, or washcloths.

8 **enameled metal pitcher**
In addition to being
decorative, a pitcher can be
used for rinsing hair or filling
a baby's bath.

9 **wooden bath mat**
A slatted rack looks good by
the bathtub and provides an
absorbent, nonslip surface.

bathroom gear

soaps, lotions, and
pampering tools for
bath time

1

1 **pure vegetable soaps**
Choose natural plant
extracts and rich, earthy
colors for bathroom soaps.

2 **pretty bottles**
Fill with a favorite cologne
or bath oil. Mine is a
delicious, spicy, orange scent
from Spain that I decant into
old liqueur bottles.

3 **soft face brush**
Made from Japanese hinoki
wood (with antibacterial
properties). Use for
exfoliating and removing
the day's accumulated dirt.

4 **natural sponge**
For a soft and lathery skin
wash. Always rinse
thoroughly after using to
prolong the sponge's life.

3

2

4

5 **moisturizing body lotion**
To pamper and feed skin dried up by air-conditioning, central heating, and water.

6 **loofah and volcanic pumice stone**
Natural products for the removal of dry, rough skin from elbows and heels.

7 **wooden back brush**
An essential item for an invigorating scrub in the inaccessible area between the shoulder blades.

8 **knitted coir bath mitt**
Use when a whole-body exfoliating and stimulating skin rub is required.

9 **decorative soap**
Made of natural oils and studded with dried rosebuds, a chunk of soap can look good as well as be luxurious to use.

bathroom linen

piles of fluffy, white cotton towels for daily bath time, and crisp linen hand towels to pamper friends who come to stay

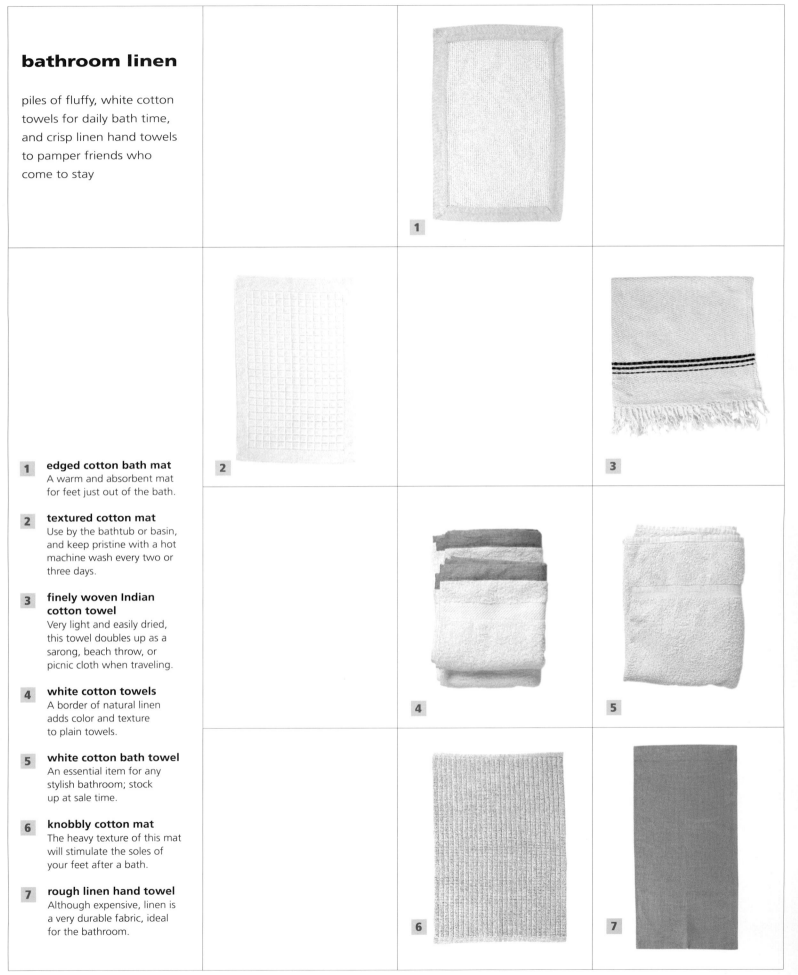

1 edged cotton bath mat
A warm and absorbent mat for feet just out of the bath.

2 textured cotton mat
Use by the bathtub or basin, and keep pristine with a hot machine wash every two or three days.

3 finely woven Indian cotton towel
Very light and easily dried, this towel doubles up as a sarong, beach throw, or picnic cloth when traveling.

4 white cotton towels
A border of natural linen adds color and texture to plain towels.

5 white cotton bath towel
An essential item for any stylish bathroom; stock up at sale time.

6 knobbly cotton mat
The heavy texture of this mat will stimulate the soles of your feet after a bath.

7 rough linen hand towel
Although expensive, linen is a very durable fabric, ideal for the bathroom.

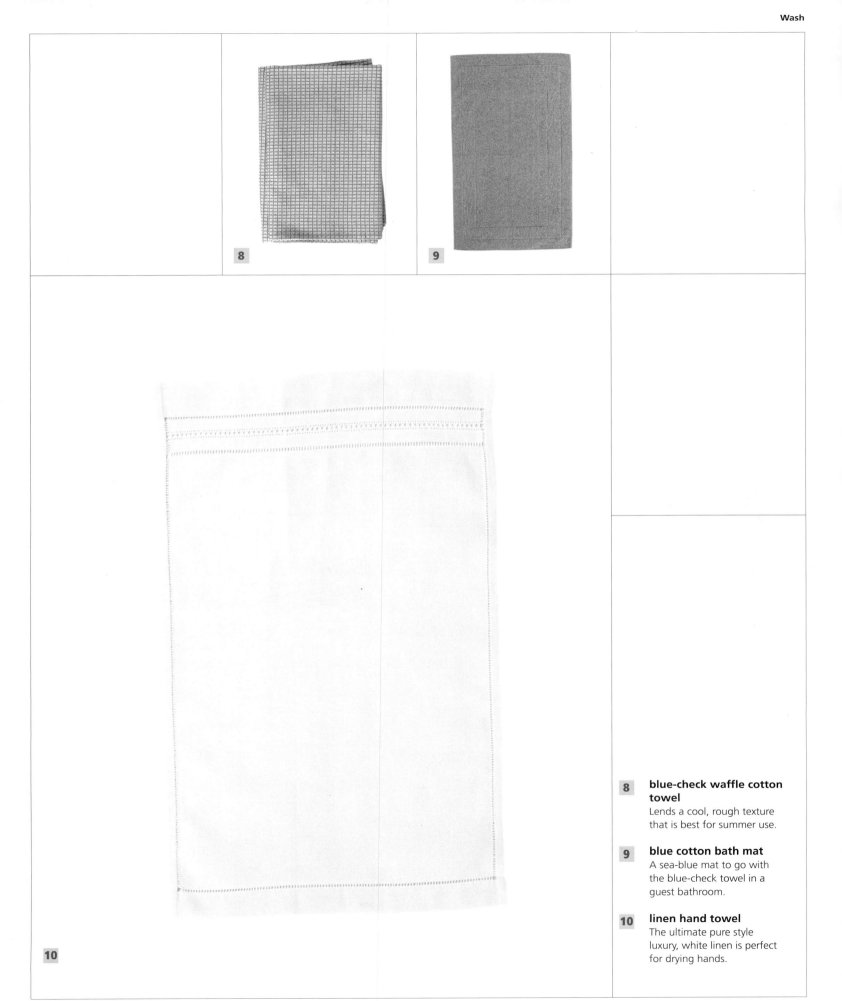

8 blue-check waffle cotton towel
Lends a cool, rough texture that is best for summer use.

9 blue cotton bath mat
A sea-blue mat to go with the blue-check towel in a guest bathroom.

10 linen hand towel
The ultimate pure style luxury, white linen is perfect for drying hands.

Sleep

beds

bedding basics

bedlinen

bedroom accessories

Sleep data

We are born in bed and die in bed. In between, beds are our havens and retreats from everyday life; a comfort zone layered with soft blankets and crisp cotton sheets. It is here that we stretch out, relax, sleep, make love, work, and play.

The earliest beds were improvised affairs: medieval people slept on handmade mattresses of straw ropes and sticks. A woman in labor was known as the "lady in the straws" – a reference to the disposable straw beds on which women delivered their babies. Sailors slept on sacks of waxed linen stuffed with feathers, which could even float if the ship went down. Contemporary bedding needs are no different, demanding practicality, durability, and comfort.

Throughout history beds have been dressed in as many different ways as sartorial fashions have varied, from elaborate four-posters draped in sumptuous brocade hangings favoured by the rich in the 17th and 18th centuries to plain, plaid-covered painted wooden beds in 19th-century Sweden.

Beds

The most basic bed is a **divan** – a mattress placed on a box spring base. Simple, painted **wooden or metal bed frames** with slats on which to rest a mattress are also comfortable. For small spaces, consider a **futon** mattress, which can be rolled up and stowed in a cupboard during the day. When friends stay, a **folding metal-framed bed** is useful, and a makeshift bed of blankets and couch pillows on the floor can be warm and cosy. Think big – larger beds are more comfortable. A **twin bed** should be at least 4–6 in longer than the sleeper and at least 3 ft wide. A 4 ft 6 in standard **double bed** – not much bigger than a child's bed – accommodates two adults 5 ft 6 in tall, which is acceptable if you like being close to your sleeping partner, but not if he or she is restless and snores. Since the purpose of a bedroom is for sleeping it might be worth sacrificing floor space for the comforts of a large bed to curl up in at night. For good **feng shui**, the Chinese recommend a shared large mattress rather than two twin mattresses lying side by side, and a bed with rounded corners is thought to take the edges off a rocky marriage. The Chinese also believe that during pregnancy you shouldn't dust under a bed or move it if you want to avoid a miscarriage; also, a bed facing east means family life will be happy, rewarding, and peaceful.

Mattresses

Buy for **support and comfort** – not just firmness – for your weight and build. We spend over 29,000 hours on a mattress during its 10-year lifespan so it's important to choose the best you can afford to keep back problems at bay. Most modern mattresses have a **spring interior**; as a rough guide, the more springs, the better the support. Spring interiors come in different types: **open springs** – rows of coiled springs joined by a helical wire, which are used mainly in budget beds; although also found in more expensive mattresses, when the spring count is usually higher; **continuous springs** – a variation on open springs that uses one length of wire to knit the spring unit together; usually found at the better-quality end of the market in mattresses with a higher spring count; **pocket springs** – small springs separately housed in fabric pockets so they operate independently for more individual support; these vary in quality and number of springs. **Foam mattresses** have a reputation for being cheap and unpleasant but have been improved in recent years; performance and price can vary depending on design and quality. **Latex mattresses** are resilient, and don't need to be turned regularly. Old-fashioned, hard-wearing striped ticking makes the best covering for most types of mattress.

Sleep

Make the bed with **natural fibers**, such as cotton and linen, which do not retain moisture and have a cooling effect; synthetics, such as nylon, don't breathe and release static. Cotton cellular blankets are good for regulating the temperature in children's and babies' rooms; wool blankets are cosy in cold weather. Invest in a good comforter and pillows – goose down is the lightest and warmest filling; hypoallergenic fillings offer an alternative for asthmatics. The **ideal room temperature** is 60–65° F; a hot, stuffy bedroom is uncomfortable and it's better to wrap up in a cool, ventilated one. **Earplugs** cut out disturbances – dogs barking, traffic, or noisy neighbors. **Exercise** to tire yourself out, but not too close to bedtime to avoid overstimulation; **don't drink or eat** late at night: alcohol sends you to sleep initially but interrupts sleep later, and digesting food is very disruptive. If you are **stressed**, take your mind off your problems and make lists of things to do the next day; **relax and have a bath**; read a good novel; keep the lighting low; listen to soothing music or a story on the radio – all good for relaxing body and mind to induce restful sleep.

beds

the best shapes for comfort and peaceful slumber in a range of traditional and contemporary styles

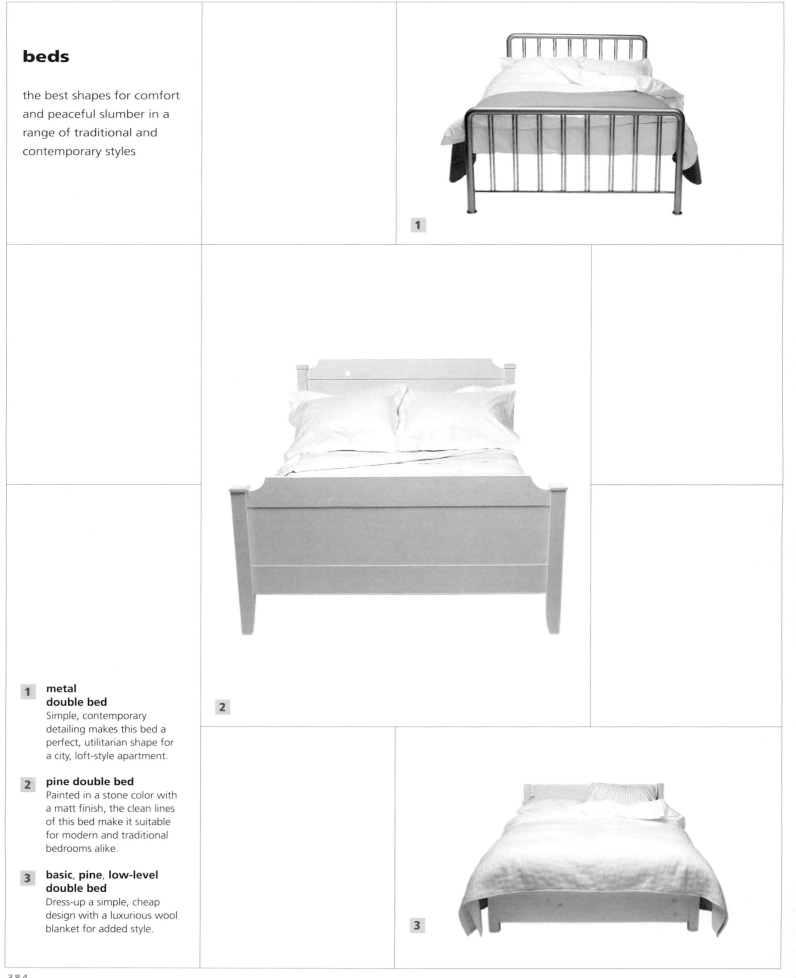

1 **metal double bed**
Simple, contemporary detailing makes this bed a perfect, utilitarian shape for a city, loft-style apartment.

2 **pine double bed**
Painted in a stone color with a matt finish, the clean lines of this bed make it suitable for modern and traditional bedrooms alike.

3 **basic, pine, low-level double bed**
Dress-up a simple, cheap design with a luxurious wool blanket for added style.

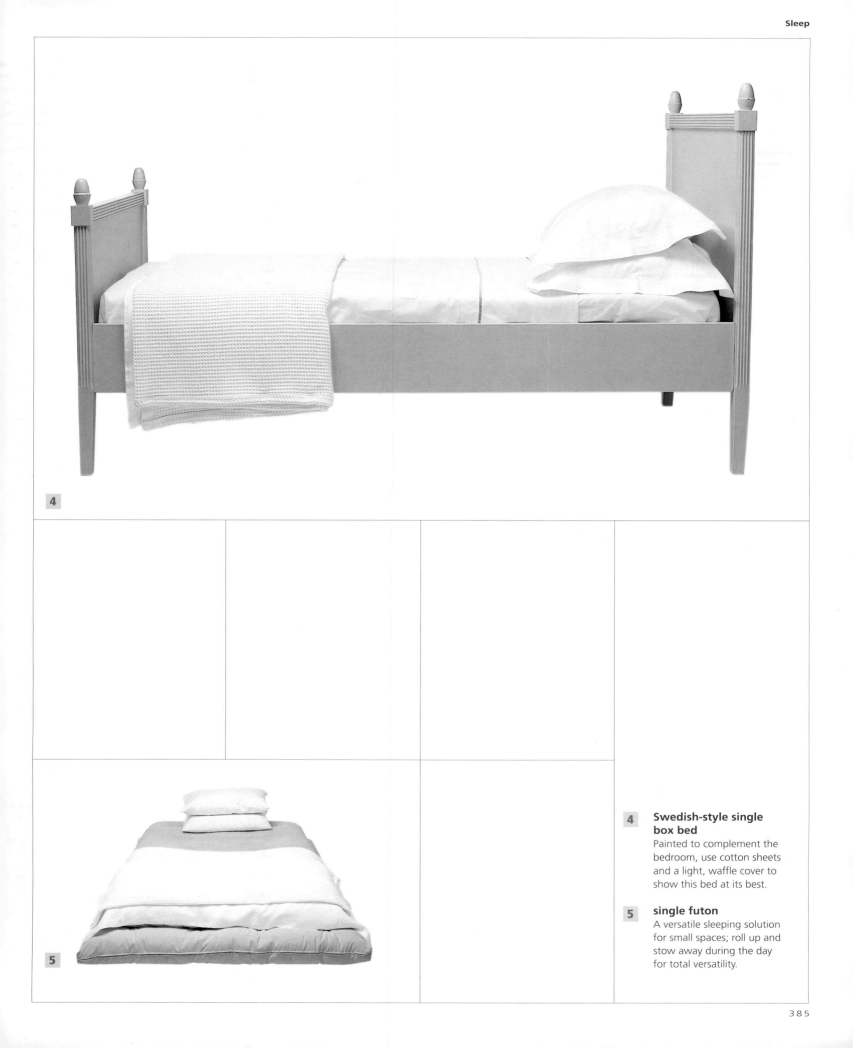

4

5

4 **Swedish-style single box bed**
Painted to complement the bedroom, use cotton sheets and a light, waffle cover to show this bed at its best.

5 **single futon**
A versatile sleeping solution for small spaces; roll up and stow away during the day for total versatility.

bedding basics

my key ingredients for
a good night's sleep are a
firm, unyielding mattress,
soft, malleable pillows, and
a light, goose-down
comforter

1

2

3

1 **duck-feather and down all-season comforter**
The ultimate in versatility, this comprises two comforters that can be used singly in warm and cool temperatures and buttoned together when it's very cold.

2 **hand-tufted, open-spring, firm mattress**
Stuffed with cotton and wool felt and covered with classic cotton ticking, this spring mattress will provide the optimum back support.

3 **pillow fillings**
A range of pillow stuffings is available to suit most needs (from top: hypoallergenic synthetic filling; goose-down and feather mix; luxurious goose down).

4 **feather and down bolsters**
Longer, thinner, and bulkier alternatives to pillows. Use during pregnancy as a good tummy support (lie sideways with the bolster wedged between your legs).

4

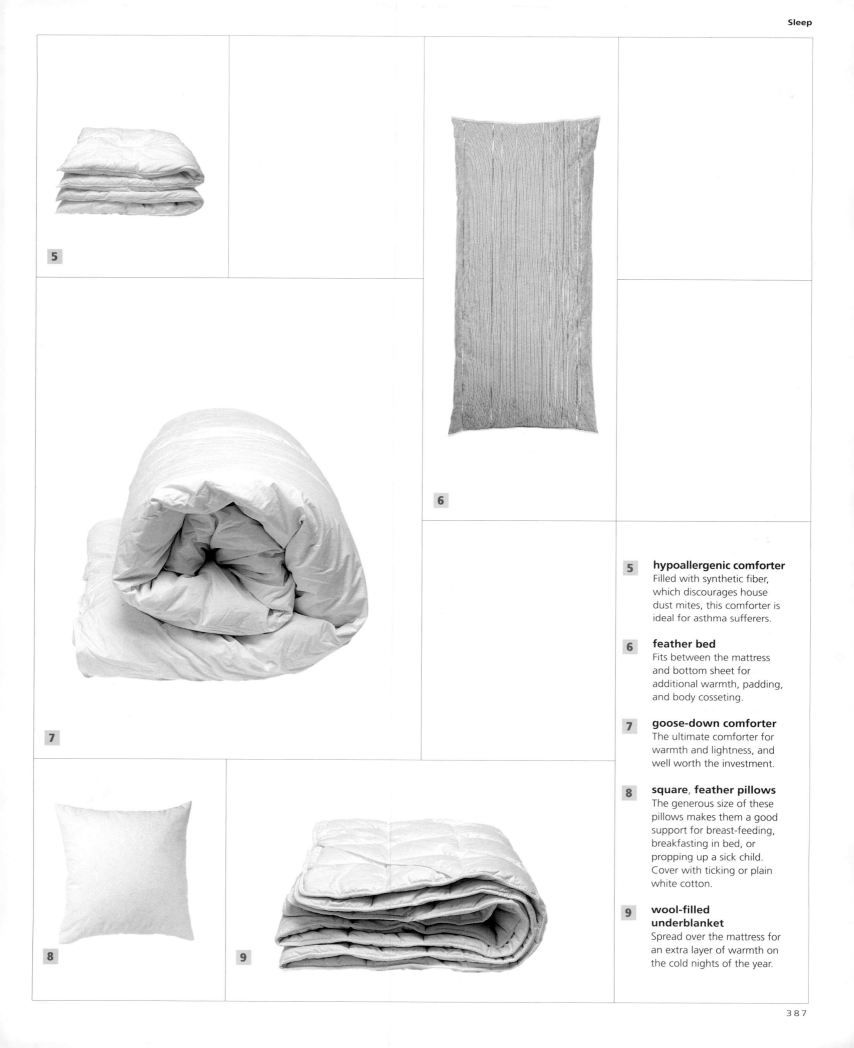

5 | **hypoallergenic comforter**
Filled with synthetic fiber, which discourages house dust mites, this comforter is ideal for asthma sufferers.

6 | **feather bed**
Fits between the mattress and bottom sheet for additional warmth, padding, and body cosseting.

7 | **goose-down comforter**
The ultimate comforter for warmth and lightness, and well worth the investment.

8 | **square, feather pillows**
The generous size of these pillows makes them a good support for breast-feeding, breakfasting in bed, or propping up a sick child. Cover with ticking or plain white cotton.

9 | **wool-filled underblanket**
Spread over the mattress for an extra layer of warmth on the cold nights of the year.

bedlinen

scrumptious bedding textures in linen, cotton, and wool are essential for bedroom comfort

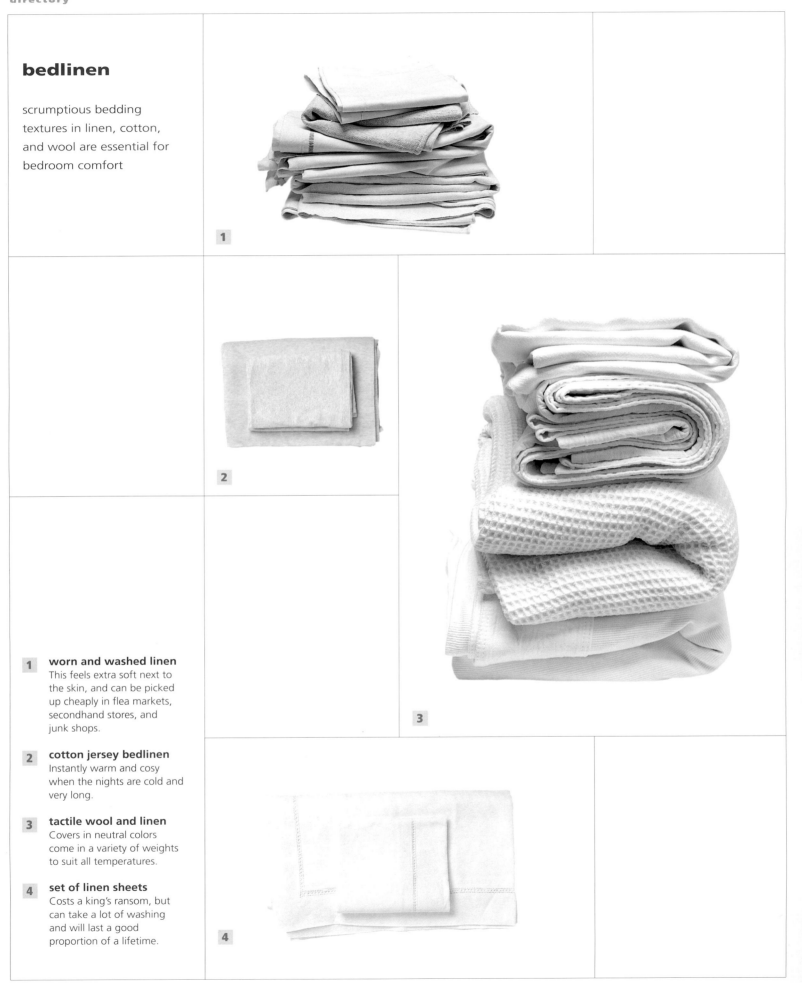

1

2

3

4

1 worn and washed linen
This feels extra soft next to the skin, and can be picked up cheaply in flea markets, secondhand stores, and junk shops.

2 cotton jersey bedlinen
Instantly warm and cosy when the nights are cold and very long.

3 tactile wool and linen
Covers in neutral colors come in a variety of weights to suit all temperatures.

4 set of linen sheets
Costs a king's ransom, but can take a lot of washing and will last a good proportion of a lifetime.

5 **wool blankets and throws**
These look good layered on the bed and can be thrown off or added to depending on individual needs.

6 **crisp, white cotton bedlinen**
The ultimate in freshness, and feels good against the skin whether the room is hot or cold.

7 **checked and striped blankets**
Use to add color and coziness to the neutral bedroom.

8 **cotton flannel sheets**
Inexpensive, warm, and comforting, flannel sheets are a favorite with children.

9 **knitted bed textures**
To give a snug, homey feel to any bedroom (from top: lambswool pillow cover; chocolate-colored blanket; linen throw; alpaca throw).

bedroom accessories

pretty, practical additions to the bedroom to make it undeniably a comfort zone

1

2

3

4

5

1. **cool white bathrobe**
   A robe in waffle cotton has a luxurious texture to keep you warm after a bath or when lounging in the bedroom.

2. **traditional hot water bottle**
   For very cold nights; only half fill, use hot, not boiling water, and wrap in a towel if you don't have a cover.

3. **bedside alarm clock**
   To wake you up in plenty of time to avoid a rushed start to the day.

4. **linen lavender pillow**
   Put under a pillow to encourage peaceful sleep.

5. **canvas boxes**
   Useful, stackable storage boxes that look good in the bedroom or can be stowed under the bed to keep the room uncluttered.

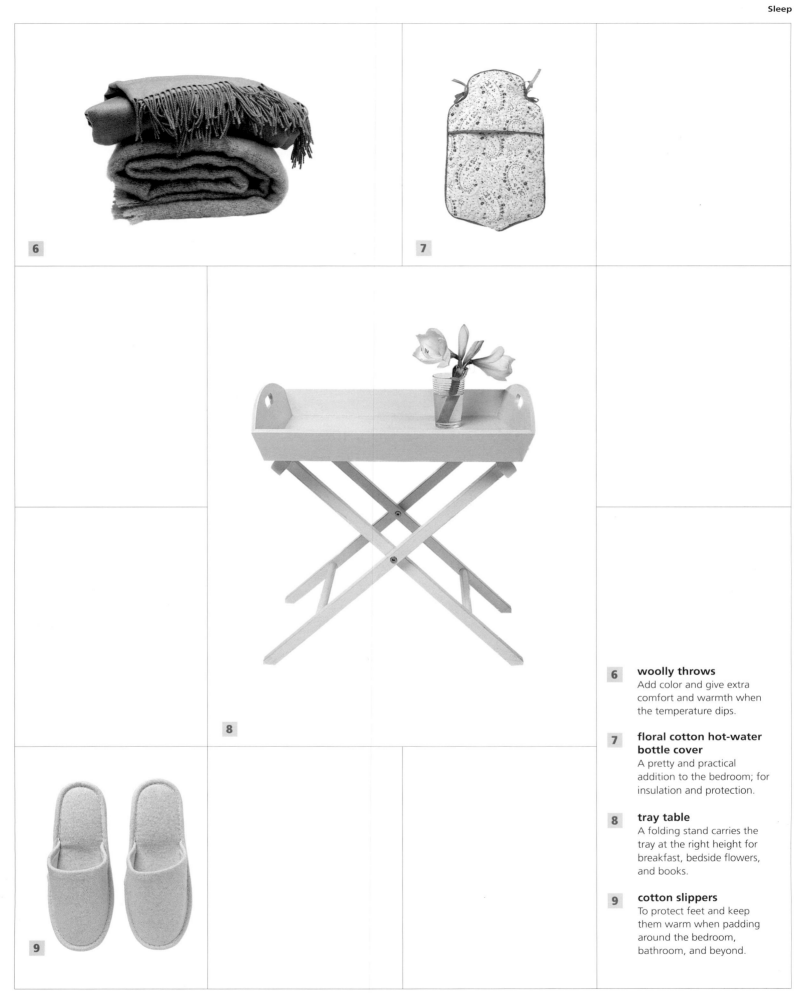

6

6 woolly throws
Add color and give extra comfort and warmth when the temperature dips.

7 floral cotton hot-water bottle cover
A pretty and practical addition to the bedroom; for insulation and protection.

8 tray table
A folding stand carries the tray at the right height for breakfast, bedside flowers, and books.

9 cotton slippers
To protect feet and keep them warm when padding around the bedroom, bathroom, and beyond.

392

Recipes Cook up feasts in the kitchen with simple-to-prepare ideas and good ingredients.

Chestnut soup
(p.97) serves 4
A soup with a smooth texture and a rich flavour that is tasty at any time of year.
1 onion, chopped; 2 sticks of celery, chopped; 1 potato, chopped; 2 tbsp olive oil; 1 lb chestnut purée; 1 quart chicken stock; single cream and parsley to garnish.

Fry the onion, celery, and potato in the oil until soft. Add the chestnut purée and stir in the stock. Bring to the boil and simmer for 1 hour, then blend with a hand-held blender. Season and add single cream and parsley to garnish. Recipe given to me by Arrabella Douglas-Menzies.

Roast chicken with a lemon and herb butter
(p.118) serves 4
Instead of a turkey at Christmas-time, chicken is just as delicious – especially with lemon and herb butter between the skin and flesh to give it extra juiciness.
3 tbsp thyme or rosemary, chopped; 2 tbsp parsley, chopped; grated zest and juice of 1/2 organic lemon; 3–5 oz unsalted butter, softened; 1 free-range chicken, approximately 1.5kg

Preheat oven to 350° F.
Mix the herbs, lemon zest and juice with the softened butter; season with salt and a little freshly ground black pepper.
Lift the skin around the breast of the chicken and ease the herb butter over both breasts, smoothing it out so it covers all the meat. Press the skin down with the flat of your hands.
Roast in the oven for about 1 hour, depending on weight; allow approximately 20 minutes per 1 lb. Baste several times to keep the bird moist.
Garnish with sprigs of fresh herbs, and serve warm with vegetables and a wonderful gravy.
Recipe ©Clare Gordon Smith

Chicken stock
(p.118) serves 4
This can be stored in plastic containers in the freezer.
1 chicken carcass; 1 bay leaf; 1 onion, chopped; 1 carrot, chopped

Place all ingredients in a saucepan or casserole dish. Cover with water and season. Bring to the boil and simmer for 1 1/2 hours. Sieve, and use the remaining liquid in soups and risottos.

Brussel sprouts with pine nuts and shallots
(p.118) serves 4
Add extra flavor and texture to sprouts with some sautéed bacon and shallots.

1 lb brussel sprouts, peeled and marked with a cross at the base; 2 tbsp butter or olive oil; 6 slices bacon cut into bite-size pieces; 8 shallots, peeled and halved; 3 oz pinenuts
Steam brussel sprouts over a pan of salted simmering water for about 7–10 minutes.
Heat olive oil or butter in a large frying pan, add the bacon and shallots and gently sauté until the bacon is soft and shallots golden – about 7–10 minutes.
Stir in the pine nuts and drained sprouts and cook for a further 5–10 minutes until the sprouts are just tender and soft and have taken the flavour of the bacon and shallots.
Season with sea salt and freshly ground black pepper.
Recipe ©Clare Gordon Smith

Sautéed leeks
(p.119) serves 4
1 lb leeks, trimmed; 2 oz butter; juice and grated zest of 1 lemon; 2 tbsp chopped chives, 4 tbsp single cream or crème fraîche (optional)

Thinly slice leeks on a diagonal; heat the butter in a large frying pan.
Add the leeks and gently sauté until soft and tender, about 7 minutes. Remove from heat and stir in the remaining ingredients.
Season with sea salt and freshly ground black pepper. Serve hot.
Recipe ©Clare Gordon Smith

Sautéed carrots
(p.118) serves 4
The combination of carrots with orange is particularly tangy and tasty.
2 oz butter; 1 lb carrots, peeled and sliced; grated zest and juice of 1 orange; parsley to garnish

Melt the butter in a saucepan. Sauté the carrots in the butter until soft and tender. Stir in the orange zest and juice, and garnish with chopped parsley. Serve immediately.
Recipe ©Clare Gordon Smith

Roast parsnips and potatoes
(p.118) serves 4
Roast parsnips and potatoes are always good with roast chicken or turkey. Make sure that the oil is hot to ensure crisp vegetables.
1 lb potatoes, peeled; 1 lb parsnips, peeled; 4 tbsp olive oil

Preheat oven to 350° F.
Cut the potatoes and parsnips into equal size pieces and parboil in a pan of salted boiling water for about 7–10 minutes.
While they are cooking, heat the oil in a roasting pan; when hot add the drained, parboiled potatoes and parsnips and toss in the hot oil until coated. Roast in the oven for 40–60 minutes;

baste every 10 minutes or so.
Alternatively, if there is space place the vegetables around the roast chicken and cook.
Recipe ©Clare Gordon Smith

Heart-shaped biscuits
(p.217) makes 12–15
Prepare a simple shortbread recipe. Use cutters to cut out hearts and stars for Christmas tree decorations.
*5 oz butter; 6 oz plain flour; 2 oz caster sugar; little drop of vanilla extract
To decorate: 5 oz confectioner's sugar; 1–2 tbsp warm water; silver balls; ribbon*

Preheat oven to 350° F.
Rub butter into flour to resemble breadcrumbs; stir in sugar and vanilla extract.
Pull together to form a smooth dough. Roll out on floured surface to about 5 mm deep. Cut out different shapes with cutters and place on greased baking sheet. Use a skewer to make a hole at the top to thread a ribbon through. Bake in preheated oven for 10–15 minutes, until just golden brown.
Cool on a wire rack. Decorate with glacé icing and silver balls.
Recipe ©Clare Gordon Smith

Mince pies
(p.119) makes 12–18
Decorate these mince pies with a simple star. If using ready-made mincemeat, stir in a little brandy or sherry for extra flavour.
8 oz shortcrust pastry; 8 oz mincemeat; 1–2 tbsp brandy or sherry; milk; granulated or confectioner's sugar

Preheat oven to 350 F°.
Roll out pastry on a floured surface; cut with an 8 cm pastry cutter and line mince pie baking tray.
Stir brandy or sherry into mincemeat; add about 2 teaspoons of mincemeat to each pastry case. With a small star cutter, cut out star shapes and place on top of mincemeat. Brush with a little milk and bake for 15–20 minutes, until golden.
Cool on a wire rack and dust with granulated or sifted confectioner's sugar.

Chocolate truffles
(p.119) makes 24
The base of the mixture is a soft and gooey chocolate ganache. Keep it firm by chilling in the fridge and use a teaspoon to help shape the truffles. Use good-quality chocolate with a minimum of 70% cocoa solids.
13 oz plain chocolate, broken into small pieces; 2 tbsp brandy; 8 oz double cream; 3–4 tbsp cocoa, sieved.

Put chocolate and brandy into a bowl over a saucepan of just simmering water, heat gently, stirring until the chocolate has melted and the mixture is quite smooth. Transfer to a bowl, add

the cream and beat with an electric mixer until cool and thick.
Chill for a few hours to thicken. Use a teaspoon to shape the mixture into balls. Roll in the sieved cocoa. Place on a baking sheet and chill in the refrigerator until ready to serve.
Recipe ©Clare Gordon Smith

Orange and almond cake
(p.107) serves 6
This moist and orangey-flavoured cake has Moorish origins and is a good choice for dessert.
*4 eggs, separated; 5 oz caster sugar; zest of 2 oranges; 4 oz ground almonds
For the syrup: juice of 4 oranges; 5 oz granulated sugar; 1 tbsp brandy*

Preheat oven to 350° F.
Beat egg yolks, sugar, orange zest and ground almonds together. In a separate bowl, beat egg whites until stiff, then fold in the yolk mixture. Pour into a greased and floured loose bottomed cake pan. Bake for 45 minutes and allow to cool in the pan.
To make the syrup: bring the orange juice, sugar, and brandy to the boil and simmer for 5 minutes.
Pierce the cake all over with a skewer; pour the syrup over and leave to soak in.
Based on a recipe from "Mediterranean cookery" by Claudia Roden; BBC Books

Sterilizing jam jars
(p.92–93)
Make sure that the jars you are using have no cracks, chips, or other flaws.

Wash well in hot soapy water, rinse, and put into a hot oven at 275F° for 30 minutes. Fill the jars while they are warm to prevent cracking.

Grapefruit, orange, and lemon marmalade
(p.92–93) makes 6 jars
Wash and dry the fruit first.
2 grapefruit, quartered and peeled; 2 oranges, quartered and peeled; 4 lemons, quartered and peeled; 3 1/2 quarts water; 6 lb sugar

Finely shred all citrus fruit zest, saving the seeds, pith, and flesh. Put the seeds and pith in a piece of muslin and tie with string (which can be tied to the pan handle).
Coarsely chop the flesh of the fruits.
Place the flesh, zest, muslin bag, and water in a large saucepan. Bring to the boil and simmer for 1 1/2 hours.
Remove the muslin bag. Add the sugar to the remaining liquid and stir until it dissolves.
Increase the heat; boil rapidly for 15–20 minutes, or until it wrinkles. Remove from the heat and let stand for 10 minutes. Stir, then ladle the marmalade into sterilized jars and cover.

Addresses Where to go to find the ingredients of **Pure Style**

PAINT

Benjamin Moore & Co.
51 Chestnut Ridge Road
Montvale
NJ 07645
tel 800 344 0400 for retail outlets
email benjaminmoore@att.net
website www.benmoore.com
*Good **period-style colors** in muted shades, available in both **interior and exterior eggshell**. Also do a range of eco-friendly paints.*

Farrow & Ball, Inc.
tel 845 369 4912 for retail outlets
fax 845 369 4913
email farrowball.na@mindspring.com
available at:
Christopher Norman Showroom
979 Third Avenue
16th Floor, New York
NY 10022
For public access to this showroom please contact
D&D Building
Designer Referral Service
Charlotte Vaslav
tel 212 231-6894
email farrow-ball@farrow-ball.co.uk
website www.farrow-ball.co.uk
*Excellent selection of **off-whites**, also good range of muted colors.*

Fired Earth products
available at:
Christians
Beverly Hills
tel 310 854 3862
fax 310 854 3836
email export@firedearth.com
website www.firedearth.com
*Range of **traditional paints in authentic 18th- and 19th-century colours**, available in the traditional finishes of Dead Flat Oil and Distemper, Latex, Oil Eggshell and Sleepy Gloss. Also a range of water-based contemporary color paints.*

ICI Dulux Paints
390 Kenmore Avenue
Buffalo
NY 13224
tel 315 446 7890
email iciduluxpaints@ici.com
website www.icipaintstores.com
for local retailer
*Vast range of colors and finishes plus a **matching service**.*

Janovic
3035 Thompson Avenue
Long Island City
New York 11101
tel 212 289 6794
fax 718 361 7288
toll free 800 772 4381
website www.janovic.com
Good color range.

Mineral-Life, Inc.
6732 SW 71st Court
Miami, Florida 33143
tel 305 661 9854
fax 305 661 6942
email minlife@ix.netcom.com
website www.mineral-life.com
Lime-based paints in a good range of muted and deep colors.

Old Village Paints
P.O. Box 1030
Fort Washington
PA 19034-1030
tel 610 238 9001
fax 610 238 9002
email info@old-village.com
website www.old-village.com
*High-quality **paint made using traditional methods**. Shades are based on original colors found in Colonial and Shaker homes throughout America.*

Pittsburgh Paints
60 James Way
Southampton, PA 18966
tel 215 322 8187
website www.pittsburghpaints.com
Over 1,800 colors to choose from. Visit the website to find your local retailer.

Pratt & Lambert
78 Route 303
Tappan
NY 100983
tel 845 359 4656
fax 716 873 6000
website www.prattandlambert.com
*Lots of colors, plus a **good range of off-whites**. The range includes both oil and water-based paints.*

Sydney Harbour Paints
12602 Ventura Boulevard
Studio City
CA 91604
tel 818 623 9394
fax 818 623 9210
website www.porters.co.au
*Traditional **limewash** for both exteriors and interiors, also milk paint, french wash and distemper.*

FABRIC

Bennison Fabrics Ltd
76 Greene Street
New York, NY 10012
tel 212 941 1212
*The diffusion range of fabrics has **pretty floral cottons** in fresh colors.*

Calico Corners
203 Gale Lane
Kennett Square
PA 19348
tel 800 213 6366
*Over 100 retail outlets that **discount top-quality fabrics**, as well as selected seconds. Call for a mail-order catalog.*

Calvin Klein Home
18th floor
1185 Fifth Avenue
New York
tel 212 696 4646
tel 800 294 7978 for branches
Fine quality linens.

Cath Kidston
8 Clarendon Cross
London W11 4AP
England
tel +44 20 7221 4000
tel +44 20 7229 8000 for mail order
fax +44 20 7221 4388
email mailorder@cathkidston.co.uk
website www.cathkidston.co.uk
Bright and fresh 1950s-inspired florals. Fabrics are available by the yard and in pretty coathangers, pyjamas, bags, sheets and other accessories.

Colefax & Fowler
19-23 Grosvenor Hill
London W1X 9HG
England
tel +44 20 8874 6484 for worldwide retailers
*Quality fabrics with a good selection of **traditional floral and checked cotton**.*

The Conran Shop
See Storage for details
Cotton and linen in plains, stripes and checks, and a great color range.

Designer's Guild
Osborne & Little Inc.
979 Third Avenue – Suite 520
New York
NY 10022
tel 212 751 3333
website www.designersguild.com
Fresh checks, stripes and florals. Light sheer organzas, cottons and linens as well as felt and wool.

Ian Mankin
at Agnes Bourne
2 Henry Adams Street
Showroom 220
San Francisco
CA 9410310022
and at
Coconut Company
129-31 Greene Street
SoHo
New York, NY 10012-8080
*Excellent stock of **utility fabrics**; tickings, checks, and stripes from fine cotton ginghams to heavy linen butchers' stripes, plain-colored cottons and linens. All fabrics are reasonably priced.*

Ikea
1100 Broadway Mall
Hicksville, New York 11801
Tel 516 681 4532
1800 E. McConnor Parkway
Schaumburg, IL 60173
tel 847 969 9700
tel 800 434 4532 for mail order
website www.ikea-usa.com
Visit the website for a list of local branches.
*Bargain fabrics in **simple, modern***

checks, stripes, and plain colors. Plus *good-value ready-made curtains, pillows, and blinds.*

Indika
Rancho Mirage
CA 92270
tel 760 321 9557
toll free 1-866 446 3452
website www.indikahome.com
email info@IndikaHome.com
*Beautiful plain-colored upholstery fabrics in natural fibers: **100% organic cotton and cotton/silk mixes**.*

Kvadrat
available at
Maharan Textiles
Maharan International
251 Park Avenue South
New York, NY 10010
tel 212 614 2901
fax 212 375 0489
email email kvadrat@kvadrat.co.uk
website www.kvadrat.dk
*Very good quality, **upholstery fabrics**. Plain fabrics in excellent color ranges with various textures from felt to boucle.*

Laura Ashley
6 St. James Avenue
Boston, MA 02116
tel 800 367 2000 for nearest store
tel 800 461 6728
website www.laura-ashleyusa.com
*Florals, **stripes and checks** in a good choice of colors.*

Liberty plc.
Regent Street
London W1R 6AH
England
tel +44 20 7734 1234
fax +44 20 7573 9876
email Fabricdirect@liberty.co.uk
for a fabric catalog
website www.liberty.co.uk
*Look among the dress fabrics for classic **pretty lightweight floral tana lawn prints** and use to make floaty curtains, pillow slips, and bags available by mail order.*

Marvic Textiles
979 Third Avenue
New York, NY 10022
*A good range of **upholstery fabrics in stylish colorings** (trade only-contact for your nearest distributor).*

Monkwell and G P & J Baker
USA retailers contact Lee Jofa
tel 516 752 7600
website www.monkwell.com
Corporate Headquarters:
call for retailers nationwide

Lee Jofa
979 3rd Avenue
New York, NY 10022
tel 212 688 0444
fax 516 752 7623
*Modern as well as traditional **good***

quality upholstery fabrics. Plain-colored fabrics in different weaves and textures from wool and cashmere to cotton voiles.

Oppenheim's
PO Box 29
120 East Main Street
North Manchester
IN 4696-20052
tel 800 461 6728 for a catalog
Denim and some print as well as remnants directly from the mill.

Osborne & Little
Head Quarters
90 Commerce Road
Stamford
Connecticut 06902
tel 203 359 1500 for retailers
website www.osborneandlittle.com
Huge range of quality fabrics covering everything from voiles to heavy linen prints.

Ralph Lauren House Furnishings
650 Madison Avenue
New York
NY 10022
tel 212 318 7000
Stylish home accessories, including cotton fabrics and bed linen in blue and white.

Romo
distributed by Arte
16758 West Park Circle Drive
Shagrin Falls
Ohio 44022
tel 800 338 278 for retailers
Excellent range of plain colors in a variety of textures. I particularly like the range of cotton velvets.

Rosebrand Textiles
517 West 35th Street
New York,
NY 10001
Great value muslin, canvas, scrim, and ticking.

Rue de France
78 Thimas Street
Newport
RI 02840
tel 800 777 0998
Curtains and accessories with a French Country look, also beautiful lace panels.

Sanderson
New York Showroom
A Sanderson & sons Ltd
Suite 409
979 Third Avenue
New York,
NY 10022
tel 212 391 7220
fax 212 593 6184
website www.sanderson-online.co.uk
London, Paris, New York
Customer service and retailers call
018995 201 509
Good stripes, checked cottons and cotton velvets.

FLOORING

Aged Woods Inc.
2331 East Market Street
York
PA 17402
toll free 1-800 233 9307
website www.agedwoods.com
Antique wood flooring.

Amtico International Inc.
The Amtico Studio
200 Lexington Avenue
Suite 809
New York, NY 10016
tel 212 545 1127
fax 212 545 8382
website www.amtico.com
Hard floor coverings available include slate, granite, ceramic, marble, wood, and metallic tile. They also offer a custom service.

Artistic Tile
79 Fifth Avenue
New York, NY 10003
tel 212 727 9331
website www.artistictile.com
Slate floor tile.

Broad-Axe Beam Company
1320 Lee Road
Guilford
Vermont 05301
tel 802 257 0064
website www.broad-axebeam.com
Wide white pine planks for flooring and paneling.

Bruce Hardwood Floors
Corporate office Bruce Hardwood Floors
Division of Triangle Pacific Corp
168 Dallas Parkway
Dallas
Texas 75248
tel 800 722 4647
website
www.brucehardwoodfloors.com
Solid hardwood and laminate flooring.

Carlisle
1676 Route 9
Stoddard
New Hampshire 03464
toll free 1-800 595 9663
website www.wideplankflooring.com
Wide planking in Eastern white pine, Southern longleaf heart pine, red and white oak, and wild black cherry. Carlisle Restoration Lumber combines recycled lumber recovered from old mills and factories with newly sawn planks to produce traditional, colonial-style hardwood flooring.

Chestnut Specialists, Inc.
tel 860 283 4209
email Chestnutspec@aol.com
website www.chestnutspec.com
Flooring created from reclaimed antique lumber from historic New England farmhouses, barns, and outbuildings. Hand selected kiln-dried woods come in wide planks, random widths, and narrow strips, and in chestnut, oak and pine.

Crate & Barrel
650 Madison Avenue
New York, NY 10022
or PO Box 9059
Wheeling
Illinois 60090-9059
(mail order)
tel 800 996 9960 for nearest store or visit the website.
website www.crateandbarrel.com
A selection of simple rugs in wool, cotton, jute and coir, both plain and stripes. 100% linen tab-top curtain panels. Plain and striped pillows.

Crucial Trading
distributed by Concept International
83 Habor Road
Port Washington
NY 11050
tel 516 767 1110 for retailers
fax 212 753 5904
Natural floor coverings such as jute, sisal, and coir.

Dodge-Regupol Inc.
PO Box 989
Lancaster
PA 17608 0989
tel 800 322 1923
fax 717 295 3414
Cork tile and recycled rubber.

Forbo Industries, Inc.
Maplewood Drive
Hazleton, PA 18201
tel 570 459 0771
toll free 1-800 342 0604
Linoleum flooring and vinyl sheet for counters.

Galileo
37 Seventh Avenue
New York, NY 10011
tel 212 243 1629
Bright striped woven plastic mats.

Garnet Hill
See Sleep for details
Jute, cotton and 100% wool hand-tufted rugs in natural tones.

Junkers
4920E Landon Drive
Anaheim
CA 92807
tel 714 777 6430
toll free 1-800 878 9663
email sales/tech@junkers.co.uk
website www.junkers.co.uk
Solid hardwood flooring available in beech, oak, ash, merbau and sycamore, which comes with a 20-year guarantee. All wood is sourced from managed forests.

Lands' End, Inc.
See Kitchen for details
100% cotton, sisal, and flatweave wool rugs.

Merida Natural Fiber Flooring
PO Box 1071
Syracuse
NY 13201
tel 800 345 2200 for nearest dealer
Natural fiber rugs: coir, jute, and sisal.

Natural Cork
1825 Killingsworth Road
Augusta
GA 30904
tel 706 733 6120
fax 706 733 8120
website www.naturalcork.com
email info@naturalcork.com
Natural cork tile and floating floors.

Paris Ceramics
150 East 58th Street
7th Floor
New York, NY 10155
tel 212 644 2782
fax 212 644 2785
tel 888 845 3487 for brochure and other branches.
email newyork@parisceramics.com
website www.parisceramics.com
Limestone flooring.

Pottery Barn
See Furniture for details
Sisal, jute, and coir rugs in neutral colors with bound edges.

Roppe Corp
1602 N Union Street
PO Box 1158
Fostoria
OH 44830
tel 419 435 8546
fax 419 435 1056
toll free 800 537 9527 for distributors
email sales@roppe.com
website www.roppe.com
Rubber tile with a smooth finish or a raised design.

Rue de France
See Kitchen for details
Blue and white striped rag rugs.

Ann Sacks
5 East 16th Street
New York, NY 10003
tel 212 463 8400
fax 212 463 0067
Terra-cotta and slate floor tile in different shades.

Safavieh Carpet
153 Madison Avenue
New York, NY 10016
tel 888 723 2843
Vegetable dyed rugs.

Sheldon Slate
Fox Road
Middle Granville
NY 12849
tel 518 642 1280
fax 518 642 9085
website www.sheldonslate.com
Slate quarried in New England and

Upstate New York State made into flooring and counters for the kitchen. See the website for other retailers.

Stark Carpet Corporation
Executive Office & Main Showroom
D&D Building
979 Third Avenue
New York, NY 10022-1276
tel 212 752 9000 stockists
fax 212 758 4342
Huge selection of carpets including various natural fibers: sisal, coir, seagrass.

Williams Sonoma
See Kitchen for details
Sisal, seagrass, and jute rugs.

Walker Zanger
8901 Bradley Avenue
Sun Valley
CA 91352
tel 818 504 0235
fax 818 504 2226
tel 877 611 0199 ext.101 for retailers and catalog
website www.walkerzanger.com
Limestone flooring.

Wicanders
tel 800 828 2675 for stockists
website www.wicanders.com
Cork and wood flooring available through various distributiors, see the website for details.

FOOD

Balducci's
PO Box 10373
Newark
NJ 07193-0373
tel 800 225 3822
and retail store at:
424 Sixth Avenue
New York
NY 10012
tel 212 673 2600
This food market has all sorts of delicious offerings: gorgeous baked goods, excellent cuts of meat and fish. Mail order is available with overnight delivery on perishables.

Balthazar
80 Spring Street
SoHo
New York
NY 10012
tel 212 965 1785
Relax in the French café-style surroundings and sample the freshly baked breads from Balthazar's bakery next door.

Dave's Organic Produce
35151 Marks Road
Barstow
CA 92311
tel 760 256 5339
fax 760 252 1241
email davesorganic@bigfoot.com

website www.davesorganics.com
Organic produce delivered to your home or business.

Dean & Deluca
PO Box 20810
Witchita
KS 67208
tel 800 221 7714
Flagship store at:
560 Broadway
New York, NY 10012
tel 212-226-6800
A fabulous store packed with fruit, vegetables, flowers, plus an excellent espresso bar, bakery, charcuterie, fish counter, and grocer.

Diamond Organics
PO Box 2159
Freedom
CA 95019
tel 888 674 2642
fax 888 888 6777
email info@diamondorganics.com
website www.diamondorganics.com
Organic supplies delivered to your door: fresh salads, fruit and vegeatables, edible flowers, mushrooms, herbs.

Foods of All Nations
2121 Ivy Road
Charlottesville
VA 24501
tel 804 296 6131
A great selection of produce sourced from more than 200 suppliers worldwide.

Jurgensen's Grocery Company
842 East California Boulevard
Pasadena
CA 91109
tel 800 344 4313
Picnic hampers packed full of fine foods.

La Tienda
PO Box 1589
Williamsburg
VA 23187
tel 888 472 1022
fax 757 565 3346
website www.tienda.com
Home delivery of fine Spanish foods: jamon serrano, olive oil, and manchego cheese.

Nash's Produce
1865 East Anderson Road
Sequim
WA 98382
tel 360 683 4642
email mailbox@nashproce.com
website www.nashproduce.com
Organic produce available directly from the farm or various farmer's markets, see the website for details.

Neal's Yard Dairy
available at
Zingermans
422 Detroit Street
Ann Arbor
MI 48104

tel 510 524 9325 for stockists
tel 734 769 1235 for mail order
website www.zingermans.com
Lots of excellent British and Irish cheeses; Applebys Cheshire, Gorwydd Caerphilly, Beenliegh Blue.

Organic Valley Family of Farms
CROPP Cooperative
507 West Main Street
LaFarge
WI 54639
toll free 888 444 6455
fax 608 625 2600
email organic@organicvalley.com
website www.organicvalley.com
Organic dairy produce and meat. Visit the website for a list of local suppliers.

PCC Fremont
716 N 34th Street
Seattle
WA 98103
tel 206 632 6811
website www.pccnaturalmarkets.com for other branches.
Groceries, meat, dairy, deli, wine, and beer with an emphasis on quality, nutrition, and organic growing methods.

Planet Organics
915 Cole Street 172
San Francisco
CA 94117
tel 800 956 5855
fax 415 648 2597
email service@planetorganics.com
website www.planetorganics.com
A weekly organic produce and grocery delivery service throughout the San Francisco Bay area.

Port Angeles Farmers' Market
8th and Chase Streets
Port Angeles, WA
Held all year round, weather permitting.

Power-Selles Imports
7206 First Avenue
NW Seattle
WA 98117
tel 206 783 5823
fax 206 783 5836
website www.psimports.net
Importers of Spanish delicacies: olive oil, olives, Blanxart chocolate, organic chestnuts, and roast peppers.

Sequim Open Air Market
2nd and Cedar Streets
Sequim, WA
Farmers' market open July through October.

Sierra Rica
C. La Julianita 7-9
Poligono Cantalgallo
Aracena 21200
Huelva
Spain
tel 00 34 959 127327
website www.sierrarica.com
Organic foods from Andalucia, Spain,

including peeled and cooked chestnuts, membrillo and cooking sauces. Visit the website for nearest retailer.

Urban Organic
230A 7th Street
Brooklyn
NY 11215
tel 718 499 4321
toll free 888 487 2260
fax 718 965 4688
website www.urbanorganics.com
Organic produce boxed and delivered weekly.

VB Farms
Certified Organic Produce
PO Box 2581 Watsonville
CA 95077
tel 831 728 9218
website www.sunshineorganic.com
Jam-making kits including fresh organic fruit, delivered nationwide except to Florida, Puerto Rico, or Hawaii.

Whole Foods Market
601 N. Lamar
Suite 300
Austin
Texas 78703
tel 512 477 4455 for nationwide stores
website www.wholefoodsmarket.com
Excellent selection of organic produce and products: cheeses, coffee, chestnuts, meat and seafood, groceries, bread, and wine.

Williams Sonoma
See Kitchen for details
Decorating sugars, pens, and confetti for cookies and cakes. Oils, speciality ingredients, herbs, and spices plus an excellent confectionery selection with good quality chocolate.

Zabar's Deli & Gourmet Foods
2245 Broadway
New York, NY 10024
tel 212-787-2000
A diverse selection of foods from around the world.

KITCHEN

Abestkitchen.com
424 West Exchange Street
Akron, Ohio 44302
tel 330 535 2811
email sales@abestkitchen.com
website www.abestkitchen.com
Commercial cookware: Bourgeat pans, steamers and pasta cookers, baking trays, cookie cutters, simple stainless steel utensils

Blanco
1000 Taylors Lane
Cinnaminson
New Jersey 08077
tel 856 829 2720
toll free 1-800 451 5782
Simple functional kitchen storage.

Bloomingdales
1000 Third Avenue
New York
NY 10022
tel 212 705 2000
fax 800 596 2116
website www.bloomingdales.com
Bloomingdale's by Mail
tel 800 777 0000
Good quality cookware, bakeware, and utensils including heavy based Le Creuset pans.

Bridge Kitchenware
214 East 52nd Street
(Between 2nd and 3rd Avenues)
NY 10022
tel 212 688 4220
fax 212 758 5387
email s.bridge@ix.netcom.com
website www.bridgekitchenware.com
Durable industrial stainless steel pans, utensils, and baking trays.

Campbell's Gourmet Cottage
127 N. Sherrin Avenue
Louisville
KY 40207
tel 502 893 6700
fax 502 895 2796
email mail@gourmetcottage.com
website www.gourmetcottage.com
Stainless steel utensils and pans, chefs knives, Le Creuset cookware and maple butchers' blocks.

Crate and Barrel
See Flooring for details
Professional nonstick bakeware, stainless steel cookware and utensils, white ceramic oven dishes, maple cutting boards, and blue-and-white dishtowels.

Dean & Deluca
See Food for details
A good selection of kitchen tools and accessories.

KitchenAid
KitchenAid Customer Satiafaction Center
Attention: Internet Communications
PO Box 218
St Joseph
MI 49085
tel 800 541 6390
website www.kitchenaid.com
1950s style food mixers, blenders, and hand mixers.

KitchenEmporium.com
32A Friendship Street
Westerley
Rhode Island 02891
tel 888 858 7920
fax 401 596 4872
website
www.kitchenemporium.com
Stovetop espresso makers, paella pans, Sabatier knives, and all sorts of pans, tools and utensils.

Knife Outlet
6640 Oak Road

Lakeville
IN 46536
tel 219 656 4127
toll free 800 607 9948
email info@knifeoutlet.com
website www.knifeoutlet.com
Sabatier knives, chunky wooden cutting boards, scissors for every task, plus a knife sharpening service.

Lands' End, Inc.
Dodgeville
WI 53595
toll free 1-800 356 4444
for nearest store
website www.landsend.com
Striped and checked dishtowels and durable twill aprons.

LL Bean Inc
Freeport
ME 04033-0001
tel 800 441 5713
fax 207 552 3080
email llbean@llbean.com
website www.llbean.com
Enamel storage containers, traditional kitchen scales, pots and pans.

Macy's
See Bathroom Accessories for details
Good quality cookware, bakeware, chefs' knives, and a whole range of kitchen tools.

Martha by Mail
See Sleep for details
Waring blenders, wooden rolling pins, white ceramic kitchen shakers, shaped cookie cutters, plus an enamel-coated, galvanized steel kitchen compost bucket.

Pottery Barn
See Furniture for details
White serving dishes, modern and classic flatware, and hemstitched linen napkins and place mats.

The Restaurant Store
One Nepperhan Avenue
Elmsford
NY 10523
tel 914 592 5200
toll free 1-800 552 5223
fax 914 592 8183
email
CustomerService@Restaurant-Store.com
website www.cookware-store.com
Quality Henckel kitchen gadgets and utensils: knives, graters, bottle openers, whisks. All-clad cookware: stainless steel pans, colanders, and utensil sets. Cookie cutters, baking pans and measuring pitchers also stock good quality chef's knives.

Rue de France
78 Thames Street
Newport
Rhode Island
New England 02840
tel 800 777 0998
fax 401 846 6821

email service@ruedefrance.com
website www.ruedefrance.com
Striped 100% cotton dishtowels and aprons with a utility feel similar to roller towels.

Williams-Sonoma
318 Christiana Mall
Newark
DE 19702
tel 302 368 7707
website www.williams-sonoma.com
Blue-and-white dish towels, classic ceramic mixing bowls in cream and duck-egg blue, all sorts of bakeware, Le Creuset pans, and Henckel knives. 1950s style mixers and chunky Dualit toasters. Shaped cookie cutters for Christmas cookies.

Zabar's Deli & Gourmet Foods
See Food for details
A good selection of kitchenware and equipment.

TABLEWARE

Area
180 Varick Street
9th Floor
New York, NY 10014
tel 212 924 7084
Linen place mats and napkins.

Crate & Barrel
See Flooring for details
Good selection of stainless steel flatware and plain white china. Simple glass pitchers and wine glasses, chunky tumblers, and milk glasses. Cotton place mats and napkins in strong plain colors.

Delco Tableware International, Inc.
Head Quarters
19 Harbor Park Drive
Port Washington
NY 11050
tel 516 625 0808
toll free 800 221 9557
fax 516 625 0859
toll free 800 328 6283
email info@delcointl.com
website www.delcointl.com
Plain white china, simple flatware and glass salt and pepper shakers.

Fishs Eddy
889 Broadway and 19th Street
SoHo
New York 10003
tel 001 212 420 9020
website www.fishseddy.com
Modern styles in flatware.

George Watts & Sons, Inc.
761 N. Jefferson Street
Milwaukee
Wisconsin 53202
tel 414 290 5700
toll free 1-888 607 9575
fax 414 276 2777
email

customerservice@tablewareamerica.com
website www.tablewareamerica.com
Retailers of Wedgwood china.

Knife Outlet
See Kitchen for details
Beautifully simple flatware by J.A. Henkels.

Koko Company
4402 11th Street
Long Island City
NY 11101
tel 718 392 7799
website www.kokocompany.com
Table linens in natural fibers.

Lands' End, Inc.
See Kitchen for details
Mix and match white ceramic tableware and 100% linen, machine washable tablecloths.

Libbey Inc.
Attn. Corporate Communications
Manager
PO Box 10060
300 Madison Avenue
Toledo
OH 43699-0060
tel 419 325 2100
website www.world-tableware.com
Simple stainless steel flatware sets, Duralex style chunky tumblers, basic white ceramics.

Macy's
See Bathroom Accessories for details
Blue-and-white striped china as well as classic white porcelain, simple flatware, chunky tumblers and elegant wine glasses.

Williams Sonoma
See Kitchen for details
Plain white china, Classic blue-and-white Wedgwood dinnerware, wooden salad bowls, and Duralex tumblers. Large selection of flatware.

Wolfman Gold & Good Co.
117 Mercer Street
New York
NY 10012
White china and silver cutlery.

ECO

Abundant Earth
762 West Park Avenue
Port Townsend
WA 98368
tel 888 51 513 2784
email service@abundantearth.com
website www.abundantearth.com
Organic cotton futons, mattresses and box springs. Composting bins and organic gardening supplies. Energy-saving appliances.

American Natural Products Co.
2103 185th St.
Fairfield
IA 52556-9232

toll free 1-800 221 7645
All natural products for gardening and lawn care, including fertilizers, insect control, disease control, deer repellents, pond cleaners and compost starters.

Conservatree
100 Second Avenue
San Francisco
CA 94118
tel 415 721 4230
fax 415 883 6264
email paper@conservatree.com
Conservatree, a project of The Tides Center, is a nonprofit organization dedicated to providing technical assistance and the most up-to-date information about environmentally sound papers.

Creative Energy Technologies
10 Main Street
Summit
NY 12175
tel 888 305 0278
website www.cetsolar.com
Energy efficient and environmentally friendly products: composters, solar panels, electrical appliances, and heating alternatives.

Energy Efficient Environments, Inc
tel 708 866 6650
tel 800 336 3749
email info@eeenvironments.com
website
www.eeenvironments.com
Eco-friendly cleaning products, laundry detergent, and water filters.

Energy Guide
Nexus Energyguide
16 Laurel Avenue
Wellesley
MA 02481
tel 781 283 9160
fax 781 283 9150
email info@energyguide.com
website www.energyguide.com
Information on how to save energy in the home including supplier comparisons.

Freeplay Energy USA Inc.
1 Ramland Road
Orangeburg, NY 10962
tel 845 680 2233 for retailers
fax 845 680 9472
website www.freeplay.net
Manufacturers of the wind-up radio, also in a solar-powered version, as well as a wind-up flashlight.

Friends of the Earth
26-28 Underwood Street
London N1 7JQ
England
tel +44 20 7490 1555
website www.foe.co.uk
Information on environmental issues.

GreenMarketplace.com
(or EthicalShopper.com)
5808 Forbes Ave., 2nd Floor
Pittsburgh, PA 15217

tel 412 420 6400
fax 412 420 6404
website www.greenmarketplace.com
Organic cotton bags, recycled denim rugs.

Light Systems, Inc.
PO Box 294
Kingsville, MD 21087
tel 410 592 2403
fax 410 592 3105
email lightsys@voiceofwomen.com
Energy efficient lighting.

**National Paint
& Coatings Association**
1500 Rhode Island Avenue
NW Washington
DC 20005
tel 202 462 6272
fax 202 462 8549
email npca@paint.org
website www.paint.org
Paint can recycling information.

Natural Home Products.com
PO Box 1677
Sebastopol, CA 95473
tel 707 824 0914
fax 800 329 9398
email nathome@monitor.net
website www.monitor.net/nathome
Cork flooring, stains and finishes for wood, bedding.

Planet Natural
1612 Gold Avenue
Bozeman, MT 59715
tel 800 289 6656 or 406 587 5891
fax 406 587 0223
email ecostore@ycsi.net
website www.planetnatural.com
Wooden clothes racks, wooden dish racks, natural pest control, organic cotton bedding, recycled trash bags, cleaning products, organic fertilizers, organic seeds and gardening supplies, natural pest control - biological pesticides, weed control, beneficial insects, barriers and repellents.

Recycler's World
RecycleNet Corporation
P.O. Box 24017
Guelph
Ontario, Canada N1E 6V8
website www.recycle.net
Information related to secondary or recyclable commodities, byproducts, used and surplus items or materials.

STORAGE

Abestkitchen.com
See Kitchen for details
Stainless steel storage canisters for the kitchen and clear plastic containers for cold storage.

The Conran Shop
Bridgemarket
407 East 59th Street

New York
NY 10022
tel 212 755 9079
fax 212 888 3008
email info@conran.com
website www.conran.com
Contemporary storage ideas.

Crate and Barrel
See Flooring for detail
Glass and stainless steel canisters for food storage, and modular shelving that is ideal in the kitchen. All sorts of baskets, white polypropylene portable storage and simple shelving. Wooden chest and storage bench painted in a creamy white ideal for storing blankets and linens.

The Domestic Paraphernalia Co. Ltd.
28 Dock Road
Lytham
Lancashire
FY8 5AJ
England
tel +44 1253 736334
fax +44 1253 795191
email sales@sheilamaid.com
website www.sheilamaid.com
Traditional wooden hanging clothes rack available to be shipped to the US.

Duravit USA, Inc.
See Bathroom for details
Simple cube wall storage.

Galileo
See Flooring for details
Bright woven plastic baskets.

Hold Everything
208 Santa Monica Place
San Francisco
CA 90401
tel 415 681 6660
Everything to do with storage from linen hampers to canvas shoe holders.

Ikea
See Fabric for details
Shelving units, shelving brackets, plastic and cardboard stackable containers, which are very reasonably priced, white box files.

Macy's
See Bathroom Accessories for details
Carts with removable canvas drawers, ideal for bathroom storage.

Martha by Mail
See Sleep for details
Powder-coated steel storage boxes in the style of vintage enamelware and glass kitchen storage jars.

Metro International
Wilkesbarre
tel 800 433 2232
email sales@slingsby.com
website www.slingsby.com
Chrome racking which looks great in the kitchen and can be built to suit your

storage requirements.

Pottery Barn
See Furniture for details
Clever Elm trunks which double as coffee tables. Tall white column cabinets make good bathroom storage. Open shelving, units both floor standing and wall mounted can be used to display or house boxes and baskets.

Rue de France
See Kitchen for details
Woven wicker totes with braided leather handles and wicker laundry hampers.

Waterworks
See Bathroom for details
Simple white side table, white cube shelving unit, ideal for storing towels in the bathroom.

Williams Sonoma
See Kitchen for details
Farmhouse-kitchen-style armoire in solid beechwood, painted white; perfect for storing china and linens. Wooden bookcases and collapsible metal shelving.

Workbench
1574 North Kingsbury Street
at North Avenue near Old Navy
Chicago, IL 60622
tel 312 640 0753
tel 800 380 2370 for nearest store
website www.workbenchfurniture.com
Great shelving; one of which, on wheels, looks good against a wall or can be used as a room divider.

OUTSIDE

Anthropologie
1801 Walnut Street
Philadelphia
PA 19103
tel 215 564 2313 for branches
Garden accessories including an assortment of pots and planters.

Bamboo Fences
179 Boylston Street
Boston
MA 02130
tel 617 524 6137
*Bamboo fencing and gates.
Mail order available.*

Barbara Israel
21 East 79th Street
New York
NY 10021
tel 212 744 6281
Period garden furniture from both Europe and America.

Brown Jordan Co.
9860 Gidley Street
El Monte
CA 91731
tel 818 443 8971

ext. 221 for local dealer
Metal garden furniture: stacking chairs, café tables.

Colonial Williamsburg
Department 023
PO Box 3532
Williamsburg
VA 23187-3532
tel 800 446 9240
Traditional garden accessories.

Chelsea Garden Center
321 Bowery
New York, NY 10003
tel 877 846 0565
fax 212 353 8919
website
www.chelseagardencenter.com
Good quality aluminum tools with easy-grip rubber handles plus handthrown terra-cotta and weathered clay pots.

Crate & Barrel
See Flooring for details
Folding metal garden tables and chairs.

Cultus Bay Nursery
See Plants, Seeds, and Bulbs for details
Handmade wooden trugs for carrying essential tools.

Ethan Allen
Ethan Allen Drive
PO Box 1966
Danbury
CT 06813-1966
tel 800 228 9229
Aluminum furniture which can be used both indoors and outdoors.

French Wyres
PO Box 131655
Tyler
TX 75713
tel 903 597 8322
Trellises, plant stands, and window boxes made from fine wire.

Gardener's Eden
PO Box 7307
San Francisco
CA 94120-7307
tel 800 822 9600 for branches
Good quality garden tools and accessories also available via mail order.

Hold Everything
See Storage for details
Wicker picnic baskets and shelving to keep the garden shed organized.

Ikea
See Fabric for details
Wooden, ceramic and galvanized pots and planters. All the essential picnic gear: plastic plates, containers, baskets and rugs plus outdoor furniture which will fold away when not in use.

Lands' End, Inc.
See Kitchen for details
Acrylic plates and glasses.

Smith and Hawken
2 Arbor Lane
PO Box 6900
Florence
KY 41022-6900
tel 800 776 3336 for branches and mail order
A good selection of plants and tools; also have natural insect repellents and gardening remedies.

PLANTS, SEEDS, AND BULBS

Blue Meadow Farm
184 Meadow Road
Montague, MA 01351
tel 413 367 2394
Unusual annuals and perennials.

Burpee Seed Company
300 Park Avenue
Warminster
PA 18991-0001
tel 800 888 1447
Full color catalog packed full of plants, bulbs, and seeds.

Chelsea Garden Center
See Outside for details
Good selection of bulbs: triumph tulips, large cupped and trumpet daffodils.

Cultus Bay Nursery
4000 E. Bailey Road
Clinton
WA 98236
tel 360 579 2329
Good selection of herbs and vines.

Jackson & Perkins
1 Rose Lane
Medford, OR 97501
tel 541 776 2000
Beautiful varieties of roses.

Johnny's Selected Seeds
305 Foss Hill Road
Albion
ME 04910
tel 207 437 9294 for mail order
A variety of flowers, herbs, and unusual vegetables.

Old House Gardens
536 Third Street
Ann Arbor
MI 48103
tel 313 995 1486
Bulbs and tubers for spring flowers: tulips, narcissus, crocus.

Park Seed Company, Inc.
1 Parkton Avenue
Greenwood
SC 29647
tel 800 845 3369
Full color catalog containing an excellent range of seeds.

John Scheepers
23 Tulip Drive
Bantam
CT 06750
tel 860 567 0838
Bulb specialists with a particularly good selection of narcissus and amaryllis.

Select Seeds Antique Flowers
180 Stickney Road
Union
CT 06076
tel 860 684 9310
Roses and other old-fashioned English flowers.

Shady Oaks Nursery
112 Tenth Avenue SE
Waseca
MN 56093
tel 507 835 5033
Specializes in plants that prefer the shade.

K. Van Bourgondien and Sons
245 Route 109
PO Box 1000
Babylon
NY 11702-9004
tel 516 669 3500
All types of bulbs available mail order.

Wayside Gardens
1 Garden Lane
Hodges
SC 29695-0001
tel 800 845 1124
Perennials including day lilies and peonies plus plants, shrubs, and bulbs.

White Flower Farm
Route 63
PO Box 50
Litchfield
CT 06759-0050
tel 800 503 9624
website www.whiteflowerfarm.com
Delphiniums, old-fashioned peonies and container-grown roses plus herbs and vegetable varieties.

Winterthur Museum and Gardens
Winterthur
DE 19735
tel 800 767 0500
A great place to visit for inspiration and unique buys.

FURNITURE

The Conran Shop
See Fabrics for details
Upholstery in modern shapes including big couches for sinking into.

Designer's Guild
See Fabrics for details
Modern-shaped couches and chairs, upholstered in contemporary fabric and colours.

Crate & Barrel
See Flooring for details
Simple wooden desks, folding wooden chairs, and upholstered dining chairs with slipcovers available.

Full Upright Position
1200 NW Everett
Portland
Oregon 97209
tel 800 431 5134 for a free catalog
website www.fup.com
A good source for modern furniture classics.

H55
17 Little West 12th Street
New York 10014
tel 212 462 4559
open by appointment
The best in American and Scandinavian design.

Ikea
See Fabric for details
Inexpensive trestle tables, folding chairs, and stools.

Lands' End, Inc
See Kitchen for details
Solid poplar tables painted in winter white. Folding metal bistro tables and chairs, great for indoor and outdoor use.

LL Bean
See Kitchen for details
Painted maple cabinets, chests, and bookcases in periwinkle, sage, and milk white, plus painted nesting tables in milk white or sage.

Machine Age
354 Congress Street
Boston
NY 02210
tel 617 482 0048
website www.machineage.com
A retro store that will source, restore, and revive furniture from the 1920s through to today.

Palecek Imports
2514 Florida Aavenue
Richmond
CA 94804
tel 510 236 7730
Painted wicker furniture.

Pottery Barn
67th & Broadway
1965 Broadway
New York
NY 10023
tel 212 579 8477
and mail order
PO Box 7044
San Francisco
CA 94120-7044
website www.potterybarn.com
Simple, solid beech dining table with a sleek stainless steel top also available as a breakfast bar.

Shaker Workshops
14 South Pleasant Street

Ashburnham
MA 01430
tel 800 840 9121
fax 978 827 6554
website
www.shakerworkshops.com
*Call for a catalog of **Shaker** furniture and accessories.*

Sturbridge Yankee Workshop
PO Box 9797
Portland
ME 04104
tel 800 343 1144
fax 207 774 7809
website www.sturbridgeyankee.com
*Traditional **Shaker-style furniture**.*

Troy
138 Greene Street
SoHo
New York
NY 10012
tel 212 941 4777
Reproduction furniture and ceramics.

Williams-Sonoma
See Kitchen for details
*Simple kitchen and dining tables: solid maple traditional trestle tables, **stainless-steel topped tables** plus simple maple stools and bar stools.*

Wolfman Gold & Good, Inc.
117 Mercer Street
New York, NY 10012
tel 212 431 1888
Furniture and accessories both old and new.

Workbench
See Storage for details
*Simple, **clean-lined wooden dining tables**, plus upholstered dining chairs.*

UPHOLSTERY

B & B Italia U.S.A. Inc.
150 East 58th Street
New York, NY 10155
tel 800 872 1697 for retailers
email bbitalia@nyct.net
website www.bebitalia.it
*Contemporary Italian design, **timeless couches**, and sofa beds.*

Coach
342 Madison Avenue
New York
NY 10173
tel 212 599 4777
tel 800 307 0040
for retailers nationwide
website www.coach.com
Great armchairs and pillows in leather.

Ligne Roset
FR Resources
155 Wooster Street
New York
NY 10012
tel 212 2535629

fax 212 253 5375
tel 800 297 6738 for retailers nationwide
website www.ligne-roset-usa.com
Simple contemporary upholstery.

Crate & Barrel
See Flooring for details
Big deep couches with slipcovers for easy cleaning.

George Smith
73 Spring Street
New York
NY 10012
tel 212 226 4747 for branches and retailers
fax 212 226 4868
website www.georgesmith.com
Traditionally made couches and chairs.

Hitch Mylius Limited
Available at
Property
14 Wooster Street
New York
NY 10013
tel 917 237 0123
fax 917 237 0124
website www.hitchmylius.co.uk
Couches and chairs made mainly for contract use, should be very long-lasting.

Ikea
See Fabrics for details
Affordable upholstery in modern styles.

LL Bean
See Kitchen for details
Simple couches with plain slipcovers plus metal day beds.

Mitchell Gold Co.
6736 Millersville Road
Taylorsville
NC 28681
tel 800 789 5401
fax 828 635 5701
website www.mitchellgold.com
*Comfortable, **affordable couches and chairs**, both contemporary and slightly more traditional.*

Pottery Barn
See Furniture for details
*Couches in **traditional styles with slip covers** as well as modern, square shapes. Many of the styles are available as sofabeds.*

Crate & Barrel
See Flooring for details
*Both **traditional** and **modern** styled couches and chairs.*

Workbench
See Storage for details
*Modern couches in **simple shapes**.*

FIRESIDE

The Conran Shop
See Fabric for details

Baskets for logs, plus pokers, tongs, and brushes..

Dovre
Distrbuted by:
Heatilator
1915 West Saunders Street
Mount Pleasant
IA 52641
website www.dovre.co.uk
*Cast-iron **wood-burning stoves**.*

Lands' End, Inc.
See Kitchen for details
Canvas log carrier with sturdy handles.

LL Bean
See Kitchen for details
*Fatwood - effective **natural kindling** - natural resin in the sticks ignites quickly and burns for a long time.*

LIGHTING

Artemide
1980 New Highway
Farmingdale
NY 11735
tel 631 694 9292
fax 631 694 9275
website www.artemide.com
Contemporary lighting in simple designs.

Best & Lloyd
available at
Louis Baldinger & Sons
1902 Steinway Street
Astoria
NY 11105
tel 718 204 5700
fax 718 721 4986
website www.bestandlloyd.co.uk
*Classic, **anglepoise desk and floor standing lamps**.*

The Conran Shop
See Fabrics for details
*Modern lighting; **spun aluminum pendants, white ceramic pendants,** aluminum desk lights.*

Colonial Williamsburg
Department 023
PO Box 3532
Williamsburg
VA 23187-3532
tel 800 446 9240
Glass hurricane lamps and candlesticks.

Crate & Barrel
See Flooring for details
*Glass tealight holders, hurricane lamps, chunky ivory pillar candles, basic white candles and tealights, plus simple table lamps and **anglepoise desk lamps**.*

Ikea
See Fabrics for details
*Fisherman's pendants, paper shades and children's night lights, and a large selection of **energy-saving bulbs**.*

Lands' End, Inc.
See Kitchen for details
*Table lamps with turned **wooden bases, painted in cream and sage**; linen shades.*

Pottery Barn
See Furniture for details
*Candlesticks and hurricane lamps, **turned wooden table lamps,** and simple metal bases.*

D'Ac Lighting Inc.
420 Railroad Way
Mamaroneck
NY 10543
tel 914 698 5959
fax 914 698 6061
Industrial pendant fixtures.

Lighting By Gregory
158 Bowery
New York
NY 10012
tel 212 226 1276
fax 212 226 2705
A huge selection of lighting from a variety of manufacturers.

SMELL

Aveda
252 A Salon
2452 Broadway
New York
NY 10025
tel 212 875 1853
website www.aveda.com
for local store
*Cosmetics, skincare, hair products, and **scented candles made with natural flower and plant essences**. Try the Valencia candle that smells like a Spanish olive grove.*

The Conran Shop
See Fabric for details
Bath oils, scented candles, cedar balls, and incense.

Crabtree & Evelyn
1310 Madison Avenue
New York
NY 10128
tel 212 289 3923
website www.crabtree-evelyn.com
for retailers nationwide
*Traditional English fragrances such as **rose and lavender** in a range of products.*

Campbell's Gourmet Cottage
See Kitchen for details
*Crabtree & Evelyn products including **scented drawer liners**, hydrating body mist and mineral bath **in spring rain and savannah garden** fragrances.*

Fredericksburg Herb Farm
402 Whitney
PO Box 927
Fredericksburg, TX 78624
tel 830 997 8615

toll free 1-800 259 4372
fax 830 997 5069
email herfarm@ktc.com
website www.fredericksburgfarm.com
*Sensual **aromatherapy candles** in lavender, rose, geranium, cedarwood and
ylang-ylang, also **various potpourri
blends and room scents.***

Linenplace.com
See Sleep for details
*Pure vegetable **soaps scented with
essential oils.** Scented candles in green
tea, lavender, verbena, and cinnamon
orange, plus linen water in wild rose and
verbena.*

L'Occitane
10 East 39th Street
New York
NY 10016
tel 212 696 9098
telefax 212 213 0803
toll free 1-888 623 2880
email
customer.serbice@loccitane.net
website www.loccitane.com
*Beautiful soaps, lotions, incense, and
burning oils.*

Lush
40 Carnaby Street
London W1V 1PD
UK
tel +44 1202 668 545 for branches
and mail order
fax 01202 661 832
email sales@lush.co.uk
website www.lush.co.uk
*Wonderful handmade cosmetics made
with **vegetable products:** soaps, bath
balls, moisturizers and cleansers. Will
ship to the US visit the website for
details.*

Waterworks
See Bathroom for details
*Lavender and rose sachets: place in a
closet, drawer, or under your pillow for
wonderful scent.*

MATERIALS

Atlantic & Gulf Fishing Supply Corp.
7000 NW 74th Avenue
Miami
FL 33166
tel 305 888 9646
fax 305 888 6027
toll free 1-800 327 6167
email webmaster@atagulf.com
website www.atagulf.com
*All sorts of **rope and twine**, great for
making drawstring bags, or guy lines for
a sun shelter.*

Dick Blick Art Materials
14399 Michigan Avenue
Dearborn
MI 48126
tel 313 581 7063
website www.dickblick.com

for nationwide branches.
*Art materials including a large selection
of papers, paints, fabric paint, plus
big **packs of ribbons and trim**
which contain an assortment of colors
and widths.*

Fabrics to Dye For
Two Rivers Road
Pawcatuck
CT 06379
tel 860 599 1588
fax 401 596 1570
email jennifer@fabricstodyefor.com
website www.fabricstodyefor.com
*Wide range of **fabric dyes and paints**
including Procion dyes, used to dye
the duvet on page 252-253. Available
at a number of retail and specialty
stores call or visit the website for details.*

Hyman Hendler
67 West 38th Street
New York
NY 10018
tel 212 840 8393
*An Aladdin's cave of **ribbons and trimmings** both new and old.*

Kate's Paperie
561 Braodway at Prince street
SoHo
New York
NY 10012
tel 212 941 9816
website www.katespaperie.com
*Wrapping and writing papers made
with herbs and rose petals, plus
stationery, ribbons, books, and
albums.*

Paperchase
in branches of:
Borders
830 Michigan Avenue
Chicago, IL 60611
website
www.go.borders.com/paperchase
for other branches
*Decorative notebooks and sketchpads,
wrapping papers, cards, and ribbons.*

Pottery Barn
See Furniture for details
*Shadow box frames for displaying pre-
cious things, and a great **magnetic chalk
board** with a white wooden frame; use
magnets to pin up messages or let the
children doodle.*

Meininger
499 Broadway
Denver
CD 80203
tel 1-800 950 2747
or 303 698 3838
fax 303 871 8676
website www.meininger.com
*Serious art materials as well as lots
of **fun kits for kids**, also holds a **Free
Art Club for Kids** on Friday afternoons,
details on the website, or print out the
activity sheets from the website.*

BATHROOM

American Standard, Inc.
1 Centennial Avenue
Piscataway
NJ 08854
tel 732 980 3000 for retailers
website www.ideal-standard.co.uk
*Sanitary ware, fixtures and accessories
in contemporary styles.*

Ann Sacks
See Flooring for details
*Modern bathroom fixtures. **big shower
roses** with fixed exposed pipes.*

Bisque
15 Kingsmead Square
Bath
Bath and North East Somerset
BA1 2AE
UK
tel 01225 469244 for retailers
fax 01225 444708
tel 020 7328 2225 for export inquries.
website www.bisque.co.uk
*Modern radiators and towel warmers.
Will ship directly to clients in the US.*

Building Resources
See Reclamation for details
*Reclaimed **plumbing, sinks, and
bathtubs.***

Duravit USA, Inc.
1750 Breckinridge Parkway
Suite 500
Duluth
GA 30096
tel 770 9313575
for nationwide retailers
toll free 1-888 387 2848
fax 770 931 8454
website www.duravit.com
*Contemporary sanitary ware, fixtures
and accessories: simple designs with
clean lines from designers such as Philippe
Starck.*

Hansgrohe
available at
A Better Bath & Kitchen
1817 130th Avenue NE
Bellevue
WA 90005
tel 425 881 1133
tel 800 334 0455 for nearest retailer
website
www.hansgrohe-usa.com
*Good selection of contemporary shower
heads and faucets.*

Historic Home Supply Corp
See Reclamation for details
*Roll top bathtubs, sanitary ware,
and plumbing salvaged from historic
buildings.*

Irreplaceable Artifacts
See Reclamation for details
*Reclaimed **bathtubs, sinks** and other
interesting **fittings and accessories.***

Omega Too
2204 San Pablo Avenue
Berkeley, CA
tel 510 843 3636
*Salvage yard which specializes in
complete finished items: **special bathtubs and showers, bathroom fixtures.***

Samuel Heath
111 East 39th Street
Suite 2R
New York
NY 10016
tel 212 599 5177 for retailers
fax 212 818 9552
email mail@samuel-heath.com
website www.samual-heath.com
*Traditional and modern **bathroom
fixtures and accessories.***

The Sink Factory
2140 San Pablo Avenue
Berkeley, CA 94702
tel 510 540 8193
toll free 1-800 563 4926
*Vintage and reproduction pedestal
sinks, roll top bathtubs, new and
old faucets. Also does repair and
reconditioning work.*

Twyfords
available at
Barclay Products
4000 Porett Drive
Gurnee
IL 60031
tel 847 244 1234
fax 847 244 1259
website
www.twyfordbathrooms.com
*Bathroom fixtures in **clean lines and
simple shapes.***

Vitra USA Inc.
6855 Jimmy Carter Boulevard
Suite 2450
Norcross, GA 30071
tel 770 453 9301 for retailers
*Sanitary ware, fixtures and accessories
in mainly modern styles, but some
traditional.*

Waterworks
225 East 57th Street
New York
NY 10022
tel 212 371 9266
fax 212 371 9263
tel 800 998 2284 for nationwide
retailers
website
www.waterworks.com
*Simple, modern chrome fittings,
including big shower roses as well as traditional style taps.*

BATHROOM
ACCESSORIES

Area
See Sleep for details
Pure linen and cotton towels.

Bonjour of Switzerland
tel 908 238 0006 for nationwide retailers
fax 908 238 0016
toll free 1-877 266 7948
email info@bonswit.com
website www.bonswit.com
Thick and thirsty cotton bath towels.

The Conran Shop
See Fabrics for details
Wooden bath racks, duckboards, good soaps, simple fixtures, cotton bath robes, linen and cotton towels.

Crate & Barrel
See Flooring for details
White toweling shower curtains, loop bath mats, and traditional bathroom scales.

Dean & Deluca
See Food for details
Fine black glycerine soap from Spain.

Ikea
See Fabrics for details
Great value cotton bath mats, towels in good colors, shower curtains, cabinets, and toothbrush holders.

Lands' End, Inc.
See Kitchen for details
Egyptian cotton towels and rugs, hooded waffle robes and toweling slippers. Waffle weave and canvas shower curtains, and an excellent wooden wall cabinet with towel rails in solid poplar, painted white.

Linenplace.com
See Sleep for details
100% Egyptian cotton extra-thick towels and bath mats. 100% cotton heavy weight canvas striped shower curtains.

LL Bean
See Sleep for details
Wicker laundry hampers.

Macy's
420 Fulton Street
Brooklyn
New York
NY 11201-5214
tel 718 875 7200
website www.macys.com
for nearest store
Thick cotton towels, "cotton twist" bath mats and luxuriously soft cotton bath robes.

Martha by Mail
See Sleep for details
Traditional style bathroom scales, towels, bath mats, and natural sisal scrubbers.

Pottery Barn
See Furniture for details
Loop bath mats and chenille robes, rattan laundry hampers and a range of wooden wall cabinets, painted white, with towel racks or pegs.

Takashimaya
3010 41st Avenue
Long Island City
NY 11101
tel 212 350 0115
fax 718 786 8884
Exquisite soaps and lotions.

The White House
C/o 6400 Highlands Parkway
Suite F
Smyrna
GA 30082
tel 888 942 7528
email sales@the-white-house.co.uk
website www.the-white-house.com
100% cotton towels with waffle detail, bath mats, and waffle robes.

Waterworks
See Bathroom for details
Thick classic white towels, simple bathmats in neutral colors and various textures, robes, and shower curtains.

SLEEP

Area
180 Varick Street
9th Floor
New York
NY 10014
tel 212 924 7084
Bed linen in pure natural fibers; neutral plain colors and striped flat sheets.

Bloomingdales
See Kitchen for details
Good quality bed linen and towels by Calvin Klein and Ralph Lauren.

Cath Kidston
See Fabric for details
50s inspired floral bedding, pyjamas, nightgowns and robes.

Chambers
PO Box 7841
San Francisco
CA 94120
Bedroom and bathroom accessories.

Charles Beckley, Inc
New York
NY
tel 212 759 8450
Custom manufacturer of mattresses, box springs, and day beds.

The Conran Shop
See Fabrics for details
Lots of luxurious throws and bed linen.

Crate & Barrel
See Flooring for details
Plain white sheets, linen-cotton blend neutral bed linen in textural weaves.

Designer's Guild
Bed & Bath
Westpoint Stevens

20th Floor
1185 Avenue of the Americas
New York
NY 10036
tel 212 840 3100
Beautiful bed linen in fresh colors and modern designs.

Eddiebauer.com
Customer Care
PO Box 97000
Redmond
WA 98073-9700
tel 800 625 7935
fax 425 869 4629
website www.eddiebauer.com
Quality mattresses, feather beds, quilts, and pillows.

Featherpillow.com
2233 Philadelphia Drive
Lincoln
NE 68521
tel 402 450 6984
fax 603 288 0595
email info@featherpillow.com
website
www.featherpillow.com
Feather-filled mattresses, pillows, and comforters.

EcoPlanet – EcoChoices
PO Box 1491
Glendora
CA 91740
fax 530 231 5312
email service@ecochoices.com
website
www.ecolivingcentre.com
Natural mattresses: latex, organic cotton and pure wool mattresses with box springs. Mattresses for futons. Beautifully simple wooden bed frames and bunk beds. Under bed wooden storage drawers. Pure wool comforters, organic sheets, and pillow cases, blankets and mattress pads.

Garnet Hill
PO Box 262
Main Street
Franconia
NH 03580
tel 800 870 3513 for mail order
fax 888 842 9696
website www.garnethill.com
Inflatable mattresses for an extra bed when you have guests. Wool plaid blankets, warm flannel sheets, and quilts made with vintage floral patches. Duck down duvets, pillows, and feather beds.

Ikea
See Fabrics for details
Good value 100% cotton bed linen sets, pillows, duvets, and simple modern beds including children's beds and bunks.

Indika
See Fabric for details
Organic cotton sheets in muted colors. Hemp/silk and organic cotton robes.

Lands' End, Inc.
See Kitchen for details
Board and batten bed in ash or painted white. A simple style bed with upholstered head and footboard, comes with 100% cotton drill slipcovers. A great range of cotton and wool blankets, striped bed linen, comforters, and feather beds.

Laura Ashley By Post
See Fabrics for details
Floral print bed linen.

Linenplace.com
350 Fifth Avenue
Suite 717
New York
NY 10118
tel 212 629 0300
email support@linenplace.com
website www.linenplace.com
100% cotton white bedding, pretty floral bedding and classic wool blankets with satin edges in muted plain colours. Goose down duvets, pillows, and feather beds.

LL Bean Inc.
See Kitchen for details
Simple metal beds in white painted finish. Goosedown pillows. Checked and striped 100% cotton blankets and washable wool blankets both plain and checked.

Macy's
See Bathroom Accessories for details
Good quality white sheets, gorgeously soft wool and cashmere blankets, feather beds, and down comforters.

Martha by mail
11316 North 46th Street
Tampa
FL 33617
tel 800 950 7130
email
marthabymail@customersvc.com
website www.marthastewart.com
Washable wool blankets, hot water bottles, Welsh plaid blankets, and gingham bed linen.

Melin Tregwynt
available at
Modern Age
New York
tel 212 966 0669
email info@melintregwynt.co.uk
website
www.melintregwynt.co.uk
Wool blankets, throws and pillows in contemporary checks, stripes and colors.

Nancy Koltes at Home
31 Spring Street
New York 10012
tel 212 219 2271
Fine table and bed linen as well as table accessories.

Paula Rubenstein
65 Prince Street
New York 10012
tel 212 966 8954
Quilts, blankets, and bedcovers.

Portico Bed & Bath
72 Spring Street
New York
NY 10012
tel 212 941 7800
website
www.porticonewyork.com
White linen bedding, towels, and beautiful throws.

Pottery Barn
See Furniture for details
Wooden sleigh beds, Victorian style metal beds and day beds, plus gingham and striped sheet sets, simple plain colored quilts, bolster cushions, and comforters.

Rose House Antiques
See Secondhand for details
Great place to find old metal beds.

Takashimaya
See Bathroom Accessories for details
Beautiful bed linen.

Williamsburg Catalog
The Colonial Williamsburg Foundation
Department 023
PO Box 3532
Williamsburg
VA 23187
Checked blankets.

Workbench
See Storage for details
Simple, modern beds in a choice of wood veneers.

The White House
See Bathroom Accessories for details
100% cotton and linen bedlinen with classic pinstitch detail.

RECLAMATION

Admac Salvage
111 Saranac Street
Littleton
NH 03561
tel 603 444 1200
website
www.musar.com/trader/admac.html
Barn boards and beams, flooring, and lumber plus lighting, office furniture, and cabinets.

Anderson Fine Carpentry
and Salvage
228 W 4th Street
Kansas City, MO 64111
tel 816 531 5976
email TheThaine@aol.com
Reclaimed lumber.

Berkeley Architectural Salvage
1167 65th Street
Oakland
CA 94608
tel 510 655 2270
Old hardware: door pulls, locks, hinges. plus a large selection of doors, moldings, and windows.

Building Resources
701 Amador
San Francisco
CA 94124
tel 415 285 7814
Nonprofit making business with one and a half acres of mixed doors, windows, hardware, tiles, lighting, and lumber.

C&K Salvage
718 Douglas Avenue
Oakland
CA 94603
tel 510 569 2070
Mainly recyled and demolition lumber: douglas fir, redwood, posts, beams, and plywood.

Eco-Timber
1020 Heinz Avenue
Berkeley
CA 94710
tel 510 549 3000
A full line of wood products, hardwood and softwood, flooring, decking, plywood, and panel.

Gardner Construction & Salvage
731-D Loma Verde Avenue
Pola Alto
CA 94303-4161
tel 650 856 0634
Warehouse
1805 Bay Road
East Palo Alto
CA 94303
email pgard0634@aol.com
Salvaged building materials.

Historic Home Supply Corp
213-215 River Street
Troy, NY 12180-3809
tel 518 266 0675
email homesupply@earthlink.net
website www.homesupply.com
Hardware, windows, lighting, doors, garden accessories, and plumbing supplies.

Irreplaceable Artifacts
14 Second Avenue
New York
NY 10003
tel 212 777 2900
fax 212 780 0642
email
info@IrreplaceableArtifacts.com
website
www.irreplaceableartifacts.com
All sorts of interesting finds: fireplaces, doors and fixtures, furniture, lighting, mirrors, railings, and staircases.

Salvage One
1524 South Sangamon Strett
Chicago
IL 60608
tel 312 733 0098
email salvoone@aol.com
Architectural salvage.

Seattle Building Salvage
202 Bell Street
Seattle, WA 98121- 1716
tel 206 632 9957
Reclaimed building materials.

United House Wrecking
535 Hope Street
Stamford
CT 06906-1300
tel 203 348 5371
fax 203 961 9472
website www.united-antiques.com
Antique furniture for the bedroom and dining room, architectural salvage and garden ornaments.

Vermont Salvage
2 Lumber Lane
Manchester
NH 03102
tel 603 624 0868
email hael@vermontsalvage.com
and
Gates Street
White River Junction
VT 05001
tel 802 295 7616
and
75 Webster Street
Worcester
MA 01603
tel 508 755 2870
website
www.vermontsalvage.com
Lighting fixtures, hardware and brackets, stone and columns, and plumbing supplies.

SECONDHAND

English Country Antiques
Snake Hollow Road
Bridghampton
Long Island
NY 11932
tel 631 537 0606
Period country furniture in pine, plus decorative blue-and-white china.

Brimfield Market
Massachusetts
Held the first week of May, July, and September; thousands of dealers and great antique buys.

Hope & Wilder
454 Broome Street
New York, NY 10013
Decorative old furniture.

Rose House Antiques
1703 Montauk Highway
Bridgehampton
Long Island
NY 11932
tel 631 537 2802
Painted furniture, old white china, and kitchenware.

Sage Street Antiques
Sag Harbour
NY 11963
Decorative period furniture and tableware.

Sammy's
484 Broome Street
New York
A good source of junk tables and chairs.

Index

Credits

Page 15 Bulb vase and hyacinth, Clifton Nurseries.
Page 24 - 25 Wool blanket, John Lewis. basket, handmade in Spain
Page 28 - 29 Espresso Maker, Heal's.
Page 34 Changing rooms at Tooting Bec Lido.
Page 35 London flat, Jane Cumberbatch; solid oak flooring, Drysdale Timber Moldings.
Page 38 Kitchen, Sierra Rica, Aracena, Spain.
Page 44 - 45 Box files, Ikea. Kilner® jars, John Lewis
Page 48 - 49 Ribbons, John Lewis; cork based basket, handmade in Spain. Cotton for skirts, Wolfin Textiles; rick-rack braid, John Lewis.
Page 51 Emulsion-proof green fabric, Russell and Chapple.
Page 54 - 55 Dried rose buds, Clifton Nurseries. Bag made by Kate Storer using tana lawn fabric, Liberty.
Page 56 - 57 From the top: homemade cushion covers in cotton by Laura Ashley, Colefax & Fowler, Ikea; checked cloth, Divertimenti; striped bag, market stall.
Page 60 White duck egg, Selfridges.
Page 61 Enamel jug, The Conran Shop.
Page 65 Terra-cotta pot, Clifton Little Venice.
Page 67 Green chairs, outside a Spanish café.
Page 73 Kitchen lights, Spitalfields house, London.
Page 77 Bertoia chair, Lifestyle; seat pad made by Kate Storer from Davina felt, Kvadrat.
Page 82 - 83 Quinces and wild mushrooms, Selfridges.
Page 84 - 85 Kitchen, London flat, Jane Cumberbatch; cabinets painted in Bollom white eggshell; Kilner® jars, John Lewis; white tiles, Aston Matthews; solid maple worktop, Junkers; checked tea towel, Divertimenti.
Page 87 Folding plate rack, Habitat; white bone china plates, Wedgewood.
Page 88 Kitchen, The Battery, Whitstable, England.
Page 90 Kitchen, London, designed by Alastair Hendy.
Page 91 Kitchen, London flat, Jane Cumberbatch.
Page 92 - 93 Seville oranges, Selfridges; bowl and ladle, Divertimenti; recycled jam jars.
Page 94 - 95 Napkins, The Conran Shop; cutlery and china, Ikea; tablecloth and glasses, Habitat.
Page 96 London flat, Jane Cumberbatch; cupboard doors made by Steve Toms; vase and tulips, Paula Pryke; table, Ikea; chairs, secondhand.
Page 97 Bone china soup bowl, Wedgwood.
Page 99 Kitchen, Spanish House, Jane Cumberbatch; custommade table and cupboards from chestnut; folding chairs, Habitat.
Page 100 - 101 Cotton fabric, John Lewis; velvet ribbon, VV Rouleaux; plates,Wedgwood; chair, Habitat.
Page 103 Green cloth homemade using Malabar Quara 13; white chair, Habitat.
Page 104 - 105 Patio, Spanish house, Jane Cumberbatch; chairs, Habitat; sheet used as tablecloth, Peter Reed @ John Lewis.
Page 108 Beach house, Portugal, Nick and Hermione Tudor; chair cover made by Kate Storer, cotton fabric, The Cloth Shop; tablecloth in cotton, Laura Ashley; fisherman's pendant light and tealights, Ikea; basket from a Spanish market.
Page 112 Enameled tin plate, Blacks; table-cloth, Divertimenti.
Page 116 Table, Ikea; cotton tablecloth, Habitat.
Page 122 - 124 Workroom, London home, Tessa Brown, custom clothes maker.
Page 126 Chairs, Habitat.
Page 127 Workroom, Spitalfields house, London.
Page 128 - 129 Raw cork, C. Olley & Sons Ltd.; painted baked bean tin; bulletin board and shelving constructed by Steve Toms; secondhand filing cabinets painted in white eggshell, J W Bollom.
Page 131 Trestle table and shelving, made by Steve Toms
Page 132 - 133 Blue felt, J W Bollom; ribbon, VV Rouleaux; push pins, Muji.
Page 134 Clothes rack, Domestic Paraphernalia Company; linen tea towel, John Lewis.
Page 136 Utility room, London home, Simon and Liz Brown.
Page 144 - 145 Cotton pyjama top, Cath Kidston
Page 150 - 151 Garden, Marianna Kennedy, Spitalfields, London.
Page 153 Roof terrace, A. Gold, Spitalfields, London.
Page 154 - 155 Secondhand chair; eggshell paint, Farrow & Ball; sandpaper, brush and primer, Homebase.
Page 157 Village house, Spain
Page 160 - 161 Téte à téte daffodil bulbs, Clifton Nurseries.
Page 164 - 165 Urban garden, London, John Matheson.
Page 170 - 171 Sun shade made by Kate Storer in cotton fabric, The Conran Shop; rope, London Yacht Centre Ltd; tent pegs, Blacks.
Page 172 - 173 Mattress, made by Kate Storer in cotton fabric, The Conran Shop; foam, Pentonville Rubber; cushions in emulsion-proof green fabric, Russell & Chapple
Page 175 Awning made by Kate Storer from emulsion-proof green waterproof canvas, Russell & Chapple; tablecloth, Tobias and the Angel.
Page 176 Cotton curtain, Ikea; homemade cotton cushion covers.
Page 178 - 179 Striped cotton, KA International; interlining, John Lewis.
Page 180 Sofa, George Sherlock; loose cover fabric, Ian Mankin; coffee table, Habitat; director's chair, Heal's.
Page 181 Table, The Dining Room Shop; director's chair, Heal's.
Page 182 - 183 Folding side table, junk shop; lamp, John Lewis; Chesterfield sofa, second-hand; throw, Colefax & Fowler; large folding table, Ikea; blinds, John Lewis; small couch, David Seyfried; large couch, secondhand.
Page 184 Cushion cover fabric, Designers Guild.
Page 186 - 187 Blind, John Lewis; Bertoia chairs, Lifestyle; table, junk shop.
Page 188 - 189 Chair, secondhand; loose covers made by Kate Storer; floral cotton, Cath Kidston; cotton ticking, Ian Mankin; green cotton, Malabar; white cotton, Designers Guild.
Page 190 - 191 Couch, George Sherlock.
Page 195 Log baskets, handmade in Spain; shadow box frames, Atlantis.
Page 197 Shadow box frames, Atlantis; specimen jars, LASSCO.
Page 209 Chalkboard paint, J W Bollom.
Page 214 - 215 Acrylic paints, Atlantis; card, WH Smith; paper bags, Gardners.
Page 220 - 221 bathroom, London, designed by Alastair Hendy.
Page 224 Bathroom, London flat, Jane Cumberbatch; heated towel rack, Aston Matthews; towel, The Conran Shop.
Page 225 Bathroom, Spanish house, Jane Cumberbatch; bath rack, Habitat.
Page 226 - 227 Canvas, Z. Butt; rope, London Yacht Centre Ltd; striped cotton ticking, Ian Mankin.
Page 228 - 229 Chair and duck board. Habitat; bath rack, The Conran Shop; basket, Spain; sink, faucets and bath, Aston Matthews; wood paneling, by Steve Toms; light, The Conran Shop.
Page 231 Bathroom, Spitalfields house.
Page 232 - 233 Tea light glasses, The Conran Shop.
Page 234 - 235 Bathroom, Spitalfields house, Jane Cumberbatch.
Page 237 Bathroom, Scotland, Lachlan and Annie Stewart.
Page 242 - 243 Bed, Ikea; orange blanket, Designers Guild; bed linen, Peter Reed @ John Lewis; checked cotton curtain, Ikea.
Page 244 Bed and bedspread, Habitat.
Page 248 Bedroom, The Battery, Whistable; striped flannel bed linen, Cologne and Cotton; blankets, Melin Tregwynt.
Page 250 - 251 Children's bedroom, London flat, Jane Cumberbatch; side table, junk shop; trestle table, by Steve Toms; anglepoise lamp, Ikea; blanket, Anta.
Page 252 - 253 Cotton sheeting, Wolfin Textiles; rubber gloves, Homebase; Procion dye & soda ash fixer, Suasion; Velcro®, John Lewis.
Page 255 White cotton bed linen, John Lewis.
Page 256 - 257 Bedroom, London home, Tessa Brown.
Page 258 Bedroom, London, fashion consultant Vanessa de Lisle.
Page 259 Bedroom, Spitalfields house, Jane Cumberbatch.
Page 260 - 261 Canvas, Z Butt; trim, VV Rouleaux.
Page 263 Bed, made by Jim Howitt; bed spread, Judy Greenwood.
Page 272 - 273
1. Off-White U/C1 latex, Farrow & Ball.
2. Strong White U/C1 latex, Farrow & Ball.
3. Lime White U/C1 eggshell, Farrow & Ball.
4. Oyster White Lt. 4-14P eggshell, Sanderson.
5. Blackened U/C1 floor paint, Farrow & Ball.
6. New White U/C1 eggshell, Farrow & Ball.
7. Great White U/C1 eggshell, Farrow & Ball.
8. 70BB 83/013 exterior eggshell, Dulux.
9. 10BB 83/014 latex, Dulux.
Table painted in 70BB 83/013, Dulux.
Page 274 - 275
1. 20YY 39/419 eggshell, Dulux.
2. 20YY 65/285 eggshell, Dulux.
3. 20YY 47/344 latex, Dulux.
4. 30YY 61/300 eggshell, Dulux.
5. 45YY 66/512 eggshell, Dulux.
6. 25YY 85/108, eggshell Dulux
7. Dorset Cream U/C1, eggshell Farrow & Ball.
8. Olive Yellow 3-16M latex, Sanderson
9. Cloudy Amber-w 4-3M eggshell, Sanderson.
Crate painted in 30YY 61/300, Dulux
Page 276 - 277
1. 50YR 23/365 latex, Dulux.
2. Mexicana 9-24D eggshell, Sanderson.
3. Porphyry Pink U/C49 eggshell, Farrow & Ball.
4. 90YR 38/239 Weathershield quick drying satin, Dulux.
5. 70YR 25/349, eggshell Dulux.
6. Brick Pink-w 16-22M, eggshell Sanderson.
7. Orange Buff 9-17M exterior eggshell, Sanderson
8. Fowler Pink U/C37 masonry latex, Farrow & Ball.
9. Orange Rust 10-11M latex, Sanderson.
Table painted in Dulux 90YR 38/239.
Page 278 - 279
1. Mayan Green 41-6D latex, Sanderson.
2. Colour World E9-23 latex, J.W. Bollom.
3 Chatham Green 41-23M eggshell, Sanderson.
4. 10GY 54/238 eggshell, Dulux.
5. Powder blue U/C22 exterior eggshell, Farrow & Ball.
6. 76GY 73/137 latex, Dulux.
7. Springtime 41-3M latex, Sanderson.
8. Olive Mist 41-9M latex, Sanderson.
9. 30GY 75/105 eggshell, Dulux.
Terracotta Vase painted in Colour World E9-23, J.W.Bollom.
Page 280 - 281
1. 16BB 41/268 eggshell, Dulux.
2. Blue Day Lt 24-14P eggshell, Sanderson.
3 54BB 41/237, eggshell, Dulux.
4. 30BB 47/179 Weathershield quick drying satin, Dulux
5. Regatta 24- 7M eggshell, Sanderson
6. Swiss Blue 25-4M latex, Sanderson.
7. 10BG 63/156 Weather sheild quick drying satin, Dulux
8. Phantom Blue 31-15M, exterior eggshell Sanderson.
9. 10BG 63/156 eggshell, Dulux.
Drawers painted in Swiss Blue 24-17M, Sanderson
Page 282 - 283
1. 10RR 25/437 eggshell, Dulux.
2. 86RB 47/274 latex, Dulux.
3. 07RB 43/231 latex, Dulux.
4. 10BB 47/149 eggshell, Dulux.
5. 64RR 45/245 exterior masonry, Dulux.
6. 41RB 58/162 latex, Dulux.
7. Chic Pink 18-16M eggshell Sanderson.
8. 24-3M eggshell, Sanderson.
9. Delicacy Lt 22-2P latex, Sanderson.
Tin can painted in 10RR 25/437, Dulux.
Page 288 - 289 1. Muslin, Russell & Chapple; 2. Medium-weight canvas, Russell & Chapple; 3. Tandragee White F494/01, Designers Guild; 4. Flax 14oz. , Wolfin textiles; 5. Iona, Monkwell; 6. 10 oz cotton duck, Wolfin Textiles; 7. Silk muslin, The Cloth Shop; 8. Tonus 2000 100, Kvadrat;
9. Jute, The Cloth Shop; 10. Linen FD170 White, Wolfin Textiles Ltd.; 11. Natural linen, International Textile Company; 12. Bamboo Zinc, Malabar.
Page 290 - 291 1.Tonus 2000 630 blue, Kvadrat; 2. Cotton drill, The Cloth Shop; 3. Dyed muslin, Z. Butt.; 4. Springfield felt, J.W. Bollom; 5. Divina 712, Kvadrat; 6. Dyed muslin, The Cloth Shop; 7. Linara Lavendar RF 2494/36, Romo; 8. Dyed muslin, The Cloth Shop 9. Divina 732 lilac, Kvadrat. 10. Tippo lime, John Lewis; 11. Lamonta Sky Suedette, Meredith Design; 12. Buchan KC307, G.P.& J. Baker.
Page 292 - 293 1. Spanish Green Check, International Textile Company; 2. Beige Square Check, International Textile Company; 3. Linum Nisha, The Blue Door; 4. 100% cotton ticking 6, Ian Mankin; 5. Checkmate 2 Green, PVC, John Lewis; 6. Azores Cuadritos Amarilla, KA International;
7. Azores Gales Azul. KA International; 8. Blue check, Ikea; 9. 100% cotton ticking 1, Ian Mankin; 10. 100% cotton ticking 2, Ian Mankin; 11. Linen/cotton ticking Union 14, Ian Mankin; 12.100% cotton ticking 2, Ian Mankin
Page 294 - 295 1. Rose Sprig Cath Kidston; 2. Ditsy, Laura Ashley; 3. Rosie Print, Cath Kidston; 4. Rose Paisley, Cath Kidston; 5. Morello, Laura Ashley; 6. Felbrigg, Bennison Fabrics Ltd. Diffusion range; 7. Abbeville, Laura Ashley; 8. Rose Wiggle, Cath Kidston; 9. Hearts, Laura Ashley; 10. Wickmere, Bennison Fabics Ltd. Diffusion range; 11. Tana Lawn, Liberty; 12. Rose gingham, Cath Kidston
Page 300 - 301 1. Antique oak boards, Lassco Flooring; 2. Oregon reclaimed pine boards, LASSCO Flooring; 3. Muhuhu parquet, LASSCO Flooring; 4. unsealed cork tile, Siesta Cork Co.. 5. "Vert d'eau" rubber tile, Dalsouple @ First Floor; 6. "Bleu Pastel" rubber tile, Dalsouple @ First Floor; 7. "Ton Pierre" rubber tile, Dalsouple @ Pentonville Rubber; 8. Antique Pammet terracotta tile, Fired Earth; 9. Pietra Laro, Stone Age; 10. Portland Blue, Stone Age.
11. Vidraco Crème, Stone Age
Page 302 - 303 1. Mat, John Lewis; 2. herringbone coir, Natural Flooring Direct; 3. basketweave seagrass, Natural Flooring Direct; 4. mini boucle sisal, Natural Flooring Company; 5. woven rug, The Conran Shop; 6. African woven plastic rug, Graham & Greene; 7. rag rug, Ikea; 8. checked rug, author's own.
Page 308 - 309 1. Wooden spoon, hardware shop; 2. bowl, Divertimenti; 3. Sabatier knife, Divertimenti; 4. balloon whisk, Divertimenti; 5. colander, Woolworths; 6. corkscrew, The Conran Shop; 7. griddle pan, Spanish hardware shop; 8. chopping board, Muji; 9. ladle, Divertimenti; 10. kitchen scissors, Muji; 11. Le Creuset casserole, John Lewis.
Page 312 - 313 1. Fly net, Divertimenti; 2. vegetable cart, Muji. 3. cutlery tray, junk shop; 4. enamel cookie tin, market stall; 5. stainless steel container with plastic lid, Muji; 6. enamel bread box, Brick Lane market; 7. Kilner® jar, John Lewis; 8. plastic clip handled containers, Muji; 9. basket, author's own; 10. plate rack, Habitat; plate, Ikea.
Page 314 - 315 1. Bistro cutlery, The White Company; 2. stainless steel cutlery, Divertimenti; 3. small Duralex glass, Spanish supermarket; 4. espresso maker, Jerry's Home Store; 5. salt shaker, hardware shop; 6.pepper shaker, hardware shop; 7.1930's jelly bowl, junk shop; 8. glass, Habitat; 9. sugar shaker, After Noah; 10. secondhand cutlery, The Dining Room Shop; 11. wine glass, Habtiat; 12. Duralex glass jug, hardware shop.
Page 316 - 317 1. White china mug, Habitat; 2. White china plate, Wedgwood; secondhand cutlery, The Dining Room Shop; 3. Striped linen cloth & napkins, Cath Kidston; 4. Ceramic mug with blue stripe, After Noah; 5. Oilcloth, John Lewis; 6. Checked cloth & napkins, Divertimenti; 7. Ceramic cup & saucer, After Noah; 8. White ceramic serving bowl, The Conran Shop; 9. Traditional ceramic pitcher, Divertimenti; 10. Cornishware mug, The Conran Shop; 11. White cloth & napkins, Jerry's Home Store; 12. Ceramic egg cup, Divertimenti.
Page 318 - 319 1. Secondhand oak desk, junk shop; 2. Metal folding table, Muji; 3. Slatted folding table, Habitat; 4. Pine table, Ikea; 5. Folding table, Ikea; 6. "Bra" table top & trestle legs, Ikea; 7. "Estel" table, Habitat; 8. Beech table with zinc top, Jerry's Home Store.
Page 320 - 321 1. Sun hat, author's own; 2. Camping kettle, Black's; 3. Basket, Spanish market; 4. Greek barbeque, Young & D; 5. Cool blocks, Black's. 6. Plastic cups, Habitat; 7. Deck chair, Habitat; 8. Blanket, Melin Tregwynt; 9. Camping kettle, Buy Green by Mail; 10. Cutlery, Ocean.
Page 326 - 327 1. Drying rack, The Domestic Paraphernalia Company; 2. Candles, hardware

shop; 3. Cotton duster, hardware shop;
4. Door mat, hardware shop; 5. Wicker basket,
Tobias and the Angel; 6. String, hardware shop;
7. Laundry basket, Ikea; 8. Cotton tea towel,
Divertimenti; 9. Galvanized garbage can, Aero;
10. Broom, hardware shop

Page 328 - 329 1. dish washing brush & spare
heads, Buy Green by Mail; 2. Milk bottle, milkman; 3. Freeplay radio, Buy Green by Mail;
5. Water filter, Natural Collection; 6. Wash balls,
Buy Green by Mail; 7. Cushion made by Kate
Storer from fabric samples; 8. Newspaper log
(logmaker from Buy Green By Mail); 9. Recycled
jar; 10. organic cotton bag, Natural Collection

Page 330 - 331 1. Canvas collapsible boxes,
Muji; 2. Wire mesh lockers, Action Handling
Equipment Limited; 3. Victorian open shelving,
Castle Gibson; 4. Square grass baskets with lids,
The Holding Company; 5. Rattan lidded baskets,
The Holding Company; 6. Pulp board shelving,
Muji; 7. 19th-century shelved cupboard, Castle
Gibson; 8. Fold-up cardboard drawers, Muji; 19.
Plastic basket boxes, The Holding Company.

Page 332 - 333 1. Bertoia chair, Lifestyle;
2. Folding wooden chair, After Noah;
3. Folding slatted chair, Habitat; 4. Wooden
stool, Habitat; 5. Old sewing factory chair,
author's own; 6. Upholstered dining chair, Jerry's
Home Store; loose cover made by Kate Storer,
canvas, Z.Butt; 7. Robin Day chair, Habitat; 8.
Secondhand stool, junk shop.

Page 338 - 339 1. Antique hoe & fork, The
Conran Shop; 2. Besom broom, Clifton
Nurseries; 3. Ssieve, Clifton Nurseries; 4. Enamel
watering can, House of Steel; 5. Cast aluminium
tools, Clifton Nurseries; 6. Shears, Clifton
Nurseries; 7. Terra-cotta pots, author's own; 8.
Compost container, Queenswood;

9.Cane sticks, Homebase.

Page 344 - 345 1. Painted planter, Ikea;
2. Terracotta pot, Clifton Little Venice;
3. Galvanized bucket, hardware shop;
4. Galvanized window box, Homebase;
5. Terra-cotta pot, The Conran Shop; 6. Tin can,
recycled baked beans can.
7. Cedarwood window box, Clifton Nurseries. 8.
painted terra-cotta pots, author's own.

Page 350 - 351 Secondhand armchair, junk
shop; loose cover, The Cotton Tree; cushion,
Heals; 2. Hitch Mylius sofa, Aero; 3. Couch with
loose covers, George Smith; 4. "Man Ray" sofa,
The Sofa Workshop; 5. Secondhand chair, junk
shop; loose cover, The Cotton Tree; 6. 'Man Ray'
footstool, The Sofa Workshop; 7. Sofa, David
Seyfried; blanket, Designers Guild @ Heals;
cushions, Heals; 8. Sofa bed, Muji.

Page 352 - 353 Pither stove, Mr W. Tierney; 2.
Toasting fork, found stick; 3. Poker, tongs &
shovel, Valantique; 4. Stripped bucket, House of
Steel; 6. "Mayasticks", Buy Green by Mail;
7. Chestnut roaster, Spanish hardware shop;
9. African log basket, Albrissi; 10. Hearth brush,
market stall.

Page 354 - 355 "Pigsty" pendant, Aero;
2. "Miss Sissi" lamp by Philippe Starck, Aero;
3. Reconditioned 1930s "chroom" anglepoise
lamp, After Noah; 4. "Constanza"floor lamp,
Aero; 5. Metal desk lamp, Habitat; 6. "Hector"
pendant, The Conran Shop; 7. Wooden lamp,
Heals.

Page 356 - 357 Linen water, The Flower Room;
2. Acqua di Parma scented candle, The Conran
Shop; 3. Rose buds, Laura Ashley;
4. Cedarwood blocks, The Holding Company; 5.
Incense sticks & holder, Muji; 6. Lavender
pillows, Couverture; 7. Melissa potpourri,

The Flower Room; 8. Ceramic oil ring, The
Flower Room; 9. Rosemary, home grown.

Page 358 - 359 Hanging tea light holders,
Habitat; 2. Glass hurricane lantern, Heals; 3. Tea
light lantern, Habitat; 4. Tea light glass, The
Conran Shop; 5. Cube candle, Heal's;
6. Ceramic candlestick holder, junk shop;
7. Stick in the ground tea light holder,
The Conran Shop; 8. Tea light holder, Habitat.

page 360 Wax crayons, Ikea.

page 364 - 365 1. Stick-on stars, WH Smith; 2.
Ribbons & braid, John Lewis and VV Rouleaux; 3.
Felt-tip pens, Woolworths;
4. Brown paper, WH Smith; 5. Luggage tags, WH
Smith; 6. Paints, stationery shop; 7. Tissue
paper, Paperchase; 8. Legal ribbon, stationery
shop; 9. Paper bags, Gardeners.

Page 366 - 367 1. Adhesive paper squares;
childrens' scissors, both stationery shop;
2. Homemade tea light holder, recycled jam jar;
3. Salt dough, homemade; 4. Metal bucket, Ikea;
plastic spade, market stall;
5. Wooden clacker, Ikea; 6. Cotton pillow case,
John Lewis; fabric pens, Suasion;
7. American rag doll, author's own; 8. Tennis
ball, sporting goods store; 9. Jump rope, junk
shop; 10. Block paints, Ikea.

Page 372 - 373 1. Reclaimed roll top bathtub,
LASSCO RBK; 2. Shower tray, Aston Matthews;
3. Reclaimed sink, LASSCO RBK; 4. Mosaic tiles,
Criterion Tiles; 5. Reclaimed shower, LASSCO
RBK; 6. Refurbished light, LASSCO RBK; 7.
Heated towel rack, Aston Matthews;
8. Bathtub, Aston Matthews; 9. Reclaimed
faucet, LASSCO RBK.

Page 374 - 375 1. Bath rack, The Conran Shop;
2. Glass, hardware shop; 3. Ceramic soap dish,
The Conran Shop; 4. Chrome wire rack, Heal's;

5. Laundry bag, made by Kate Storer;
6. Bathrobe, Heal's; 7. Wire soap dish, author's
own; 8. Pitcher, The Conran Shop; 9. Duck
board, The Conran Shop.

Page 376 - 377 1. 100% pure vegetable soaps,
The Flower Room; 2. Recycled liqueur bottle
filled with Godas De Oro cologne; 3. Face brush,
Muji; 4. Natural sponge, The Conran Shop; 5.
Body lotion, Immaculate House; 6. Circular
loofah, & pumice stone, Muji; 7. Back brush,
Muji; 8. Bath mit, The Conran Shop;
9. "Flower Garden" soap, Savonnerie.

Page 378 - 379 1. Waffle mat, The Conran
Shop; 2. Bath mat, Heal's; 3. Towel, The Conran
Shop; 4. Linen-edged towels, linens select; 5.
White towel, John Lewis; 6. Bath mat, Heal's; 7.
Linen towel, Ocean; 8. Waffle towels, The
Conran Shop; 9. Bath mat, Heal's; 10. Linen
guest towel, Linens Select

Page 384 - 385 1. Bed, Daniel Spring;
"Florence" pillow cases, Habitat; percale duvet
cover, Cologne & Cotton; "Seafoam Crepe"'
blanket, The Conran Shop; secondhand linen
sheet, The Cloth Shop; 2. "Suffolk" bed, Laura
Ashley; "Madeira" bedspread, The White
Company; pillow cases, Cologne & Cotton;
3. "Shaker" bed, Warren Evans; "Domino"
blanket, The Conran Shop; striped flannel pillow
cases, cotton duvet cover, both Cologne &
Cotton; 4. "Anna" bed, Nordic Style; antique
french monogrammed sheet, The Cloth Shop;
waffle blanket, The White Company; 5.Futon
mattresses, both Yakamoto Futon Centre;
natural linen sheet, Toast; herringbone sheet,
The Linen Mill; Waffle blanket, The White
Company.

Page 386 - 387 1. All weather duvet,
The Iron Bed Company; 2. "Orthos" mattress,

Hypnos; 3. Hypoallergenic pillow, Debenhams;
goose down pillow, The Feather Bed Company;
goose down & feather pillow, Debenhams;
4. Bolster & body pillow, The Feather Bed
Company; 5. Hypoallergenic duvet, Debenhams;
6. Feather bed, The Feather Bed Company; 7.
Goose down duvet, Debenhams;
8. Square pillow, The Feather Bed Company;
9. Underblanket, The Linen Mill.

Page 388 - 389 1.Secondhand linen pillow
cases, monogrammed French linen sheet, antique
heavy linen sheet, all The Cloth Shop;
2. Jersey duvet cover & pillowcases, Muji;
3. Herringbone duvet cover, The Linen Mill;
"Empress" bedspread, waffle blanket, "Madeira"
bedspread, all The White Company; 4.
"Victoria" duvet covet & pillowcase,
Linens Select; 5. Striped "Etienne" throw, The
Conran Shop; cream cellular blanket, The White
Company; soft wool blanket, Linens Select;
6. Percale pillow case and duvet cover, Cologne &
Cotton; 7. Plaid blanket; fine checked blanket,
both Melin Tregwynt; secondhand Welsh
blanket, The Cloth Shop;
8. Flannel duvet cover & pillow cases,
Cologne & Cotton; 9. Cushion cover, Melin
Tregwynt @ Earth Tones; alpaca throw; Shaker;
knitted linen throw, Eastern Trading Alliance;
alpaca throw, Shaker.

Page 390 - 391 1. Waffle bath robe, Linens
Select; 2. Cherry stone hottie, Toast;
3. traditional alarm clock, Aero; 4.Lavender
pillow, Cologne & Cotton; 5. Canvas collapsible
boxes, Muji; 6. Gray mohair blanket, lilac
cashmere throw; both Couverture; 7. Hot-water
bottle cover, Cath Kidston; 8. Tray table, Nordic
Style; 9. Canvas slippers, Muji.

Author's acknowledgments

Putting together *Pure Style Living* has been a team effort, and I am grateful to everyone who has
helped to make it such a beautiful and informative book.

I am indebted to the commitment, creativity, and enthusiasm of the multitalented Kate Storer, and it
has also been a joy to collaborate with such a creative designer and art director as Vanessa Courtier,
who has clearly and stylishly interpreted my vision. Many thanks too, to her assistant Gina Hochstein.

Thank you to all the suppliers (see above) who have loaned me products for photography.

I would like to thank the photographers Steve Gorton, assistant Andy Komorowski,
Pia Tryde. I would also like to extend special thanks to Henry Bourne, Simon Brown,
and James Merrell.

Thank you to the following people for allowing me to photograph in their homes:
Ian and Safia Thomas, A.Gold, London; Marilyn Phipps, The Battery, Whitstable; Simon and Liz Brown;
Jon White and Tessa Brown; Vanessa De Lisle, Fashion Consultant; Alastair Hendy, food writer and

stylist; Richard Naylor and Sidonie Winter, Jones Dairy, London; Marianna Kennedy and Charles
Gledhill; John and Colleen Matheson; Annie and Lachlan Stewart, Anta, Scotland; Nick and Hermione
Tudor, Finca el Moro, Spain; Emma and Damon Heath; David and Carolyn Fuest; Pia Tryde.

Thank you to food writer and stylist Claire Gordon-Smith for her styling and recipes to illustrate
Christmas food ideas, and to Emma Heath for her marmalade recipe.

A big thank you to Christopher Davis who commissioned me, and to the editorial and design team at
Dorling Kindersley, Judith More, Janis Utton, and Neil Lockley.

Thank you to Clare Conville, my agent, who has always been a voice of creative reason and support.

Photographs by: Steve Gorton – all cut out images – and Pia Tryde except for the following:
©Henry Bourne for pages 234-235, 239 far right, 259; ©Simon Brown for pages190-191;
Jane Cumberbatch pages 168, 222-223; James Merrell pages 61, 139 far right.